A HISTORIAN LOOKS
AT HIS WORLD

SIR CHARLES PETRIE BT
from an oil painting by A. C. Davidson-Houston

A Historian Looks at His World

SIR CHARLES PETRIE, Bt.
C.B.E.

SIDGWICK & JACKSON

LONDON

ISBN 0 283 97850 3

Printed in Great Britain by
William Clowes & Sons, Limited
London, Beccles and Colchester
for Sidgwick and Jackson Limited
1 Tavistock Chambers, Bloomsbury Way
London WC1A 2SG

Contents

List of Illustrations   viii

Foreword   ix

PART ONE

FIRST LOOK 1895–1920

I Liverpool   3

Birth. Family Background. Robert Petrie of Portlethen. George and Margaret Petrie. The Irish Petries, James and George. My Grandfather. Liverpool at the Turn of the Century. My Early Recollections of the City. Coming of the Internal Combustion Engine. The Wales of Those Days. Political and Social Divisions. Men's Clothes. Manners and Customs. Heavy Eating. Taboo on Sex. Opening of the Adelphi Hotel. The Provincial Sunday. Local Patriotism. My Relations with My Parents. No Feeling of Frustration. A Reminiscence of Kaiser Wilhelm II. Liverpool Politics. Sir Robert Houston and Sir Archibald Salvidge. The Seventeenth Earl of Derby. Bonar Law. Some Stories of F. E. Smith. Municipal Socialism. A Glimpse of Queen Victoria. A Self-Contained Community.

II Ireland and Abroad   19

Life at Carrowcarden. Uncle Peter. Boyhood Recollections of Connacht. An Eccentric Doctor. The Pery-Knox-Gores and the Gore-Booths. The Countess Markievicz. Her Part in the Easter Rising. The Witticisms of Father Healey. Crossing Swords with Gladstone. Politics in Mayo and Sligo. The Home Rule Agitation. The Orangemen and the Southern Unionists. Bitter Feelings. Contrast between the Irish and the English. Birrell as Chief Secretary. Early visits to Norway and France. Russia under the Tsar. Impressions of Moscow and St Petersburg. The Moroccan Crisis. A False Rumour. Lunch at Lübeck. The Spa Life of Europe. King Edward VII at Marienbad. Politics and Cures. The Marienbad Golf Course. A Sight of the Emperor Francis Joseph. The End of an Era.

III The First World War   34

The Royal Regiment of Artillery. Tynemouth and My Impressions of Northumberland. Experiences with Irish Reservists. Anti-Aircraft and its Drawbacks. A False Alarm of Invasion. Learning Spanish. Defeating the Zeppelin. The Air-Raids on London. Popular Attitude towards the War. A Contrast in Colonels. A Wartime Officers' Mess. The War Cabinet Office. Colleagues and Responsibilities. Meeting with Curzon and Trenchard. Cabinet Procedure. Wartime London. Lord Swinton. Sudden End of the War. British Unpreparedness. An Unsatisfactory Settlement. Preparing the Third Reich. Armistice Day, 1918. Saturnalia. The Peloponnesian War of Modern Europe.

IV Oxford   49

London After the Armistice. A World of Illusions. Demobilization Troubles. A Revolutionary Mood. My Return to Oxford. The Undergraduate of Those Days. Irreligious Outlook. Wartime Corpus. Tolerance of the Authorities. The College Soviets. Thomas Case. Some Stories about Him. Robert Bridges and G. K. Chesterton. R. B. Mowat. His Intellectual Honesty. Sir Richard Livingstone – A Much-Loved Figure. The Union after the War. My Contemporaries. Ignorance regarding Cambridge. The Foundation of the Oxford Carlton Club. Its Original Office-Bearers. The Tragedy of Edward Marjoribanks. F. E. and the Club. Political Conventions of the Time. J. S. Sandars. A Reminiscence of Disraeli. *The Oxford Review.* How Great a Snob was Warren? A Retrospect.

v

PART TWO

SECOND LOOK 1920–1945

V   The Home Front in the Twenties   69

Death of My Father. Marriage and Divorce. Conservative Politics. Fatal Compromises. Influence of Big Business. Conservative Candidate for North Cornwall. The General Election of
1923. The Requirements of South Dorset. Thoughts of Oxford University. Two Election
Stories. Election to the Carlton Club. The Trials of a New Member. The Club in the Twenties.
An Eccentric. Entry into Journalism. *The Outlook*. Fleet Street and Its Notabilities. Gwynne
and Garvin. Some Reflections on the National Press. Inadequate Remuneration of Journalists.
Re-marriage. A House at Horley. Sir Harry Preston. Succession to the Baronetcy. My First
Book. Do Reviews Sell Books? History and Historians. The Fallacies of the Period.

VI   Some Figures of the Twenties   82

National Respect for Failure. The Case of Arthur Balfour. A Personal Reminiscence. His
Private Life. A Failure as a Leader of Men. The Dual Personality of Stanley Baldwin. The Evil
Effects of Baldwinism. Had He a Sense of Humour? Austen Chamberlain. A Great Foreign
Secretary. Resignation from the India Office. In Private Life. The Strange Case of Queen
Victoria and Joe Chamberlain's Trousers. Asquith's Blunder in 1924. His Relations with Lloyd
George. John Buchan. A Man of Strong Likes and Dislikes. Not a Good M.P. Understanding
of Youth. Ramsay MacDonald. Most Misunderstood of Prime Ministers. The Evidence of Rose
Rosenberg. MacDonald and Heriot. The Protocol of Geneva and the Pact of Locarno.

VII   France and Spain in the Twenties   97

France Again Mistress of Europe. A Reminiscence of Clemenceau. Royalism in France. Its
Weaknesses. The Comte de Paris. The Action Française. Maurras and Daudet. An Anecdote of
Charles Benoist. A Holiday at Etretat. Honeymooning in Mallorca. Some Very Odd Fellow-
Countrymen. Cheapness of Living. The Spanish Trains. Their Unpunctuality. Bobadilla
Junction and Dyer. The Adventures of Richard Chenevix-Trench. Life in Spain in the Twenties.
Some Reflections on the Spanish Character. King Alfonso XIII and the Palace Sentry. Primo de
Rivera. My Impressions of Him. His Relations with the King. A Changing Madrid. Surviving
Customs. The British General Strike of 1926 as Seen from Spain.

VIII   The Gathering of the Storm   109

The Depression of 1929. The Slump spreads to Europe. Labour in Office. Rise of Nazism in
Germany. Excessive British Reliance on the League of Nations. Its Strength and Weakness.
Insistence on Peace rather than Justice. British Youth in The Thirties. The Heyday of Paradoxes.
Temporary Upsurge of Fascism in Britain. The Influence of Oswald Mosley. His Mistakes. My
Debate with Him. Lloyd and Mosley. The *English Review* Movement. Appreciation of Douglas
Jerrold. The Indian Controversy. Its Unfortunate Effects upon the Conservative Party. The
Social Round. The Eighteen Club. Its Members and its Meetings. Some Stories it Provoked.
The Coningsby Club. The Storm Gathers.

IX   The Lighter Side   122

Lillington. The Charm of Dorset. The County's Infinite Variety. Social Life influenced by
Physical Configuration. The Townsman in the Country. Some Reflections on This Theme. A. G.
Street at a Brains Trust. Shaftesbury, Canute, and Toby O'Brien. A Memorable Celebration.
George III in Dorset. Our Week-End Guests. Local Inns and Their Frequenters. The New Inn
at Cerne Abbas and the Mermaid at Yeovil. Major H. Charlewood Turner and His Exploits.
Vyvyan Pope. His Death a National Tragedy. Wavell, a Personal Reminiscence. His Clashes
with Churchill. Sherborne and Its Pack Fair. Some Dorset Customs and Traditions. A Galaxy of
Ghosts. A very Pleasant Interlude.

X   Europe in the Thirties   135

The Convegno Volta and Its Participants. Göring and His Decorations. Two Stories of Rennell
Rodd and Cardinal Merry del Val. A Visit from Rosenberg. A Drink with a Borgia. Some
Characteristics of Mussolini. Personal Impressions of Him. An Important Discussion. Cold-
Shouldered at the British Embassy. A Situation Mishandled. Attempt to Improve Anglo-Italian
Relations. Decline and Fall of Mussolini. Roman Society. Blacks and Whites. Nostalgia for the
Old Order. Curious Behaviour of Sir John Simon. An Audience of King Victor Emmanuel III.
A Service for the Archduke Otto. Monarchy at a Discount. Visits to Rheims. Shortsightedness
of British Diplomacy in The Thirties. Tragic Failure to Effect a Danubian Federation.

XI   Some Balkan Reminiscences   147

The Tragedy of Balkan History. Meeting with King George II of the Hellenes. A Very Lonely
Man. His Devotion to His Country. A Sincere Friend of Britain. Dimitri Levidis. The Res-
toration of the Greek Monarchy. Life in Athens. A Country of Contrasts. A Second Visit to the
Balkans. Banned from Jugoslavia. My Journey to Sofia. Experiences in Bulgaria. Audience of
King Boris III. My Impressions of Him. Transition to Romania. Atrocity Stories. The Iron
Guard. My Lecture in Bucharest. Progress under King Carol II. Professor Grimm and Cluj.
Charm of Transylvania. Contrast between Vienna and Budapest. A Strenuous Day at Szeged.
The Shadow of the Third Reich. The Jugoslav Diplomatist and the Young Jewess.

XII   The Second World War   162

We Move to Dorset. Opinion in the Services. Paradoxical Coming of the War. Effect on the Public.
The Case for and Against Neville Chamberlain. The Position of Sir Horace Wilson. Impact of the
War on Dorset. My Wife's Activities. My Memorandum to the Prime Minister. Its Frigid
Reception in High Places. Disliked by the Establishment. Work for the Ministry of Information.
Air-Raid on Sherborne. My Wife's Narrow Escape. The Jolly Sailor at Saltford. Lecturing to the
Forces. Inadequate Financial Reward. Attitude of Officers and Men. The Guards Armoured, and
the 1st and 6th Armoured Divisions. A Diversity of Types. The Women's Services. The Aus-
tralians, Czechs, and Americans. Complaints of Socialist Influences in Army Education. The Air-
Raids. London at the End of the War. A Disillusioned Generation.

PART THREE

THIRD LOOK 1945–1971

XIII   London Politics in the Fifties and Sixties   185

Return to Kensington and Its Politics. Changes in the Royal Borough. A Shift of Population.
Robert Jenkins and His Work. Amalgamation of Kensington and Chelsea. The Councillors of the
Post-War Era. Local Elections and National Politics. The 1900 Club. Its Origins and Influence.
A Story of Winston Churchill. Service of the 1900 Club to the Conservative Party. Churchill as
Prime Minister. His Relations with Beaverbrook. His Greatness and His Pettiness. Death of
Oliver Stanley a Great Loss to the Party and the Country. The Strange Case of David Maxwell Fyfe.
Harold Macmillan a Misunderstood Man. The New English Review. The Disappearance of the
English Landowner.

XIV   The Twilight of the West End Club   197

Position at the End of the First World War. The Carlton Club. Changing Habits of Its Members.
The Acquisition of the Annexe. Bombing of the Club. Occupation of Arthur's Old Premises.
Kitty Fischer. The Carlton becomes Less Political. Influence of the Internal Combustion Engine.
Inflation a Real Menace. The Future of the Carlton. The Oxford and Cambridge and the Guards'
Clubs. A Story of the Duke of Wellington. The Authors' Club. Douglas Jerrold's Unjust
Aspersions. Some Outstanding Members. Its Friendly Atmosphere. Migration to the National
Liberal. Hurlingham. Its Early History. A Happy Club. The Dining-Clubs. The Story of the
Pitt Club. Hugo Wortham and Harry Brittain. Clubs a Part of the British Way of Life.

XV   Ireland Again   209

Changes Caused by the Second World War. The Tendency to Look Back. Misinterpretation of
Irish History. Why Not a National Park? Tolerance in the Republic. Low Standard of the
Politicians. Loss of Michael Collins. The Irish Army Underestimated. Foundation of the
Military History Society of Ireland. Mr de Valera's Interest in it. The Irish Sword. Outings to
Battle-Fields in Ireland and Elsewhere. Support of External Affairs. A Tribute to the Irish Diplo-
matic Service. The University Club in Dublin. Colonel McAlister an Admirable Secretary. Local
Traditions and Their Value. The Algerine Raid on Baltimore. The Propagation of Bad History.
James II at Shelton Abbey. The Attraction of County Wicklow. The Future of Ireland. A United
Ireland the only Solution.

XVI   The Latest Look Round   218

Spain and the Duke of Alba. An Outstanding Personality. His Love of England. Relations with
Winston Churchill, General Franco, and King Alfonso XIII. Spain Fortunate in her Ambassadors in
London. Anglo-Spanish Relations always Strained. Promise of the Infante Don Juan Carlos. The
Petrie Family in the U.S.A. Decline of American Self-Confidence. Effect of the War in Vietnam.
American Desire to be Liked. Different Interpretation of the Same Word. No Great Natural
Affinity with Britain. Some Reminiscences of E. P. Warren. The Average American Ignorant of
the Outside World. The United Nations – its Pros and Cons. France in the Fifties and Sixties.
Post-War Bitterness. Trial of Marshal Pétain. Political Contrasts with Britain. Is Pompidou
playing Mazarin to de Gaulle's Richelieu?

XVII   Some Conclusions   230

My Conclusions.   Necessity for a Federated Europe.   Immediate Post-War Fallacies.   Yet Prophets
of Gloom can be Wrong.   The Shadow of Inflation.   Roman and Spanish Precedents.   Ever-
Increasing Cost of the Roman Administration.   Arrival of the Police State.   Unrest in the Univer-
sities.   No New Phenomenon.   The German Students.   Sand murders Kotzebue.   The Message for
Today.   Is Authority in Modern Britain Too Remote?   The Academic and Industrial Spheres.   A
Conservative Fallacy.   The Coming of Radio and Television.   History now Read as Literature.
Four Notable Women Historians.   The Human Attitude Towards Death.   Some Examples from the
Past.   Epilogue.

Index   239

Illustrations

Portrait of Sir Charles Petrie Bt   *frontispiece*

1   Alexander Petrie of Carrowcarden, 1823–1921   *facing page*   22
2   Ivy Lodge, Liverpool   22
3   Sir Charles Petrie Bt of Carrowcarden, 1852–1920   22
4   Sir Charles as a freshman at Oxford   23
5   With Colin Coote at Etretat   54
6   Viscount Lymington, Sir Rennell Rodd, and the author in
    Rome, autumn 1932   54
7   The author at a dinner at the Hôtel de Ville, Rheims, 11 October
    1936   55
8   The Petrie family at Lillington   55
9   Sir Charles and Comte Robert de Vogüé   55
10 As President of the Oxford Carlton Club   58
11 Lady Petrie with the Queen Mother   198
12 With Professor Johnston and Don Alfonso Vallejo Franco de
    Espés   199
13 The author, with his wife, the Spanish Ambassador to the
    Republic of Ireland, and the Señora Iturralde   199
14 At the memorial to the Irish dead at Fontenoy   230
15 Sir Charles and Lady Petrie with the Alcalde of Madrid   230
16 The author and his son Peter at Epsom Races   231

Foreword

THIS is not a biography in the modern sense, for that would imply on
the one hand a series of vicious attacks upon those with whom I have
been closely associated during the greater part of my life, and on the
other a detailed and probably boring account of the people, preferably
titled, whom I have met, and of what I have drunk and eaten in distinguished company during the past sixty years. Is is rather an attempt to
recall scenes and people that might otherwise be forgotten, looked at
from the point of view of a historian, and using my own experiences as
a peg upon which to hang my narrative. This may sound very conceited
but I am not in the least a conceited person as I am sure those who know
me best will agree.

It has been my good fortune to touch life at many points though I have
rarely held any official position, and to have travelled widely and con-
tinuously. I probably ought to have regrets, but in actual fact I possess
only memories. Events now move so rapidly that much of what is written
in these pages will appear to the younger generation as ancient history;
yet unless I am grievously mistaken in my estimate of quite a large section of the youth of today that will appeal to them all the more. Soon
after the Second World War I wrote a book called *Chapters of Life*
which has long been out of print: some of what it contained is repeated
here, but this is an entirely new work, and in any case I have altered
several of my views during the past quarter of a century.

Following these lines this book falls into three sections, which are of
equal length.

The first takes the story to 1920 when my father died, and I came
down from Oxford. Unlike a great many authors I spent the early years
of my life in a provincial city, namely Liverpool, and there is to this day
a world of difference between the viewpoint of London and that of the
provinces. Against this background must be set the fact that my father
was born in Ireland and my mother in Scotland, so at no stage of my life
have my reactions to events been predominantly English. I have also

tried to show why the First World War can rightly be described as the Peloponnesian War of modern Europe.

The second section covers the twenties and thirties, as well as the Second World War. During the twenties there was a general desire to get back to the conditions existing before 1914, and it was not until the slump of 1929 that it came to be realized that things would never be the same again. In my opinion the thirties were the climacteric of the present century, with the internal combustion engine establishing its control over the destinies of mankind, a development in my opinion of infinitely greater importance in the direction of social and political change than any ideology, while the Second World War completed the damage which had been begun by its predecessor.

Finally we come to the modern, or nihilistic and exhibitionist, era, when everything is called into question, and nobody is certain of anything. In this period it seems to me that the changes in our way of life brought about by the internal combustion engine have been accelerated by those emanating from the radio and television.

I wish to express my heartfelt gratitude to my wife, who has read the book in manuscript, and who has made a number of most valuable suggestions; also to my son, Peter, for the same reasons.

CHARLES PETRIE

PART ONE

First Look
1895–1920

———————————————

CHAPTER I

Liverpool

THERE would appear to be no valid reason why I should not commence a book that is mainly about myself and my reactions over seventy-five years in any different manner from that which I am in the habit of adopting when I write about others, and that is to say why I should not start at the beginning, and proceed with my narrative, as far as possible, chronologically.

I was born in a house called New Heys, in Sandfield Park, West Derby, Liverpool, on 28 September 1895, and Liverpool was my home until the outbreak of the First World War, although we changed houses several times during that period. My family connections with Lancashire, however, were of very recent date, for they originated when my father came from Ireland to Manchester some eighteen years before I was born. The Petries originally hailed from Scotland, and the name has been spelt in several different ways down to comparatively recent times, but it seems pretty clear that it was originally a patronymic – Petri, son of Peter. The original home of the Petries was Aberdeen and Kincardine, and one of them is said to have fought at Bannockburn. There are fifteen members of the family on the burgess-roll of Aberdeen between 1399 and 1631, and in the early years of the reign of Charles II one Robert Petrie, Laird of Portlethen, was both Provost of Aberdeen and M.P. for that city from 1665 to 1667, and again from 1669 to 1674. The records show that while he was engaged on his parliamentary duties at Edinburgh the Council of Aberdeen allowed him £5 Scots a day, for the laudable custom was in force by which a Member of Parliament was paid by his constituents.

Robert Petrie certainly had a very proper sense of his own importance and of the dignity of his office, for when one Francis Irwing 'without the leist offence or provocation to him, fell out in most disdainful and re-proachfull speeches of expressions against the magistrates of the said burgh of Aberdeen, boasting that he would cause his footmane take off the provosts hatt of his heid at the croce and cause him kick him in the arse with his foott', Petrie reported the matter to the Privy Council of Scotland, and the offender was severely punished. The Provost would not appear to have had any sons, but there was a nephew who had a commission in the Scots Guards which he resigned on the death of Queen Anne, and he was later killed fighting for King James VIII at Sheriffmuir.

The only other Petrie who was a regular soldier would appear to have been my great-great-grandfather, George Petrie, but his military career does not seem to have been a particularly brilliant one. A place was found for him in the 21st Foot, commanded by his mother's brother Lord Colville; and he was a captain with them when the regiment was cap-tured at Saratoga during the American War of Independence. Promo-tion, however, was slow in those days, especially if it had to depend chiefly on merit, and it was only as a major that some twenty years later, having transferred to the Seaforth Highlanders, he commanded part of the British forces during the capture of Ceylon from the Dutch in 1796. Ten years later, already on half pay at the rate of five shillings a day, he died through the re-opening of a bullet wound in the leg, though when or where he received it history does not record. According to family tra-dition he was a man of very violent temper: on one occasion came with-in the clutches of the law for running an excise-man through with his sword in a fit of passion.

More remarkable than George Petrie was his wife, Margaret, who was born in Canada in 1750 and died in 1857. By birth she was a MacDonald of Clanranald, and her father, James, was a younger brother of Aeneas MacDonald, one of the Seven Men of Moidart. 'Out' in the Forty-Five he had been captured at Culloden, but managed to escape, and some-where on the west coast of Scotland he was picked up by a French ship which was going to Canada. Not unnaturally when Wolfe's invasion took place there was considerable apprehension among the Jacobite refugees as to what their fate might be if the British won, and several of them, including James MacDonald, served in the French militia regi-ments at the Battle of Quebec, in spite of which, however, when France went down no action was taken against them by the victorious British. My great-great-grandfather met his future wife when he was released after the American War of Independence. My father was five at the time of Margaret Petrie's death, and he remembered her telling him of these stirring events, so I can claim that there is only one life between myself and the time when Canada was French.

Then there was my collateral ancestor, another George Petrie, the famous Irish archaeologist who was born in Dublin in 1789, and died there in 1866. It was of him that the late Aodh de Blacam wrote, 'Painter, musician, and man of letters, he was ardent in each and master of all. . . . His part in the revival of Irish studies was to organize, guide, and stimulate, and it was indispensable.' His father, James, was a portrait painter, who originally came from Aberdeen, but settled in Dublin about 1780. It was here that he painted many portraits, including those of Lord Edward Fitzgerald, John Curran, and, best known of all, Robert Emmet in the dock – and it was before this picture in Petrie's studio that Sarah Curran burst into tears. The works of both James and George Petrie are to be found in the National Gallery of Ireland.

By this time my branch too of the Petrie family had left Scotland for Ireland, and had settled near the mouth of the River Moy on the borders of Mayo and Sligo, but what were the reasons for the move and when it actually happened I have no idea. Could it have been that George Petrie, the soldier, settled there because his wife's Jacobite connections were still considered too close for life in Scotland? The choice of place was probably decided by a marriage with the Coles, themselves cadets of the Earls of Enniskillen, who then owned a good deal of property in that part of the West of Ireland.

This brings us to my grandfather, Alexander Petrie, who was born in 1823 and died in 1921: this long span of life meant that when he was born there were no railways but when he died men had flown the Atlantic. He was in his own way quite a remarkable character: an elder of the Presbyterian Church, a strong Radical, and a supporter of Home Rule, he was a man who did not know what compromise meant. He was, too, a first-rate farmer, and he never pretended to be anything else: once when it was suggested to him that on some certificate or other he should describe his occupation as 'gentleman' he demurred and wrote 'farmer', on the ground that he occasionally made some money out of his farming and he had never made a penny out of being a gentleman. On the whole, however, it must be admitted that humour was not his strong point. One Sunday morning during a very hot summer in the 1870s when he arrived at Ballina Presbyterian Church he was told by the minister, Mr Duff, that instructions had come from the General Assembly, then meeting in Belfast, for prayers to be said for rain. 'All right,' replied my grandfather, 'pray away; but it isn't much use while the wind is in the east.'

Of a very different type was a cousin of my father, one of the Petries of Rosserk, who just beat the under-sheriff of County Sligo to the port, and got away to Australia: he was probably a Fenian. He made a success of his life in his new home – I am told that there is a town in Queensland called after him. He left Ireland, or so the family tradition goes, about the time that my father and mother became engaged, and as my mother's relatives, who came from Dumfries, were very strict in their views my father was much concerned lest his cousin's exploits should reach their ears.

So much for my ancestral background; now for the Liverpool in which I passed the first nineteen years of my life. It was still the second port of the empire, and its inhabitants rightly felt themselves to be citizens of no mean city. The Mersey was thronged with ships of every tonnage and of all nations, and the great Atlantic liners were one of the local sights. Visitors were always taken for a ride on the now defunct overhead railway to see the docks, and the activity to be observed along the riverside always made Liverpool electors, Tories as most of them were, a little sceptical about Joseph Chamberlain's new national remedy of Tariff Reform. The shadow of Southampton had not yet fallen across the Merseyside. Some notable buildings were put up at this time, especially the new Adelphi Hotel and the Royal Liver Building. It was of the latter that the first Lord Mersey, perhaps better known as Mr Justice Bingham, observed, in reply to a stranger who asked him what it was, 'I don't know; probably new chambers for F. E. Smith.' The foundation stone of the Anglican cathedral was also laid during this period.

Of course the Liverpool of those days was very different from what it has since become. There was no Mersey Tunnel until after the First World War, and when motor-cars began to make their appearance in any quantity the boats across the river became uncomfortably crowded, especially on Saturday nights when people had been visiting friends in the Wirral Peninsula or had been for a run in North Wales; if one missed the last ferry from Birkenhead there was nothing for it but to return home by way of Warrington. Within the city itself means of locomotion had recently improved, for about the beginning of the century the conversion of the tramway system from horse to electric traction was carried out, and by the end of 1902 the whole of the tramways had been electrified. One of my earliest recollections is a ride in one of the last horse-trams from the corner of Devonshire Road, Princes Park, where we then lived, to the Pier Head. In all my early life the trams played a prominent part, for my father was the chairman of the Tramways Committee for many years, and associated with him were A. B. Holmes, the City Consulting Engineer, and Messrs Bellamy and Mallins. Once a year there were the tramwaymen's sports, where my mother presented the prizes, and while my elders and betters were preoccupied with other matters I was relatively free to regale myself with chocolates and such like things. Apart from this, the light frockcoats and grey toppers of the City Fathers are my chief recollection of this festivity.

Much of what is now built over was then open fields. Mossley Hill church was on the edge of the country, while Allerton and Childwall were definitely rural. Even up to the time we left Liverpool in 1920 I could see nothing but fields from my study window in Aigburth Hall Road, even though the house itself no longer exists. Memories, too, were still fresh of a very different Liverpool from the progressive and well-ordered city of Edwardian days. My mother, who had come from Dumfries as a child, well remembered the great fire that destroyed the landing stage, and in her youth she had met many who recalled the cholera epidemic, when grass grew between the cobbles in Castle Street. In her childhood there were no buildings between Princes Avenue and Parliament Street. She, too, recollected the crowds that used to flock to the public hangings, presumably outside Walton Jail, and I have heard her say that on these occasions the maids at her home always asked to have time off duty to see the execution.

When one looks back on the first fourteen years of the present century it is impossible to resist the conclusion that most of the changes in our habits are due, directly or indirectly, to the internal combustion engine, which has been far more revolutionary in its influence than the theories of Marx or Bakunin. North Wales, now the playground of South Lancashire, was, it is true, unspoilt when I first knew it, but save for a few places like Llandudno it was very remote. It was still the Wales of Borrow. My father used to take a shoot there nearly every winter, and travelling by both road and rail was very uncomfortable by modern standards. Early rises on cold mornings by candlelight and hasty ablutions in lukewarm water in a tin bath in the bedroom, followed by long drives over execrable roads to the station in a wagonette, were the order of the day. In actual fact the Welsh hotels at that time left a great deal to be desired, and in the visitors' book of one of them a disgruntled guest wrote:

> *If ever you go to Dolgelly,*
> *Don't stay at the Royal Hotel;*
> *For there's nothing to put in your belly,*
> *And no one to answer the bell.*

The Wales of those days had at least as much claim as Ireland to be a 'distressful country', for at all levels the great division between church and chapel affected every social relationship. To be a Nonconformist implied the profession of Liberalism in politics and a belief in the infallibility of Lloyd George, while Churchmen were always Tories who considered him as an emanation of the infernal regions. The Conservative standpoint was well expressed in some jingling lines which were very popular about the time of the first General Election of 1910:

> Lloyd George no doubt,
> When his day is out,
> Will ride in a flaming chariot.
> He will sit in state
> On a red-hot plate
> 'Twixt Satan and Judas Iscariot.
>
> Ananias that day
> To Satan will say,
> 'My claim to precedence now fails;
> So move me up higher,
> Away from the fire,
> To make room for that liar from Wales.'

Yet in spite of internal dissensions, and the absence of amenities, then unknown, Wales was already attracting visitors, though not in any great number. Even in my parents' early married days driving tours in the Principality, lasting a week or ten days, were very popular with those who could afford the time and the money. Within a few years all this changed, and what had necessitated at least a week-end's holiday became accessible in a few hours' run in the car. The transformation was very rapid, and at the time one hardly realized that it was so complete.

When my father was Lord Mayor of Liverpool in 1901–2 heavy eating was still the order of the day, and at a dinner he gave in honour of Lord Rosebery there were no less than five main courses. Private dinner parties of eighteen or twenty people in private houses were the rule rather than the exception, and the small dinner was much rarer. Tablecloths had not yet been discarded, and luxurious table decorations, in which smilax played a conspicuous part, were still in vogue. Of the ladies' dresses I remember little, having always been somewhat unobservant in that respect, but men still wore black waistcoats with tail-coats unless they were going to a dance, in which case they wore white ones, and then gloves were also indispensable. The dinner-jacket was as yet rare, and was somewhat contemptuously referred to as a 'bum-freezer'. The older men never took very kindly to them, and many years afterwards Tommy Case, the President of Corpus Christi College, Oxford, of whom more anon, replied to me when I asked him to come in a dinner-jacket to a reception at Wadham at which the then Warden and Mrs Wells were to be present, 'Mr Petrie, I have never exposed that portion of my anatomy to any lady save Mrs Case, and I do not propose to make an exception in favour of the wife of the Warden of Wadham. I will come in a tail-coat.'

Class distinctions in the earlier Edwardian days were very strict, and even the merchant princes of a city such as Liverpool rarely mixed with what they would freely have admitted were their social superiors – they knew their place and kept to it. The local aristocracy such as the Earls of Lathom or Sefton, or the members of the old county families, were rarely seen in the city save at some formal reception at the Town Hall – at a private party hardly ever; Lord Derby was an exception, but then he had a political axe to grind. It was still extremely rare for a local magnate to have been to either Oxford or Cambridge, though they were beginning to send their sons there; they would never have thought of having their daughters presented at Court; and not many of them belonged to a London club. Comfort, rather than ostentation, was the guiding principle in their lives, and in the provinces to keep a manservant was regarded as the height of pretentiousness. King Edward VII had been on the throne for some years before there was, largely due to his influence, any general relaxation of the customs which had obtained during the later decades of his mother's reign, and then it was more noticeable in the capital than elsewhere.

During most of my youth social relationships were subject to a rigid code of etiquette. All women who had any social pretensions had 'At Home' days to which they strictly adhered: my mother's, if I remember right, were the second and fourth Thursdays in each month. In a commercial city such as Liverpool few men had time to pay calls during the week, and they did their visiting mainly on Sunday afternoons. One took hat, stick, and gloves into the drawing-room; for, although they got in everybody's way, to do otherwise was to lay oneself open to the charge of behaving as if one were in a hotel. Attendance at a dinner or dance necessitated a formal call soon afterwards. In the present permissive age all this may sound very stereotyped and precise, and so, no doubt, it was; but at any rate you knew where you were. Either behaviour was correct or it was not, and there are many advantages in having a definite code in such matters.

On the other hand the segregation of the sexes, and the taboos on all that concerned their mutual relations, were undoubtedly overdone, though this was in no way peculiar to Liverpool. Whether youth in the first decade of the century was any more moral than it is today I take leave to doubt, and it is at least arguable that the main difference is that the present generation is exhibitionist in matters of sex whereas its predecessor was inhibited. If a woman went in a hansom alone with a man who was neither her husband nor old enough to be her grandfather her reputation was irretrievably lost, presumably on account of what in such circumstances idle hands might find to do. The ruling convention was directed against unmarried men and women ever being alone together unless they were engaged, and not always then. If an engagement was broken off the girl suffered in consequence, while divorce, like cancer, was never mentioned in polite society. What the effect of these taboos was on the young women it is difficult to say in the absence of relevant evidence, but it was certainly harmful to the young men, for they were driven to somewhat sordid intrigues in other quarters. Youths of the upper middle and middle classes in their late teens were apt to rank among their fellows according to their alleged triumphs over what were generally termed 'scivvies' and as the homes from which they came all employed maid-servants such triumphs were easily obtained.

The motor-car wrought great changes in the manners and customs of all classes of society owing to the inevitable relaxation in established habits which it caused, and the outbreak of the First World War found provincial society with a very different outlook from that which had characterized it at the death of Queen Victoria. So far as Liverpool was concerned the improvement in the means of transport caused an increasing number of people to live out of the city, principally in the Wirral Peninsula. The opening of the new Adelphi Hotel was another factor operating in the same direction: its teas became fashionable, and thus was initiated the custom of entertaining away from home which had previously been unknown. The more old-fashioned denounced the hotel as a sink of iniquity where young men drank more than was good for them, but then the same thing had been said of the Crocodile and the Bear's Paw: at any rate the old bonds were gradually relaxed, and men and maidens repaired in increasing numbers to the Adelphi to eat and dance.

No illusion is more persistent, especially in the South of England, than that in the provinces the Sunday of sixty or seventy years ago was a day of gloom and misery. In reality, nothing could be further from the truth, though it was very different from what it has since become. Games were not usually played in public or in private, and no one would take his carriage out on a Sunday. Church-going was universal, and after church those with any social pretensions took a turn along Princes Avenue, while in the afternoon the young men used to call upon those of whom they had recently been the guests at dinner or a dance. In effect, Sunday was a day of rest, and as such it met a definite need, for if the business-man of those days did not work any harder than his successor today he worked longer hours: the head of a firm was at his office by nine, and he rarely left it until five-thirty, while he never took Saturday morning off as a habit, though in London this was already becoming the custom. There was no compulsory early closing; the shops did not shut before eight; and the mass of the population worked a full six-day week, so a little rest on Sunday by no means came amiss.

In short, Liverpool was a singularly pleasant place in which to live. There was nothing narrow about its life, and as it was continually being visited by people on their way to or from the New World it was by no means isolated from the main currents of international activity. We had good theatres, the Court and the Shakespeare; lectures were frequent and popular; and there were ample facilities for the study of art, music, and letters. Men and women were so proud of their city that the local patriotism recalled that of Athens or Venice. We were not prepared to take our orders from London, and with other provincial centres, such as Manchester and Birmingham, there was the keenest rivalry. Those who sneer at the alleged narrow outlook and limited opportunities of the inhabitants of a large provincial city know little of what they are talking.

The youth of today, or at any rate the more vocal section of it, never tires of telling us that it is frustrated and that it has nothing in common with its parents. That is as may be; all I can say is that I never felt frus-trated, and if my contemporaries of those days were not in their graves in Gallipoli or on the Somme I am sure they would say they never felt frustrated either. As for my parents, I was devoted to my father; his presence still seems very real to me even though he has now been dead for more than fifty years. When he died in 1920 the *Liverpool Daily Post* wrote of him, 'There were, we have no doubt, many claims upon his time and strength, but it seemed as if the city came first. Certainly he never spared himself in its service.' There is no tribute which would have pleased him more. He came to Liverpool from Ireland by way of Man-chester in the 1870s, after which the Merseyside city was the scene of his activities. None save his family knew the sacrifice he made of both money and leisure, and my mother and I often cursed the City Council heartily when holidays had to be cut short in order that he might get back for its meetings. It is no exaggeration to say that had he devoted more of his time to his business and less to public life he would have become a rich man. He was fully aware of this, but it never affected his actions.

Yet at heart he was always a countryman. He was more than an average shot, quite a good rod, and in his earlier days it had been one of his greater claims to distinction that he had been allowed to drive the four-in-hand coach which then plied between Sligo and Ballina. In private he was one of the most regular of men in his habits, but those who were associated with him in business have told me that to the very end of his life he was prepared to take the most enormous financial risks – a line of conduct which I fear I have inherited, though far less successfully. As custodian of Liverpool's finances he was, on the contrary, almost Gladstonian in his methods, and nothing gave him greater pleasure than when he was able to borrow a fraction cheaper than, say, Birmingham, where his opposite number was Neville Chamberlain, who many years later told me of their rivalry in this field. Probably the honour my father appreciated most was the Freedom of Liverpool.

He was abundantly possessed of that ready wit associated with the land of his birth. Once he was being cross-examined by the then Sir Rufus Isaacs in a compensation case against the Liverpool Tramways. The point at issue was that the conductor had rung the bell for the tram to start before the plaintiff had succeeded in boarding it, and that she had in consequence been precipitated on to her back in the street. Sir Rufus in cross-examination was pressing my father to admit that the conductor should have thought of the implications of his action before ringing the bell, but my father, looking in the direction of the judge, turned the tables on the counsel for the plaintiff by observing, 'My Lord, you cannot expect a legal mind on thirty shillings a week.'

Until the outbreak of the First World War my father placed great hopes in Anglo-German co-operation, and when the breach came it was a great blow to him. 'I never thought I would see this day,' he remarked to me as we were driving down to Lime Street station on the day that war was declared and the reservists were flocking to the trains which were to take them to their depots. As a young man he had wanted to join the Prussian army as a volunteer in 1870, being deterred only by the refusal of my grandfather to advance the necessary fare. In 1903 he was involved in an incident which throws an interesting light upon the character of Kaiser Wilhelm II. My father had gone to Kiel in a friend's yacht, and the Kaiser asked him to spend a couple of days on the *Hohenzollern*. When he arrived at Kiel he was a little surprised that there were not any letters from home waiting for him, but when he met the Kaiser before dinner the latter at once congratulated him on the fact that his name was in the Honours List which had appeared while he was still at sea: what had happened was that the Kaiser had ordered that my father's letters were not to be given to him until he personally had announced the good news.

If life in Liverpool in those days was in many ways peacefully uneventful its politics were lively in the extreme, the violence which they engendered being comparable to that of more recent times. Once, indeed, when the troops had to open fire, two men were shot dead and two hundred people injured; not that Liverpool was alone in these disturbances, for there was fighting in the streets in Cardiff, Hull, and Manchester. The idea that violence is a modern phenomenon in England is a complete illusion. Equally there was a keen interest in local affairs in Liverpool, and nearly every ward was contested each succeeding November, for in those days the municipal elections were held on the first day of that month, while when a General Election took place nobody appeared to talk of anything else. With the city's large Irish population, both Orange and Green, events in Ireland had a very considerable influence upon the Liverpool election results, particularly whenever the Home Rule controversy flared up. The issues in the municipal fights were often trivial enough – one is said to have turned on the position of a coffee-stall – but the rivalry to which they gave rise testified to the interest taken by the electors in the administration of their city. There was no sign of apathy in any quarter.

On the Conservative side there were two singularly unattractive figures: one was Sir Robert Houston and the other was Sir Archibald Salvidge. Houston was a good deal of a mystery, and many people were puzzled to account for the fact that he was regularly returned for West Toxteth when he rarely set foot in the constituency. He even held the seat in 1906, though since his time it has rarely been represented by a Conservative. His opponents used to declare that the explanation was to be found in bribery, in which free coal played a prominent part, and this may well have been the case, but all the same his critics never brought a petition against his return. The present Lord Birkenhead, in his admirable biography of his father, describes Houston as 'a shipping magnate of ruthless character and questionable methods, a bearded pirate, the type of shipowner described by Kipling in *The Mary Gloster*'. His widow, who is said to have commenced her public career as a tart on Ryde Pier, made herself notorious in Right Wing circles between the wars, much to the embarrassment of the Conservative Central Office.

Of Salvidge it is difficult for my father's son to write with anything approaching objectivity. He was an extremely formidable figure as Chairman of the Liverpool Working Men's Conservative Association, which he converted into a machine that enabled him within fairly wide limits to control the results of elections in Liverpool. He was more than a little of a rabble-rouser, and he deliberately made religion the key issue in local politics. Although a brewer by trade, he would not appear to have made brewing pay, for his financial position was always delicate – possibly because he kept up two establishments – and on at least one occasion the hat had to be taken round to relieve his embarrassments. This was done by F. E. Smith, who raised five thousand pounds for the impoverished publican, though Salvidge had been hoping to receive double that amount: of this sum Lord Derby, Alderman Cohen, and Messrs Cain contributed a thousand each, and the rest came from friends in London. Salvidge was possessed of a hectoring, not to say bullying, manner, and it must be admitted that this often enabled him to carry his point. Twice at least, however, he was badly thwarted: the first time was when he tried to browbeat Lord Woolton, then Frederick Marquis, on his first arrival in Liverpool, the second when he ventured to cross swords with Lord Beaverbrook, in which contest he very definitely had the worst of it.

My own attitude towards this repulsive figure cannot help being influenced by the fact that at the very end of my father's life, when he was far from well but still leader of the City Council, Salvidge persuaded a majority of the Conservative party to go back on a decision that had been taken at a party meeting, and vote the opposite way in the Council: all this was unknown to my father, who thus found himself in a minority, supported only by a few faithful councillors. Resignation was, of course, his immediate reaction to such treatment, and he died two years later of cancer.

Lord Beaverbrook once described Salvidge as 'Lord Derby's Sancho Panza'. But Derby himself was very far from being a Don Quixote – in fact he is very difficult to assess at all. The influence of the Stanley family in Liverpool had long been one of the outstanding features of Lancashire life, and in essence it was a case of feudalism protracted into modern times. In appearance and manner the seventeenth Earl of Derby was the bluff John Bull Englishman of tradition, but he was known to his critics as 'the smiling Judas': certainly he was a born intriguer, and on two quarto pages of backstairs intrigue which he once wrote to Walter Long the recipient noted, 'He wrote this on the day that his father died.' Haig wrote of him, 'like the feather pillow [he] bears the mark of the last person who sat on him'. Yet if Derby often appeared to poor advantage on the national stage, he was at his best where Lancashire, and in particular Liverpool, were concerned. He was in very truth their patron, and his reward was the popularity he enjoyed in his own county.

For some years Bonar Law was a local M.P. since he sat for the Bootle division of Lancashire, which then included many of the suburban districts of Liverpool. He came among us as a stranger with a great reputation, and a stranger he remained. No man ever gave a book a more fitting title than did Bobby Blake when he called his biography of Bonar Law *The Unknown Prime Minister*. He was a curious mixture of shyness and ambition, indeed in ordinary social relationships he could be extremely *gauche*. On one occasion he said to his private secretary, John Davidson, 'I've got two men coming to dinner tonight: do you think one bottle of champagne will meet the case? You know I drink next to nothing myself.' On Davidson asking the names of his chief's prospective guests he was told that they were Winston Churchill and F. E. Smith, so he suggested that half-a-dozen bottles would be nearer the mark. Bonar had no personality either on a platform or off it, yet he marshalled his facts so lucidly that he always carried his audience with him. In the great meetings at the Sun Hall his style was in marked contrast with the fiery eloquence of F. E. and Carson, and with the balanced periods of Lord Lansdowne, but it was no less effective.

Our other representatives in the House of Commons were worthy enough fellows, though not particularly distinguished, with the exception of F. E. Those who knew him only in later days as a Minister of the Crown can have little idea of what a tower of strength he proved to the Tories of the North in the years that followed the electoral disaster of 1906, a disaster in many ways even greater than that of 1945. After two decades of almost continuous office, the Conservative Party was dumbfounded by its overthrow, especially in Lancashire. Traditionally Tory since Jacobite times, this was the first time that county had been false to its old allegiance. Preston was gone, Balfour was defeated in Manchester, and even Lord Derby's son and heir had lost his seat, while no less than four of Liverpool's nine divisions were represented by Liberals or an Irish Nationalist. It seemed the end of all things.

Then with the appearance of this youthful-looking David who displayed not the least fear of the Liberal Goliath, before long the initiative in Lancashire was back in Conservative hands. His superb insolence almost took one's breath away, and he had a manner with hecklers which soon silenced the most determined opposition. To an interrupter at Preston who had kept on shouting 'liar', he retorted, 'If the gentleman who has been abusing me for the last ten minutes would go outside and abuse himself, I should be very grateful.' When a man screamed, 'The Tories want to tax my food', he instantly replied, 'No, sir: there is no proposal to put a duty on thistles.' At the first General Election of 1910 he was addressing a meeting in a theatre in Llandudno, and there were not fifty Conservatives in a packed house; one man, obviously put up by the Liberals to do so, asked if the Tories intended to tax music. 'What sort of music?' queried F. E., 'instrumental or vocal?' Thinking to score heavily the heckler replied, 'Vocal.' 'No,' was the immediate response, 'that is raw material. Under Mr Chamberlain's pledge it comes in free.'

His wit was as marked in private as in public. One day the leading bore in the Carlton Club button-holed him, and started a long-winded story. F. E. promptly rang the bell, and when a waiter appeared, said to him, 'Would you mind listening to the rest of this Member's story? I've got to go.'

In later life F. E. made many enemies among those who did not know the kindness of heart which lay behind the arrogance of manner, and his attitude towards the Irish Treaty alienated many of his earlier associates. In Liverpool he had none but friends, for his kindliness was too well known for it to be otherwise. His hand was always held out to those whom life had treated harshly, and he helped many a lame dog over a stile. Though he made more than one serious mistake in the course of his career, no man could ever accuse F. E. Smith of being either a hypocrite or false to his friends.

The Liverpool Conservatism of those days had municipalization as its basis, its leaders believing firmly that the services which primarily concerned the ratepayers should be owned by the ratepayers. The Conservatism of the North of England has always approximated to the old Toryism and it and the Conservatism of the South are often as the poles asunder: some of the policies adopted in Liverpool during the reign of King Edward VII would even today, after two World Wars and the lapse of two generations, be viewed askance by many a Conservative councillor in London. Especially is this the case with anything that resembles municipal trading, which is anathema in the South, but to which the Northern Conservative can see no special objection. It was, indeed, seriously proposed not long before the First World War to establish a municipal zoo, and no opposition was encountered on ideological grounds, though one can well imagine what an uproar such a suggestion would create in, say, some London Conservative borough. My own father, a Tory if ever there was one, in 1905 claimed credit for the acquisition by the City of the Tramways and of the Electric Supply Company as 'a daring and successful experiment in municipal Socialism'.

To pass from politics to myself, 'What is the first thing that I remember?' is a question most people ask themselves, and it is a very interesting one too. In many cases the earliest recollection is at a relatively advanced age, say seven or eight, while in others, of which Sir Compton Mackenzie is an outstanding example, it can be dated much earlier. The difference is usually ascribed to the possession of a good or bad memory on the part of those concerned, but surely this can have little to do with the matter. If a child spends the first years of its existence in circumstances in which nothing out of the ordinary ever occurs it is unlikely to remember any event in its very early years; whereas if the opposite has been the case, and there have been occurrences of a nature to appeal to its imagination in extreme youth, the memory of them is likely to remain, even though they took place at the age of three or four. Anyhow, that seems to me a more likely explanation than the other, and is supported by the experience of many to whom I have put the point.

Personally, I have no doubt of what I first remember; it was seeing Queen Victoria when I was four. I was walking with my father from Hyde Park Corner down Constitution Hill: we were on the right-hand side, about a hundred yards from Buckingham Palace, when the Queen passed in an open carriage going in the opposite direction; there was no one in our immediate vicinity, so when we took off our hats we got the royal bow all to ourselves. Other early recollections are of the Relief of Mafeking, probably because of the noise created in Sunnyside by exuberant patriots beating kettles and trays with pokers and tongs; of a visit to the newly opened Hippodrome in Leicester Square to see a highly exciting production called *Siberia*; and of being taken to see Irving in a revival of *The Bells*. While my father was Lord Mayor of Liverpool the Freedom of the City was given to Lords Roberts and Kitchener. Of the latter I remember nothing, but Lord Roberts, seeing me eye his medals with all the curiosity of a boy of six at the end of a war when soldiers were very much in the public eye, took me on his knee and told me what the medals were and how he got them, including, of course, the Victoria Cross. I would not have needed to be much older for this to be the one subject on which he would have refused to open his mouth.

My nineteen years in Liverpool were as happy as any in my life, and the memories of them are almost wholly pleasant. We were, as has been pointed out on an earlier page, a self-contained community. London might be the capital of the kingdom, but its influence was not as great then as it was later to become. Two world wars have resulted in a concentration of authority in Government hands that would have seemed impossible to the vast majority of Edwardians, and the Government is situated in London. Sixty or seventy years ago in cities like Liverpool what went on in the capital aroused little interest: there was neither television nor radio, and no great prominence was given to it in the local press. National newspapers were in their infancy, while the London ones did not reach Liverpool much before noon, and in any case they were not widely read. All this explains the creative municipal life in the provinces in the opening years of the century, which I, for one, found extremely attractive.

CHAPTER II

Ireland and Abroad

IF Liverpool was my physical home during the first nineteen years of my life Ireland has been my spiritual home during the whole of it. My earliest recollections of the country centre round my grandfather's house of Carrowcarden near Enniscrone in County Sligo, where he farmed between five and six hundred acres, which was quite a large holding for that district. There the customs of an earlier day still persisted, and to a comparatively late date he continued to plough with oxen. His domestic life was on the same plan. One rose at six, winter and summer alike, and breakfasted very substantially at seven; there were light refreshments between twelve and one, but they amounted to little more than whiskey and biscuits, so the pangs of hunger had to be repressed until five when there was a truly gargantuan repast which centred round, if the season was right, a salmon which had been boiled whole – nothing was in any case ever made up. Later in the evening tea was served, and after a last look round the farm to see that everything was all right one retired to bed at nine.

Although my grandfather was advanced in his opinions he was conservative in his habits: smoking indoors he would not tolerate, there was no lighting save lamps, no bathroom existed, and the solitary closet was of the earth variety. The old man was wonderfully active until almost the end of his life, as is attested by the fact that he drank a whole bottle of whiskey to his own cheek at midday in the Moy Hotel, Ballina, on his ninetieth birthday in 1913, when whiskey was whiskey and cost 3s 6d a bottle.

Not far away lived an uncle, Peter, at Knoxbarrett, near Crossmolina. He rarely came to England, and save for one fishing holiday in Norway had never visited the mainland of Europe; even Dublin only saw him two or three times a year, when he always stayed at Jury's Hotel. He was an extraordinarily good classical scholar, with a knowledge of Hebrew. Towards the end of his life, and in his will, he was not unmindful of me, but my gratitude for this generosity is tempered by remembrance of the fact that when my grandfather died, which was a year after the death of my father, he and my elder brother – neither of whom had sons – divided the Carrowcarden property between themselves and sold everything in the house, lock stock and barrel, without even so much as telling me what they had done. Within ten years they were both dead, leaving me the only surviving male of our branch of the family.

Up to the outbreak of the First World War I spent a good deal of time in the West of Ireland, and my memories of Connacht are uniformly pleasant. Boating on Lough Conn or Lough Gill; trips round Achill in the old *Tartar*; and the stories told by my father and uncle of their adventures in the same districts a generation earlier: all these are very fresh in my mind. Killala Bay, close as it is to Carrowcarden, was, however, an ill-omened spot, for it was there that an uncle and aunt had, with others, been drowned on a picnic party in 1885, so that although a visit to Bartra Island has always been a popular excursion with Ballina people I was never allowed to go there; indeed, I doubt if any member of my branch of the Petrie family was ever on the island between the day when my uncle's body was washed up and that on which, sixty-one years later, my wife, my son, and I landed for a picnic. Personally, I have never yet crossed the bar at the mouth of the Moy which was the real cause of the disaster.

A friend of my father who was often with us in Ireland was Dr Brannigan. He was our family doctor and also doctor to the Liverpool tramwaymen, with whom he was extremely popular, for many of them came from Ireland, as he did himself. His father was a Roman Catholic who had become a Presbyterian minister in the Ox Mountains in County Sligo, and Brannigan was always said to have been a Fenian in his youth. He was very fond of practical jokes, to which my father and mother were also considerably addicted, and he was often a victim of them. On many holidays, in Ireland, Wales, and once in Norway when he was our companion, one never knew what he would do next – a characteristic in an adult that always appeals to a boy. One favourite trick was to shoot rabbits from a wagonette, and as he would open fire without the least warning the consequences to the nerves of the horses and to the tempers of the other passengers in the vehicle can be imagined.

His wife, who probably had to put up with a great deal, was rather inclined to be prim and proper. Her efforts to restrain her husband's ex-
uberance added to the amusement to be derived from any holiday in
which the Brannigans were of the party.

When Trollope wished to stamp Laurence Fitzgibbon as an Irishman
from the back-of-beyond he made him M.P. for Mayo, but it was a slur
upon the district for there were more worthy characters to be found in
Connacht in real life. During my boyhood Canon Hannay, better known
as George A. Birmingham, was Rector of Westport, but his popularity
was never so great locally as it was elsewhere, for it was felt that his
success as a novelist was due to the fun he made of his fellow-countrymen. At Coolcronan was Mrs Pery-Knox-Gore, a great lady of the old
school and one who in many ways recalled Theresa, Marchioness of
Londonderry, though she exercised her authority on a more restricted
scale. Markree was the home of Captain Bryan Cooper, whose untimely
death in 1930 at the age of forty-six was to be a great calamity for Ireland: he was one of the very few Irishmen of his day who inspired general confidence, and had he not died so early he might have become the
rallying-point for that moderate opinion which so rarely discovers a
spokesman in Ireland, North or South, but which is far more widespread
than is commonly supposed.

At Lissadell, famous for its wealth of daffodils, lived Sir Josslyn Gore-
Booth, whose son Brian I was to know in later years as a literary agent
until he went down in H.M.S. *Exmouth* in the autumn of 1939. My
son Peter was to serve under his nephew, Paul, first in New Delhi and
later in the Foreign Office itself.

Of course the best known of the Gore-Booth family was Constance,
who married the Count Markievicz and became one of the outstanding
figures in modern Irish history. My father knew her well in the days of
her youth, when she was living the life of many another Ascendancy
daughter, being presented at the vice-regal court, and generally enjoying
herself, with no thought for politics. Even at that time she was, it is
true, a trifle eccentric, for she kept a pet monkey, and had a tame snake
which she used to wear round her neck. In men she took little interest –
'I'm not interested in men,' she once told a friend, 'for I have had the
pick of too many' – and she had her own methods of repelling their
advances. One evening during a large and formal dinner party she suddenly felt the hand of an elderly admirer on her dress under one of the
long table-cloths of those days: she picked it up from her knees like a
dropped pear, held it up for everyone to see, and said, 'Just look what
I have found in my lap.' Life at Lissadell could be very unconventional

in those days. Then the Polish Count came into her life, and at the time their marriage seemed very fitting. But before long it became obvious that they were temperamentally unsuited to one another, so Constance took to politics and her husband to the bottle – which is the worse fate must be a matter of individual opinion.

It was the Easter Rising of 1916 which gave her worldwide fame. With Michael Mallin she was in charge of trench-digging in St Stephen's Green, but it is difficult to see what military purpose was served by this particular operation: surely she and Mallin would have been better employed in seizing the high buildings dominating the Green, in particular the Shelbourne Hotel, which contained plenty of food with cooking and kitchen equipment to feed the insurgents. But it was here that the Countess first came into action, though the accounts of what she actually did vary: she was eventually sentenced to death on the evidence of a page-boy at the University Club who testified that he saw her fire at one of the windows of the building. She was reprieved and eventually released, to become the first woman to be elected to the House of Commons, though she never took her seat.

In retrospect, one cannot help wondering whether the rest of her life was not in reality anti-climax, and that it would have been better for her reputation had she met her death on St Stephen's Green where her monument stands today. So wild became her views, and at times her actions, that it is permissible to doubt whether she was wholly balanced: also, had she lived it is difficult to believe that she would have followed the processes of thought by which her leader, de Valera, finally decided to take the Oath of Allegiance and enter the Dail. She died in 1926 at the age of fifty-eight: she had had her role in the making of modern Ireland, but had she lived to extreme old age it is hard to visualize her playing any part in its development and consolidation.

It must not be imagined that my grandfather was on back-slapping terms with the Bryan Coopers, Pery-Knox-Gores, and Gore-Booths: as a Radical he regarded the county gentry as only slightly better than the aristocracy, of whom he was deeply suspicious – he certainly had nothing in common with those who lived in 'the big house'. The younger generation, however, was more broadminded in its outlook. A taste for the pleasures of life, in which sport in all its forms was a powerful factor, was bringing them together irrespective of their social background.

The witticisms of the famous Father Healey, who was Parish Priest of Little Bray, were still going the rounds. One of the best concerns a conversation he is alleged to have had with Gladstone, which so far as I am concerned rests on the authority of the late Lord Quickswood.

Alexander Petrie of Carrowcarden,
1823–1921, the author's grandfather

Ivy Lodge, Liverpool, March 1911

r Charles Petrie Bt
Carrowcarden, 1852–1920,
e author's father

Sir Charles as a freshman
at Corpus Christi College, Oxford, in 1914

During the course of this conversation the English statesman declared that on a recent visit to Italy he had seen a notice on the door of a church in which the local priest offered to rescue souls from Purgatory for twenty-five lire a time. 'I ask you,' thundered the G.O.M., 'as a clergyman of the Church of Rome, what have you to say to that?' At once came the reply, 'Tell me of any other Church, Mr Gladstone, that would do it at the price?' On another occasion when he and the Protestant Archbishop of Dublin, Lord Plunket, had been spending the night in a small provincial town on their respective duties, the following morning the Archbishop suggested that they should walk from the hotel where they were both staying to the station to catch the train back to Dublin. Father Healey doubted if they had time, but Plunket looked at his watch and said that they had. However, when they arrived at the station the train was just slipping out. 'I had great faith in that watch,' said the Archbishop sorrowfully. ' 'Twould have been better if you'd had good works in it,' replied the priest.

An aggressive Protestant was one day loudly proclaiming his utter disbelief in Purgatory. 'Well,' said Father Healey doubtfully, 'if you won't believe in Purgatory, you may go to Hell.' He hated theological controversy in everyday social intercourse, and he usually found a mild but pointed phrase with which to put an end to it. 'What, after all, is the difference between Catholic and Protestant?' asked someone of him suddenly. 'I've lived for sixty years in this world without discovering it.' 'Never mind, my dear fellow,' said Father Healey soothingly, 'You'll know all about it before you've lived sixty seconds in the next.'

But, it may be asked by someone who does not know Ireland, was not this the time when the Home Rule agitation was sweeping the country, and did not this issue set everybody by the ears? The answer is in the affirmative, but contrary to what is commonly supposed in England the Irish are interested in other things than politics, and it was these latter, of which sport in all its forms was the most important, that brought men and women together. Then again, Mayo and Sligo took their politics rather more easily than, say, Clare on the one hand and Derry on the other. Memories were still fresh at only one remove of the landing of the French at Killala, and Humbert's soldiers had not been so popular as legend would have us believe, for it was not forgotten how they had left their Irish allies in the lurch at Ballinamuck. As for the Unionists, they were far from holding to their faith with the grim fanaticism of the Black North, and later, when Ulster decided to accept exclusion many among them became very bitter in regard to what they considered to be the betrayal of the cause of the Union. In short, for a variety of reasons tolerance was the order of the day in Mayo and Sligo, and with the exception of some occasional cattle-driving there was no political crime worth the name.

All the same the situation was changing, though very few people realized the fact. When the Liberal government of Sir Henry Campbell-Bannerman came into office in 1906 there was a momentary hope that it might do something to satisfy Irish nationalist aspirations, though long experience had shown that there was little to choose between the two English parties where these were concerned, and John Redmond well put the Irish point of view when he said, 'The sooner that this government understands that to us Whig, Tory, Liberal, Conservative, are but as names, and that British governments are judged by us by what they do and not by their professions of sympathy, the better it will be for them and for everyone concerned.' Mindful of their defeats in 1886 and in 1895 on the subject of Home Rule the Liberal leaders were fearful of introducing any measure with that end in view, and as they possessed an independent majority in the House of Commons they were under no necessity of placating Redmond and his followers: they went, however, so far as to introduce a Bill to establish an Irish Council having wide administrative functions but with no power to make laws or to control finance. This emasculated form of autonomy was referred by the Irish Party to a convention in Dublin which contemptuously flung it back in the Liberal government's face. As a contemporary parody of an old Irish patriotic song ran:

> *Is it this you call Home Rule?*
> *Says the Shan Van Vocht.*
> *Do you take me for a fool?*
> *Says the Shan Van Vocht.*
>
> *To be sending round the hat*
> *Five-and-twenty years for that*
> *Isn't good enough for Pat,*
> *Says the Shan Van Vocht.*
>
> *And the Lord-Lieutenant too,*
> *Says the Shan Van Vocht,*
> *Is he still to be on view?*
> *Says the Shan Van Vocht.*

> *And all them big police,*
> *Monumentally obese,*
> *Must I go on feeding these?*
> *Says the Shan Van Vocht.*

Nevertheless there was another Ireland – the Ireland of the future – coming into existence, and it was in more ways than one a reaction against Lords-Lieutenant, political action at Westminster, and all that these things implied. While the old Queen was still on the throne Arthur Griffith had started Sinn Fein and Douglas Hyde had founded the Gaelic League, and to them were turning the young people who felt themselves frustrated by the fact that Irish ambitions had so obviously become the plaything of English politicians. As for the parliamentary party,

> *Faith it's growing clear to me,*
> *Says the Shan Van Vocht,*
> *That ye like being absentee,*
> *Says the Shan Van Vocht.*

> *At Westminster to appear;*
> *On two hundred pounds a year;*
> *Ye'd have empty stomachs here,*
> *Says the Shan Van Vocht.*

> *All your promises were vain,*
> *Says the Shan Van Vocht.*
> *I'm turning to Sinn Fein,*
> *Says the Shan Van Vocht.*

Apart from a certain amount of cattle-driving there was a deceptive calm until the two General Elections of 1910 deprived Asquith of his independent majority in the House of Commons: if he wished to retain office it would now only be with the help of the Irish vote. After a slight hesitation the Liberals agreed to pay the price: the Parliament Act deprived the Lords of their veto, and the Third Home Rule Bill was duly introduced. It represented the last hope of survival for John Redmond and his followers: if their efforts did not secure autonomy Ireland would turn to Sinn Fein.

At once the Orangemen were up in arms, and all the old slogans of the eighties and nineties were trotted out again, 'Home Rule means

Rome Rule' being the most prominent, for there was no hesitation in appealing to sectarian prejudice. This went so far that I distinctly remember seeing carried in an Orange procession in Liverpool a large banner with a picture of the Pope on one side and of the Sultan of Turkey on the other with a caption 'Rather the Sultan than the Pope'. Two arguments in particular were stressed by the more extreme Protestants of the North in their opposition to Home Rule – one was that they were fighting on behalf of their co-religionists in the South and West of Ireland who would assuredly be persecuted under a Dublin government, and the other that they alone were loyal to the British Crown.

This agitation by no means failed of its purpose for a time, but in due course the British Government showed itself not unwilling to compromise by the exclusion from its Home Rule proposals of the six Ulster counties where there was a Protestant majority: this modification was duly accepted by those affected, and in due course resulted in the formation of Northern Ireland as we know it today. Whether it was even temporarily a satisfactory compromise must be a matter of individual opinion, but it made nonsense of the claim that the Protestants of the North had the interests of their co-religionists elsewhere at heart. This *volte face* has been neither forgotten nor forgiven by the old Unionists of the South and West, more particularly as they came to find that their immunity from persecution was due to the tolerance of their Republican rulers, not to the efforts of their self-styled champions north of the border.

As for the 'Loyal Ulster' claim, no doubt it was sincerely held by the vast majority of those who voiced it, and who, in consequence, unhappily turned the Union Jack into a party flag: but there were others who were more cynical. One day a year or two before the First World War my father and I were being entertained at the house of a prominent Ulsterman who was also an Irish Privy Councillor. Father asked him what his fellow-Ulstermen would do if Asquith's government used troops against them in an effort to enforce Home Rule. 'Appeal to the Kaiser for help,' came the reply. 'One William saved us, and so will another. A couple of good German divisions would go through the British Army like a knife through butter.' After we had left the house I expressed my surprise at the sentiments expressed, only to be told by my father, 'That's nothing: when I was at Wesley College in the sixties the boys from the North always talked about kicking the Queen's crown into the Boyne if the British Government did something Ulster didn't like.'

In those days I travelled with my parents a good deal in what is now Northern Ireland, and I think there is one fundamental difference in the general outlook then and now. In those days everyone was an Irishman first and an Ulsterman afterwards – today only the Catholics are. Not long before he died Carson confessed to me in the Carlton Club that he was worried at the course events were taking in the North, remarking, 'I fought to keep Ulster part of the United Kingdom, but Stormont is turning her into a second-class Dominion.'

Yet the Irish are, as President de Valera once remarked to me, essentially a conservative people, and it is not their fault that they have been driven to acquire revolutionary habits. By instinct an Irishman respects tradition as much as he dislikes authority, and it is the Englishman's insistence upon regarding both with equal affection that has much to do with the lack of understanding between the two races. Rarely has an English government made any appeal to Irish sentiment. Had Queen Victoria spent half the time in Ireland that she passed in Scotland the future of the British Isles might have been very different. Then came the fierce controversy over Home Rule when the extremists on both sides obscured the issue, and English politicians twisted it for their own ends; but, even so, one last chance of a peaceful settlement came with the First World War. That was wrecked by Lord Kitchener, an Irishman by birth but not by interest, first when he refused John Redmond's offer of the Irish Volunteers and then when he placed obstacles in the way of the formation of a distinctive Irish force: had circumstances permitted Lord Roberts to carry out his intention of coming to Ireland himself the results might easily have surpassed all expectations. It was not to be, and it is no use crying over spilt milk now, though I personally still feel that Arthur Griffith's solution was probably the ideal one.

Birrell, too, has a great deal for which to answer. Whether he was the right man to have been sent to Dublin as Chief Secretary in the first place is a moot point, but Campbell-Bannerman had little choice. Birrell, to give him his due, was not so sure of his own adequacy that he did not make several efforts to resign, and on one occasion the Chief Secretaryship was even offered to Winston Churchill – it is indeed an interesting speculation what would have been the future of Ireland and of Winston himself had he accepted the post. When Birrell first took office he was by no means blind to the changes that were taking place in Ireland, but in his later days as Chief Secretary he seems to have drifted out of touch with the facts of Irish life: after the outbreak of the First World War he spent increasingly less time in Ireland, and he was unquestionably taken by surprise by the events of Easter Week, 1916.

There can be no denying that the regime which it was his duty to uphold was characterized by a great deal of make-believe, and the centre of make-believe was the vice-regal court, for which, to give him his due, Birrell had very little use at all. Many of those who appeared at it were longer in the pedigree than in the pocket with the result that at official functions victuals of all kinds had a habit of disappearing into pockets and hand-bags for future consumption. So prevalent did thefts of this nature become at one time that the chickens at the buffet were secured to the dishes with elastic, and the story was told of one old dowager whose hand-bag shot back to the counter together with the bird which she was endeavouring to conceal in it.

Dr O'Broin in his recent biography of Birrell tells a story of a Chief Secretary (although he does not vouch that it relates to Birrell), his wife, and a lady friend spending a night in a Donegal hotel. When they started off on the following morning a crowd of people pushed into the hall to get a glimpse of the great man. One more inquisitive than the others asked the boots which of the two ladies was the Chief Secretary's wife. 'Well, thon's a question,' came the answer, 'A'm not rightly able to answer you, but all ah can tell you is that last night the Chief Secretary slept with the one in the red hat.'

It has always seemed to me a mistake to take a child abroad too young, for it receives no impressions of any value: in my opinion fifteen or sixteen is the right age to begin seeing the world. I was taken to Norway when I was five or six, where we spent a few days in Christiania, as Oslo was then called; after that we stayed up country at a place in the woods of which I have forgotten the name, and of which all I remember was being told that there were bears in the neighbourhood; then we moved to an island called Hanko in Christiania Fjord. Those were the days when Norway and Sweden were united in a dual monarchy; I was given a Norwegian flag with the Swedish colours in the corner. Some years later when I went with my parents to Paris, we returned to England – for some unknown reason – by way of St Malo and Jersey: all I remember of this trip is that some of the people in St Malo could only speak Breton; that at the Hotel Chateaubriand where we were staying all the guests sat at one long table; and that in Jersey there were thirteen pence to a shilling.

Not until the age of fifteen, when I was taken abroad regularly, did I derive advantage from the experience, though I little realized how soon the whole scene was to be changed. Talleyrand's observation that only those who had lived before the French Revolution knew how pleasant life could be could well be made with equal truth about the First World War, especially where travelling was concerned, for travelling then was a great deal more comfortable than it is today. In the very hot summer of 1911 we went to Russia by sea. We sailed from Grimsby to St Petersburg by way of Copenhagen, to visit Moscow and Nijni Novgorod. During the whole trip the daytime temperature rarely sank below ninety-five in the shade. Moscow was then a very provincial city, in which life moved extremely slowly; neither was it any too clean – though the Slaviansky Bazar where we stayed was free from bugs, the Hotel Metropole was not, as some friends who put up there sorrowfully informed us. The Kremlin was little more than one large museum.

In those days Russia and Turkey were the only countries in Europe for which passports were required, though what use they were I do not know, as one's photograph was not required to appear on them; anyhow I was very proud of mine in which Sir Edward Grey recommended me to the special care and protection of the Tsar of All the Russias. St Petersburg, compared with Moscow, was clean and very well laid out, but my chief recollection of our stay there was of a review of boy-scouts by the Tsar at which the Tsarevitch was present, although I was not very close to either of them. To what extent we were subject to police supervision I would not like to say, but one had to be very careful what use one made of a camera, especially in the case of any building outside which there was a sentry; but this could often be got round, if one had a Russian speaker in attendance, by offering to include the sentry in the photograph. It was extremely rare to come across anyone who could speak English, but in society and the hotels a sort of bastard French was spoken and understood. The general impression one received was that Russia was a fairly free-and-easy place so long as one kept clear of politics.

That was the summer of the Moroccan crisis, when the First World War was nearly anticipated by three years. An incident in connection with this crisis is impressed on my memory. Our boat, a British one, was proceeding from St Petersburg to Stockholm, when one scorching hot afternoon a Russian cruiser, her funnels belching the blackest of smoke, suddenly appeared over the horizon, signalled to us that war had broken out between Great Britain and Germany, and raced off for the shelter of the guns of Cronstadt. Our ship had no wireless, so we were compelled to await the progress of events with such patience as we could muster. It was therefore a definite relief when a German man-of-war, which hove in sight not long afterwards, displayed no interest in us. Of course in the civilized world of those days we never thought of internment or anything unpleasant of that nature; the worst we feared was some delay and inconvenience in our return home. Only cads like

Napoleon interfered with the comfort of British travellers on the Continent, and that was more than a century ago.

A week or two later the Burgomaster of Luebeck gave a lunch to my father at which my mother and I were present, and I think a good many of the lunchers wondered how much longer the toasts to Kaiser Wilhelm and King George V (both of which we duly honoured that day) would continue to appear on the same menu. It was on that occasion that I acquired the invaluable piece of information that for as long as I kept the lid of my beer mug up the mug would be duly replenished. The international tension was, however, never far from us that August, for as we came through the Kiel Canal our boat was held up for twelve hours to allow the German Fleet, less its heavier vessels, to pass from the Baltic into the North Sea. The battleships and the battle-cruisers still had to go round the north of Denmark, but the widening and deepening of the Kiel Canal was already proceeding apace, and the pundits declared that there would be no war until this work was completed. In other ways, too, that was a disturbed summer, for at home there had been the long drawn-out constitutional crisis, and when we landed at Grimsby it was to find the country in the grip of its first railway strike. A few days earlier there had been the violent scenes in Liverpool to which I have alluded on an earlier page.

In the following year, 1912, my mother had to undergo a cure at Marienbad, on which my father and I accompanied her. So far as I know no history has yet been written of the spa life of Europe, which had its origin in the reign of Louis XIV and to all intents and purposes died with the outbreak of the First World War. Its origins are obscure, but there can be little doubt that its demise was due to the ingenuity of the members of the medical profession, especially in England, who came to realize that it was much more profitable for them to put their patients on a diet at home under their immediate supervision than to send them abroad to some watering-place when the fee would have to be split with a foreign physician. The example, at any rate in the earlier years of the present century, was to no small extent set by King Edward VII, of whom the Duke of Windsor has written:

'King Edward would meanwhile repair to his favourite watering-place, Marienbad, in Bohemia, for his annual cure. There in the company of friends he would submit to a Spartan regime: drinking the waters, eating only boiled food, and walking off the effects of a year's fine living. Much reduced in girth, he would rejoin my grandmother at Balmoral, where, succumbing to the irresistible genius of his French chef, he would in about two weeks undo all the drastic and beneficial effects of the cure.'

What lasting purpose these cures at Continental watering-places served so far as those who took them were concerned is, indeed, a moot point. The regime, at least at Marienbad, was strict for those accustomed to the delights of upper-class life in the earlier years of the century. The first waters, and very nasty they were (though the connoisseurs in such matters declared that those of Carlsbad were even more unpleasant) had to be taken at eight, the second at twelve, and the third at six; as the springs were a mile apart this ensured that everyone walked a few miles a day, since any form of vehicular transport was frowned upon by the doctors. The mornings were spent in undergoing various forms of treatment, mostly repulsive, in which the application of mud-packs played no inconsiderable part. The afternoon was devoted to golf or driving, and by ten o'clock bed was very definitely indicated. The menu at all meals was of the plainest for those taking the cure (among whom my father and I were fortunately not numbered), which generally lasted three weeks.

Those cosmopolitan gatherings at Marienbad and other Continental spas served a political as well as a medical and social purpose, for they enabled the statesmen of Europe to meet and exchange views in an atmosphere of calm and relaxation. In three weeks quite a lot of business could be done in the most unostentatious manner – I myself distinctly remember seeing the Austrian Chancellor and the Turkish Grand Vizier chatting amicably over a glass of Marienbad waters at eight o'clock in the morning. It is true that today the world's leaders are continually meeting one another, but it is not quite the same thing; for they come together with the maximum amount of publicity in circumstances of considerable tension, and for two or three days at most, which is very different from the leisurely sojourning which characterized spa life in the days before the First World War.

King Edward VII, however, regarded his visit to Marienbad as relaxation, and he resented any interference on the score of official business. One year, however, Sir Edward Grey urged upon him the advisability of a meeting with the German Kaiser, who was very desirous of seeing him, to which the King reluctantly agreed, only insisting that it should be as informal as possible. It took place at a wayside station in Bavaria; but when the British royal train approached, the King observed, much to his annoyance, that not only were there what seemed to him to be an excessive number of troops present, but that his nephew was on the plat-

form wearing the full-dress uniform of the Royals of which he was honorary colonel. As King Edward descended from his carriage his delighted
suite heard the following exchange,

'Willie, you've got the wrong trousers on.'
'But Uncle, they're the ones Grandma sent me.'
'Possibly, but we've changed the width of the stripe since then.'

For the rest of the time that the two monarchs were together, so eye-
witnesses have averred, the Kaiser was clearly discomposed, which may
well have been the object of the original observation. This story, I may
add, rests on the authority of the late (third) Lord O'Hagan, who was a
lord-in-waiting to King Edward VII.

In those days the Marienbad golf course was a notable social centre,
much patronized by King Edward. He was dead by the time my mother
took her cure, but the golf club was still flourishing, and my father used
to play there with Lloyd George and T. P. O'Connor. The players were
cosmopolitan in the extreme, and there was a fine collection of dubious
Russian princes and Polish counts. The management of the club, however, was in local hands, for the committee consisted of Prince Trauttmansdorff as President; the Abbot of Tepel, whose monastery owned
Marienbad; the Burgomaster; two aldermen of the town; and two hotel-
keepers. There were probably more amusing *contretemps* on the links
than is usual at golf clubs. One day, for instance, a Russian nobleman
appeared with a mashie which had prongs like a hayfork, claiming that
with it anyone could easily play a ball in long grass as the prongs went
through the grass like a comb. Unfortunately for his theories, however,
on this occasion he had impaled his ball on one of the prongs, and the
question arose whether he should drop the ball with the penalty of one
stroke or just shake it off and go on playing. A crowd collected, and the
point was argued in all the leading languages of Europe: finally it was
settled with the disqualification of the Russian for using an illegal club.

Other places I visited in those days were Hamburg, Berlin, Vienna,
Budapest, and Leipzig, which last was *en fête* because the Kaiser and
the King of Saxony were about to unveil the monument to commemorate
the defeat of Napoleon a hundred years previously. Of the Austrian
capital my most distinct recollection is that of saluting the old Kaiser
Franz Josef as he returned from his morning ride in the Prater: there
were no guards or police escort, only an equerry a horselength behind.
How many heads of state today would care to show themselves in their
capital cities thus unprotected? As for Budapest, the difference between

it and the Vienna of those days was that between a *demi-mondaine* and a *grande dame*. Another holiday was spent in the Engadine, but that was somewhat prolonged as my mother developed appendicitis in the train, so to be nearer to the hospital my father and I moved from Pontresina to Samaden, but this had its compensations for at the Hotel Bernina I met Bergson, who was to the youth of that generation what T. S. Eliot was to be to a later one, while my father played golf with the Grand Duke Nicholas of Russia at St Moritz. In the summer of 1914 we had our passages booked for the United States, but the Peloponnesian War of Europe intervened, and it was many years before I set foot in the New World.

CHAPTER III

The First World War

THE outbreak of the First World War found me at the age of eighteen still residing with my parents in Liverpool, being educated by a tutor, and about to go up to Oxford. After vainly trying to get into the Army and being rejected because of my sight, I went into residence at Corpus Christi College and remained there for twelve months. By the autumn of 1915 the military authorities were not so particular, and as I had had a year's training in the Oxford University Officers' Training Corps I was given a commission in the Royal Garrison Artillery. Those were the days when the Royal Regiment was divided into Horse, Field, and Garrison, 'yet', as the parody of the Athanasian Creed went, 'there were not three Artilleries, but one Artillery'. The R.G.A. had had a good deal of fun poked at it before the war, and horse and field gunners were wont to say that 'its guns were always in oil, its men in beer, and its officers on leave'. When war came, however, it showed itself the equal of the other three branches of the Royal Regiment, for if the Navy were to render coast-defence work a sinecure for the soldier, there were siege, heavy, and anti-aircraft batteries to be provided, and all these were manned by the R.G.A.

I was posted to Tynemouth, and a very bleak spot it was in winter. My quarter was in the castle, which had been built by William Rufus, and which appeared to have remained unchanged since his time. The first night I was there my window blew in. Sometimes the wind was so strong that a rope had to be stretched across the barrack square to enable the men to get from one side to the other, and on more than one occasion a parade had to be dismissed because it was impossible to preserve any sort of formation. Nevertheless such discomforts were amply compen-

34

sated for by the unfailing kindness of the people of Northumberland at
all social levels, and by the beauty of the scenery on the upper Tyne.
After I had been some months at Tynemouth the medical authorities
decided that my sight was not good enough to allow me to be sent
overseas, so the military powers-that-be somewhat paradoxically decided
that I should go to anti-aircraft. Accordingly, I was sent for a course to
Shoeburyness, where I remained for a month, and at the end of this
period I was sent to gun stations at, successively, Halifax, Rugby, and
Banbury. While I was at Shoeburyness the Easter Rising took place in
Dublin, but those of us who had relatives in Ireland were allowed to
opt out of service there.

My men were mostly Reservists from Cork and Kerry, and my feelings on first taking command of them was something akin to those of
Parnesius, in Kipling's *Puck of Pook's Hill*, when he led his detach-
ment out of Anderida. Although my own Irish background soon enabled
us to understand one another and mostly all went well, in a typical
English countryside there were, all the same, some awkward moments.
Christmas 1916 found us outside Rugby at Clifton-on-Dunsmore, where
the local inhabitants got up a concert for us. The day before it was due
to take place the sergeant-major asked me whether the National Anthem
was going to be sung; on my replying that this would certainly be the
case he told me that the men would refuse to sing it. No ordinary argument would have been of the least avail, so I decided to appeal to the
innate courtesy of the Irish. When I had all the men collected in the
barrack-room I asked them if they would join in 'God Save the King'
out of compliment to their English hosts if 'The Wearing of the Green'
was also sung, and I put it to them on these lines, never mentioning
politics at all. To a man they said they would, and so it was settled,
after I had perjured myself by assuring those who were arranging the
concert that far from having a political significance 'The Wearing of the
Green', of which they had fortunately never heard, was just a sentimental
tune which would remind the men of home.

In those days anti-aircraft was still very much in its infancy, and the
enemy was the Zeppelin rather than the aeroplane. At Shoeburyness we
were trained on a variety of guns, both fixed and mobile, and there
were not a few accidents owing to the different lengths of the recoil,
which varied from 45 inches in the case of the 13-pounder to 11 inches
in that of the 3-inch naval gun. All these guns were converted, and
many of them left a good deal to be desired. For nearly a year I had a
6-pounder Nordenfeldt, which I am glad to say I never had a chance
to fire. The only time a Zeppelin came within range we had no ammuni-

tion and were constrained to admire her beauty in the moonlight; perhaps, however, the lack of shells did not matter so much as we imagined at the time, for when they did arrive they were filled with nothing more deadly than salt. Indeed, the position of many gun stations seemed to be dictated by political rather than military considerations. Lack of ammunition was the rule rather than the exception, but all the same officers and men had to pretend that the guns were ready for action, presumably to impress the civilian population, and each night we were compelled to stand by as if we were in a position to open fire. It was a sorry and somewhat demoralizing piece of make-believe.

What made anti-aircraft so onerous was not the amount of work there was to do but the necessity of being at call or short notice, as they say in the City. For twelve months I had no other officer with me and no leave at all; once a week I was allowed to be away from the gun station for three hours, but the rest of the time I had to be within ten minutes' reach by day, while by night it was forbidden to leave the compound. The men were in no better plight: they got one late pass every ten days or fortnight, though in defiance of the regulations I used to allow those on duty to go one at a time to the village pub for a 'quick one'.

To those of use at home the war seemed a distant affair, and we had our daily routine. While I was at Clifton the Lord of the Manor and his wife, Dr and Mrs Townsend, very kindly gave me the run of their library, which was an extensive one, and I read widely, while during my few hours off duty each week I roamed the countryside on horseback: once or twice I even managed to go out with the Pytchley, but I was soon convinced that my sight was not good enough for serious hunting. The men had little to do off parade, and they were often profoundly bored. The war seemed to have been always going on, and there appeared no likelihood that it would ever cease. We were mere pieces in a game, moved about the board for no apparent reason. No initiative of any sort was required of us, and the result was that the most important events made little impression upon minds which were half atrophied. The only occurrence that I remember stirring me personally from my general indifference was the Russian Revolution, which I profoundly mistrusted.

One other incident from those rather dull and uneventful days which sticks in my memory occurred on Easter Sunday, 1917. I was then on a gun-station a mile or two outside Banbury with two other officers and about fifty other ranks. Just as we were falling in for Church parade we got a message to say that Hindenburg had landed near Scarborough with 70,000 men. But the effect of this news was complete anti-climax, for no one was in the least perturbed: Scarborough is a long way from Banbury, the Fleet would come down from Scapa and interfere with the German landing, and it would take a long time to get the horses ashore – these were the immediate reactions of us all. Nor was it only in rural Oxfordshire that the tidings of the German invasion were received calmly, for although the Guards were confined to barracks for three nights Lady Cynthia Asquith has told us in her *Diaries, 1915–1918* that she was far more interested in what she calls 'Russian gossip talk' at 'a very nice little party'. Years afterwards, in the Second World War, the officer commanding at The Verne on Portland showed me the identical message which his predecessor had received on that occasion, but attached to it was the further information that the Navy at Scapa would be unable to interfere seriously with Hindenburg's operations for seventy-two hours. This would seem to have been one of those occasions when ignorance was bliss, for had we known the full facts we would not have taken the news so lightly. Anyhow, by the time we returned from Church parade we were informed that the alarm was false, but as evidence of the differences in the general attitude towards the First and Second World Wars respectively it is difficult to believe that on the latter occasion a similar scare would have been treated so lightly.

It was in that same spring of 1917 that an event occurred which was to have a very important bearing on my subsequent career. The Conde de Romanones, the Prime Minister of Spain, was strongly pro-Ally, and the British Government came to the conclusion that he was going to follow the example of President Wilson and bring his country into the war, which would have been uncommonly useful as the sinkings by submarines were at their height and Spanish troops could have been brought overland to the Western Front. Accordingly, one day at Banbury we received orders to send in a return of all officers who could speak Spanish. I knew a few words, so I sent in my name, and then rushed off to Blackwell's in Oxford for a phrase-book, from which I proceeded to acquire some sentences of the-pen-of-my-aunt-is-in-the-garden type. In due course orders came for me to report at a certain room at the War Office for an interview. When I got there I was cross-examined by a general and a civilian, but not a word was said to me about Spain or Spanish; I was asked if I could ride a horse and told to translate aloud the opening lines of the second book of the *Iliad*. I then went back to Banbury, and a week or two afterwards was told to report at King's College, Strand, for a three months' course of Spanish.

I had always been interested in foreign affairs, and Spain had a special attraction for me, but my selection for this course definitely decided my vocation. There were about twenty-five of us, drawn from all arms of the Service, and no instruction could have been more thorough than that which we received from Señores Villasante and Plá, the latter a retired officer of the Spanish Marines, and the best company in the world. We were taught not only the language but also the literature, history, and customs of the country, presumably with the idea of fitting us to become liaison officers should Spain join the Allies. I write 'presumably' because neither then nor at any other time were we told why we had been sent on the course.

I took up my quarters at Bailey's Hotel in Gloucester Road, and thoroughly enjoyed my three months in London. The spring of 1917 was late, but May and June were exceptionally good months, though the rain came when the British Expeditionary Forces took the offensive in Flanders in July. Those were the days of the daylight air-raids on London. During the one on 7 July I was riding in the Row, and somewhat optimistically pulled up under a tree until the enemy had passed. Of my colleagues on the course my chief friend was Crichton-Browne, of the King's Own Scottish Borderers; he and I tied for the first place in the examination, but he was killed not long afterwards. As soon as the course was over we were all returned to duty, and not a word did any of us ever hear on the subject of it again. It is true that Spain did not enter the war, but one would have thought that somewhere in the Government Service use might have been made of men who had been trained with so much care and at such expense.

Autumn found me back on anti-aircraft on the outer defences of London at Much Hadham in Hertfordshire, where poor Arnold Wilson afterwards lived. The raids during the summer had galvanized the authorities into action, and the whole of the A.A. (anti-aircraft) services were on a much more business-like footing than had been the case earlier in the war. To the command of the London defences had been appointed Major-General E. B. Ashmore, who years later was to help me with the British-Italian Luncheon Club in the early days of Grandi's embassy. From the very beginning he inspired confidence, and proper measures of defence were soon taken. The Zeppelin was being defeated with comparative ease, though its real Waterloo did not come until this same autumn, when of eleven airships that flew over on one raid only four returned safely to Germany. It was clear that no country could stand losses at that rate. The aeroplane was another matter. At Much Hadham we had two of the then new 3-inch guns, and during the moonlight raids at the end of September 1917 we were in action nearly every evening. It was a curious change to be having tea at Rumpelmeyers at five in a relatively carefree London and to be in the middle of a battle only twenty-five miles away three hours later.

It was rarely that we could see our target, and mostly we were employed on barrage work, when we used to fire something like thirty rounds a minute from each gun. Anything up to two hundred rounds a gun an evening was the usual procedure. Of course height and direction were in those days largely a matter of guesswork, but we managed to keep the enemy up to over ten thousand feet, and in the First World War accurate bombing at that height was impossible. One night a German plane shut off its engines, glided under the barrage, and machine-gunned us. At first we thought the patter of bullets on the fallen leaves betokened a thunderstorm, but we were soon undeceived. We had no tin hats; but fortunately the enemy did not persist in his attack, and our only casualty was one man slightly wounded in the arm.

As will have been gathered, while I was on anti-aircraft I moved about England a good deal. The countryside during the First World War was very much more like what it must have been in the eighties or nineties than what it was to be during the next conflict. The private motor-car was never seen, but that was no great hardship since the horse was very far from having been driven from the roads by August 1914. For instance, I remember once having to go to Chelmsford at very short notice from a camp near Chipping Ongar. The only way to do this was to hire a dog cart, which I did without difficulty and drove myself over. It now seems passing strange to be living in the space age, having at one time driven into the yard of the Saracen's Head at Chelmsford and called for the ostler to take my horse. Official cars there were in plenty for the staff, but the ordinary regimental officer had to get across country as best he could, using horses, bicycles, the slowest of trains, and his own feet in the process. It was often a nuisance at the time, but one realizes now that one was seeing the last of Victorian England, the England of Trollope and Whyte-Melville.

Save in a few of the larger centres of population the war seemed far away. Men still went to it in the way they had done for generations, and even the introduction of compulsory military service had not brought the conflict home to the ordinary man and woman in the way that the threat of invasion had done in Napoleon's time. The air-raids were on too small a scale to affect the mass of the people, while the victory of the Marne seemed to have removed any possibility of defeat almost before it had been realized that the country was at war. It was not until the great German offensive of 21 March 1918 that feelings akin to those of the next war began to be aroused, but from that date until the Armistice every man, woman, and child had his or her eyes glued upon events across the Channel.

The autumn of 1917 saw me away at last from anti-aircraft, for which my poor sight had never really fitted me, and at a desk in the R.G.A. (Royal Garrison Artillery) Record Office at Dover. The office was on the seafront, and as I lived in the castle I got plenty of exercise walking to and from my work four times a day. My quarter, which I shared with another subaltern, looked out over the Channel, but use of the bathrooms, which were in short supply anyway, was forbidden to those below field rank, so we junior officers had to be content with a tin bath in our quarter. The Mess was a pleasant enough place, though this was in no way due to the C.R.A. (Commander, Royal Artillery), a Lieutenant-Colonel Breakey, who was a very unpleasant piece of work indeed, and whose only pleasure in life appeared to be to make it intolerable for the subalterns. His knowledge of human nature, too, left a great deal to be desired. On one occasion, for instance, he came to the conclusion that too much whisky was being consumed, which, as far as some half-dozen officers were concerned, was true. Accordingly he gave orders that no officer was to have more than two doubles a day. The only result, however, was that the consumers of whisky drank more than ever, for they 'borrowed' the two doubles from those – the vast majority – who did not drink whisky, and settled up when the mess bill came in. Such is often the fate of ill-conceived sumptuary legislation. From time to time, I may add, the scene was enlivened by bombs from the air or shells from the sea, though not to anything like the extent that was to be the case in the next war, and there was always the distant thunder of the guns in France.

The officer in charge of Records was Lieutenant-Colonel Tremaine, who was in marked contrast to Colonel Breakey in every way, and one of whom all who served under him can have only the most pleasant memories. He had a house at Folkestone, to which one of us subalterns would be invited every weekend, and a very welcome change this was after a week in the garrison town of Dover. He also possessed an equally charming wife and daughter. It was under his roof that I met Lady Irving, the widow of the great actor, whom, so the story goes, her husband always had excluded from the theatre when he was playing. (If the story is true all my sympathies are with Sir Henry judging from what I saw of his widow.) Colonel Tremaine was very strict in all matters connected with the work of the office, but he was reasonable in the granting of leave. As we did not work on Saturday afternoons or Sundays it was always possible, without any dereliction of duty, to go up to London at mid-day on Saturday and to return the next night, so that Dover had other advantages in addition to the society to be found in the town itself and in the neighbourhood. Getting about locally was certainly a difficulty, but I was lucky enough to make the acquaintance in the Mess of the A.D.C. to an Infantry Brigadier-General. In those days Brigadier-Generals had horses, and as this particular one liked as quiet a mount as possible, I was allowed to ride it at all times when the General was not requiring it, which was never if he could possibly avoid it.

My experience in a big Mess like that at Dover led me to the conclusion that, at any rate at home, there was less camaraderie in the First World War than there was to be in its successor, nor is this surprising in view of the fact that English society as a whole was much more formal in 1914 than it became as a result of the struggle against Hohenzollern Germany. The senior officers in the main were very stiff towards their juniors, who, if they were only serving 'for the duration', were given the impression that try as they might they would never become soldiers in any real sense. The 'spit-and-polish' brigade were firmly entrenched in the seats of the mighty, and those who had not been in the Army before the war were too often regarded as 'temporary gentlemen', irrespective of their personal character and social background. This has always been my impression, and it was confirmed in the autumn of 1940 when I was lecturing to the Australians on Salisbury Plain, for those who had fought in the First World War all commented on the increased friendliness among both soldiers and civilians. A good many of the pre-1914 regular officers, never having seen a shot fired in anger, as the saying goes, were inclined to regard the Army as their own special preserve from which intruders should be barred, or, if this was impossible, admitted only on sufferance. The dividing line between Regulars, Special Reservists, Territorials, and New Army also strengthened the centrifugal influences in military circles.

In the spring of 1918 I was, to my great satisfaction, attached to the Historical Section of the War Cabinet, of which the offices, long since pulled down, were in Whitehall Gardens. They constituted a veritable rabbit warren, for they spread over several large houses, and all the time I was there the only part of the labyrinth with which I was thoroughly acquainted was the way from the entrance to the room in which I worked. My immediate colleagues in the Historical Section, to give them the rank they then held, were Lieutenant-Colonel the Hon. E. I. D. Gordon of the Royal Scots Fusiliers (my great-great-grandfather's regiment); Captain E. C. Lentaigne of the Gurkhas; and Captain

FitzM. Stacke of the Worcesters. A great many people came in and out of the office, among them some, such as Austen Chamberlain and Leo Amery, whom I was to know better in after years. We were generally regarded by politicians and soldiers alike as an encyclopaedia on all that had hitherto happened in the war, and our main job was to keep such information up-to-date. Gordon always impressed me as seeming to know everybody and everything, while Stacke, in addition to being a very gallant fighting soldier, was a repository of knowledge on all that related to military history or heraldry: he could give the battle-honours of any regiment in the leading armies of the world, and he took a positive delight in blazoning the most complicated coat-of-arms.

The last-joined member of the Historical Section was made responsible for what were known in the office as the three Beasts – Black, Pink, and Red. The Black Beast contained the minutes of earlier War Committee meetings, while the Pink and Red Beasts were fortnightly publications giving the disposition of troops at home and abroad respectively. All three were highly confidential. They were kept in a most imposing safe, of which the key was locked in a smaller safe; the key of the second safe was kept in a drawer, of which the key in its turn was placed each evening in an ornament on the mantelpiece, because, as the custodian was brightly informed, 'The Hun will never think of looking for it there. He'll think you've got it on you, so that he may cut your throat when you're in bed, but he won't find the key.' There were also secret papers, respectively termed P. and W.C., for which the same luckless officer was responsible; they were private and War Council papers.

Once during my time at Whitehall Gardens I saw the 'Purple Emperor' himself, namely Lord Curzon, then Lord President of the Council. Hankey had told me to take some highly confidential documents to the Persia Committee over which Curzon was presiding, but not to let them out of my sight, and to come back with them when they were no longer required. I did as I was bidden, but although I had to remain in the room for an hour Curzon never had the courtesy to offer me a chair. It is to be feared that such treatment of those whom he considered to be his inferiors was typical, not exceptional, and it explains his widespread unpopularity. Very different was the behaviour of Trenchard, to whom Hankey sent me on a similar mission at about the same time. The great airman was then in command of the Independent Air Force at Nancy, but he had come to London for consultation, and was staying at his flat at the bottom of St James's Street. As soon as he had glanced at the documents he said, 'This will take at least half-an-hour. There's whisky on the side-board, and here's an evening paper, so make yourself comfortable while you're waiting.' When he had finished we had a chat, during the course of which I remember he said of Americans, 'Before the war I didn't care much for them personally, I admired their powers of organization and I respected their foreign policy; as a result of having them under me I like them personally very much, I have a low view of their powers of organization and I profoundly mistrust their foreign policy.'

Of course, the whole idea of Cabinet minutes and a Cabinet secretariat was new in those days, and for the form in which I encountered it Lloyd George was responsible when he displaced Asquith in 1916: nevertheless there were precedents of sorts for the minutes. George III chose his own Cabinet during most of the earlier part of his reign but that body had no right to meet as a Cabinet and to tender advice to him, except at his request and by his authority. George laid this down in writing in 1782 in a document which still exists, and his ruling was accepted without demur. He used to say to his Cabinet, 'Here is such and such a question. Meet, and tell me what you think,' or they said, 'May we meet?' In times of crisis they might go so far as to say, 'We have summoned a meeting; please sanction it.' Having met, the Cabinet submitted its opinion in the form of a minute of Cabinet, which began with a list of the members present, place (as often as not a private house), and time, and then proceeded to the resolution. Such minutes were drawn up by the Minister for the Department concerned, sometimes so hastily that words were omitted, sometimes ungrammatically and almost illegibly. In consequence the only person who had a file of these minutes was the King, to whom alone were copies sent. When, in the nineteenth century, the choice of the Cabinet was for all practical purposes transferred from the Crown to Parliament, and the Sovereign was excluded from all share in administrative business, there was no further need for minutes, and the practice lapsed, only to be revived in different circumstances and in a different form during the First World War.

What is often forgotten about the war is how, in contrast to its successor, it ended so unexpectedly. In the middle of July 1918 the Central Powers were spread all over the map; Russia and Romania were out of the fight, and the Allies were everywhere on the defensive. Yet by the middle of November the Allied troops were in Cologne and Austria-Hungary had ceased to exist. We know now that Ludendorff had prophesied disaster at the beginning of the war, but all we saw then were the apparently invincible German armies flushed with the series of offensives which had begun in March. When a secret report came into the office to the effect that the apparent might of Germany was a mere façade, behind which was a growing chaos and despair, we dismissed it as what a later generation would have called wishful thinking, for the wish seemed father not merely to the thought, but to its whole ancestry.

Even when Turkey and Bulgaria had collapsed, the belief of those best qualified to express an opinion was that the war would last well into 1919, and men talked gloomily of the Germans desperately defending every hill, river, and town all the way back to Berlin. There had been so many disappointments and disillusionments that we no longer dared to hope, and it was not until the middle of October that we became convinced that the great military machine, which had been the wonder and terror of Europe for nearly fifty years, was really on the verge of collapse.

Such being the case I settled down at the War Cabinet Office in the expectation of remaining there for a year or two. I was elected to the Oxford and Cambridge Club, and I took a furnished flat at 28 Alexandra Court, Queen's Gate, S.W.7, consisting of a bedroom, sitting-room, and bathroom at a rent of four-and-a-half guineas a week. One of my more interesting jobs at the office was to keep track of the various German divisions and to follow any changes in their composition; where the information came from I was not told, but from inside the Reich it was not easy to obtain. (Apparently while Russia was in the war this presented no such problem as the British secret service was largely dependent upon the Russian which was kept remarkably well posted as to what went on in Germany itself.)

While looking through some old files I came across an instance of misapplied military information which might have had the most serious consequences, and which was eloquent of the danger of jumping to conclusions. On a desolate part of the Salonika front a British airman spotted a squadron of German cavalry which he machine-gunned. He was subsequently able to land and identify them from a corpse as the 23rd German Dragoons, a fact which he duly reported to his own headquarters. There the unit was found to belong to the 3rd German Cavalry Division, and this piece of information was added to the message; at Corps, however, the name '23rd Dragoons' was omitted by some bright staff officer as being of no particular importance, and by the time the message reached G.H.Q. it was to the effect that the 3rd German Cavalry Division had been located on the Salonika front. At once all was confusion, as it was naturally assumed that this presaged a big German offensive. The telegraph wires to Whitehall buzzed; Haig was asked if he could spare the cavalry from France, but he replied that he could not—then it occurred to someone to see if the Russian C.-in-C., the Grand Duke Nicholas, could throw any light on the matter. Back came the message that on the date in question the 3rd German Cavalry Division was near Kiev, less the 23rd Dragoons which was acting as divisional cavalry to a Landsturm division which had been in the Balkans for the past six months.

Another of my chores was to keep in touch with the Italian and Serbian military missions and with the Russian exiles, whose headquarters were at Whitehall Court. There was a spaciousness about the Russians which the Italians and Serbs lacked, but they were much more difficult to deal with, for they themselves did not know what they wanted, whereas the others knew only too well.

There were many disillusionments to be experienced by a young man at the War Cabinet Office in those days, and some of the worst were contained in a box file labelled *The War Aims of the Allies.* One evening when we were on late duty with nothing much to do, Stacke and I got this file out, took a few blank maps, and set about tracing on them those war aims. We had not gone very far before we discovered that vast areas, particularly in the Near and Middle East, had been promised to at least two separate Powers, so we put the cards back in their box, tore up the maps and returned to our work, sadder, if wiser, men.

This was my second experience of wartime London, and there can be no doubt that the lot of the capital in the First World War was far happier than it was to be in the Second, during which I also had to spend a good deal of time there. Air-raids did occur, it is true, but they were relatively insignificant: the difficulty was to find accommodation of any sort. Money was flowing into London from all over the kingdom, and civil servants, far from being evacuated to Blackpool, were being recruited from the provinces to staff the new Government Departments which came into being owing to the needs of the war or the whims of Lloyd George. Even the lake in St James's Park was drained, and huts erected in its bed, to house them. Indeed, the period of the First World War is one of the most important in the recent history of the capital, for the pressure lasted not only throughout the conflict, but continued after its conclusion. This was partly owing to the short-lived boom, but chiefly because large numbers of demobilized officers and men, regarding London as the best centre from which to re-enter civil life, decided to remain there. The capital, too, largely escaped the subsequent slump, and it did not begin visibly to be affected by the international situation until the Munich crisis.

In the period of which I am writing the chief centres of attraction for the officer off duty or on leave were the Berkeley, Hatchett's, and the

Piccadilly Grill. It was the heyday of the revues, and of those that stick in the memory the best known were *The Bing Boys* (with George Robey and Violet Loraine), *Theodore and Co.*, and *Cheap*. Also there was always *Chu Chin Chow*. To London there flocked in their tens of thousands not only soldiers on leave but their relatives and friends, and never can any city have been so thronged with men and women solely intent on enjoying themselves as was the English capital during the First World War.

Naturally I came in contact with a number of very interesting people, often through my colleague Gordon, who seemed to know everything and everybody. One of those to whom he introduced me was John Buchan, then Director of Information, of whom more anon; another was Denys Reitz, son of the State Secretary of the Orange Free State and himself the author of that delightful book *Commando*. It was through Gordon, too, that I met Lord Swinton, then Philip Lloyd-Greame, the possessor of as pretty a wit as is to be found in these degenerate days, and one that has improved with keeping. In addition to meeting interesting people I also saw some interesting documents: one was a Treasury memorandum on the general subject of war finance in which occurred the words, 'in the case of an offensive war, such as the South African War', on which Austen Chamberlain, then Chancellor of the Exchequer, had minuted, 'Possibly, but you should not say so to my father's son'. Another was a memorandum by Lloyd George himself, on which King George V had written in the margin, 'Isn't this waving the Union Jack a bit too much?'

As September passed into October and it became clear that the collapse of Germany was imminent, the one subject of conversation in Whitehall was what sort of peace we were likely to have. Although those of us who worked at the War Cabinet Office had naturally more idea of the real situation than had the general public, even we imagined that the Government had some plan for a final settlement other than the above-mentioned contradictory promises that had been made to various allies. In these circumstances it is hardly surprising that we should have been wildly out in our forecasts. Also, until a few days before the Armistice, it was never anticipated that there would be an internal revolution of any magnitude in Germany. What was expected was that the Kaiser would be forced to agree to a much more democratic constitution which would bring the army under the control of the Reichstag and that the influence of Prussia in the Reich would be greatly weakened. Perhaps had these modest expectations been fulfilled, the future of Europe might have been happier.

What none of us anticipated was that the Allies, in opposition to their own interests, would carry the work of Bismarck to its logical conclusion and complete the unification of Germany, thereby paving the way for Hitler and the Third Reich. The strongest centrifugal force lay in the dynasties which ruled the various kingdoms and duchies, and which were always restive under the tutelage of Berlin. Yet the German people were deliberately encouraged to overthrow their ruling houses, to many of which they were deeply attached, as the price of peace; the last obstacle to a unified Reich was thus removed by those concerned in its retention. Once the dynasties had gone there was no reason for the continued existence of their former dominions as separate units, and so the path was cleared for that complete Prussianization of Germany which was to be the outstanding accomplishment of the Nazi regime.

Few voices were raised at the time against this mistaken policy, but now that more than fifty years have elapsed it is difficult to disagree with the late Jacques Bainville that the Allies lost the war in the first clause of the peace treaty, in that the settlement should not have been made with Germany as a whole, but rather that there should have been separate treaties with Prussia, Bavaria, Saxony, and the other states which had composed the Hohenzollern Empire. Unhappily the French were so determined to reverse the verdict of 1870 that they forgot this in its turn had been rendered possible only by the victory of Prussia over Austria four years before, while the British Government does not appear to have thought about the matter at all, having drifted into peace almost as inconsequently as it had drifted into war.

With the arrival of November events began to move so fast that their effect was numbing. The Kaiser's flight into Holland was the only incident of itself to strike the imagination, for it seemed inconceivable until it had happened, since at that time we knew nothing of the drama that had been enacted at Spa. For the rest one heard, almost without grasping its significance, the daily list of places captured by the advancing Allies – places that only a week or two before seemed outside the scope of any possible offensive until the following year at the earliest. Those of us who knew what was going on behind the scenes were horrified at the discourteous treatment meted out by the French to the German delegates negotiating the Armistice, and I would certainly have been astonished to have been told that one of them, the Graf von Oberndorff, was to be the grandfather of my daughter-in-law in years to come. Then the rumour began to go round that if the Germans delayed signing the Armistice preparations had been made for the bombing of Berlin, for that city had hitherto been too remote a target

for the aeroplanes of those days, and such was the prevailing climate of
public opinion that most people hoped this would take place.

The actual events of 11 November 1918 must always remain fresh in
the memory of any who were in London at that time. The day began in
the normal way, and people went to their work as usual. As eleven
o'clock approached it was as if the population of the capital were coming
out of a trance – a trance that had lasted for more than four years. The
war was nearly over: in a few minutes the last shot would have been
fired. The moment for which millions had been waiting, and which had
been so long delayed that they had almost ceased to hope for it, had
arrived. Soon all pretence at work was abandoned, and in the West End
a great crowd surged into Downing Street to salute Lloyd George. The
Prime Minister duly appeared and said a few words, chiefly to the effect
that the time had come to relax: after this there was a stampede to
Buckingham Palace, where the crowd cheered itself hoarse. Thus ended
what we now know to have been the Peloponnesian War of modern
Europe.

After these relatively orderly proceedings the scene was soon transformed into something reminiscent of the Roman Saturnalia. In the
main streets wheeled traffic eventually became impossible, but before
this was the case taxis by the dozen were carrying excited patriots on
their roofs up and down Piccadilly and the Strand, while East of Temple
Bar the normally staid magnates of the City were dancing on the tables
in the restaurants. By one o'clock it was only with the greatest difficulty
that one could get a drink anywhere, and as the afternoon progressed
the disorder grew worse. The King and Queen received an ovation as
they drove through the packed streets. Older people recalled Mafeking
night. The lights were on again, and that itself was an inducement to
come into the streets. In Trafalgar Square a huge bonfire was started
at the foot of the Nelson Column, and was fed with the notice-boards
from the buses. An old gentleman asked a policeman the quickest way
to Charing Cross Hospital. 'Call for three cheers for the Kaiser,' was the
immediate reply. I went to the Savoy that evening, and the first thing I
saw was a girl in evening dress being sick in the gutter in Savoy Court;
no one minded or appeared to think it odd. Inside the hotel a number of
young officers were trying to burn a German flag in spite of the protests
of the management. As I was going home on the District Railway, a
rather drunken workman got into the carriage and kept on repeating,
'We've won the bloody war, but we'll lose the bloody peace. You see if
we don't'. *In vino veritas?*

CHAPTER IV

Oxford

SOON after the Armistice I was asked to stay on at the War Cabinet Office for a couple of years at quite a good salary, and at first I was attracted by the proposition, but my father strongly urged me against it. He pointed out that by the time the two years had come to an end everybody else would have settled down, that the job would be dead-end, and that it would be much better to go back to Oxford and take my degree. The more I reflected on the matter the sounder the advice seemed, so I duly took it.

I did stay on until Easter 1919, but the immediate post-war period of London was depressing in the extreme. For two or three nights after the Armistice the authorities had very wisely tolerated the rowdyism mentioned in the previous chapter, and then it was stopped. After that there was a reaction, and people began to wonder just what the victory really meant. There were some major excitements such as the surrender of the German Fleet at Scapa Flow, which I should have witnessed but for an inopportune attack of measles, and the visit to London of Foch and Clemenceau; and one or two minor ones such as the General Election, in which, however, no one took much interest. The war was over, and the one desire of officers and men alike was to get back to civil life. Few stopped to realize that there was no magician's wand to put everything back where it was in July 1914 and the Government, with slogans such as 'A Land fit for heroes to live in', did nothing to dispel the illusion that the golden age was at hand. No hint was ever dropped in official circles that the period of adjustment after the war was likely to be as difficult to win through as the war itself had been. People were definitely encouraged to

49

believe that without any effort on their part all would soon be for the best of all possible worlds.

The first disillusionment came when it was discovered that there was a shortage of everything required for a quick return to normal conditions. Houses and flats in the more fashionable parts of London were only to be had on payment of a colossal premium, while houses for the working classes just did not exist in anything like sufficient quantity to meet the demand. Those were the days when men used to jump on the running-board of one's car in a traffic block and ask what one would take for the vehicle. Coal supplies had fallen off badly; retailers had, at the best, only 75 per cent of their normal supplies, and in fact had very often less than that, while gas and electric light supplies were compelled to work on heavily curtailed stocks of fuel. When the crowds had cheered first the French leaders, then Haig and his generals, and lastly President Wilson, they went home to face a New Year that promised little but threatened much.

The fact was that the Government, both at home and abroad, was as unprepared for peace in 1918 as it had been for war in 1914, and it was heart-rending to see the rapid dissipation of all those centripetal forces that had contributed so much to the winning of the war. In their place grew up a spirit of envy and malice, an attitude of every man for himself, which foreboded ill for the future, and which characterized every class of the community. Demobilization bases in France grew increasingly difficult to handle, even when they did not break out into actual disorder, while at home there were riots in more than one camp.

There were demonstrations of troops outside the War Office, and one morning as I was crossing the Horse Guards Parade on my way to Whitehall Gardens I found it thronged with mutinous soldiers from Osterley. With both sets of gates at the Horse Guards closed to prevent the mutineers from joining the demonstrators in Whitehall, for a time the situation looked very ugly indeed, as revolution of the most violent type was everywhere the order of the day. There were even rumours that the Guards themselves could not be relied upon, and to those of us who knew of the behaviour of *corps d'élite* on similar occasions – that of the Gardes Françaises in the French Revolution and of the Preobrazhensky Guards in the Russian – this did not seem impossible, but when a company was brought up to overawe the rioters these stories happily proved unfounded. It was as unpleasant an incident as I have ever witnessed. Elsewhere things were worse: when the Canadians mutinied in Kinmel Park order was not restored until five men had been killed and over twenty injured, while in the industrial world there were numerous strikes. Such was the world which at enormous cost had been made safe for democracy.

In consequence of the war my Oxford career was thus considerably prolonged, for although I first went up in October 1914 I did not come down until June 1920, so that I was in residence with what would in normal circumstances have been several generations. Indeed, some of my best friends, such as Ralph Clitheroe, are much younger than I am, which is a great blessing, for one of the tragedies of being a man in the middle seventies today is that one has so few contemporaries – they lie in their graves in Gallipoli or on the Somme. Every other man on my staircase in Gentlemen Commoners when I first went up to Corpus was killed, and of the other members of the college at that time very few are still alive. In quality, owing to the delay in introducing compulsory military service, it has always been my belief that Great Britain suffered more in the First World War than did any of the other belligerents.

Before that war Corpus normally had some eighty men in residence, but at the beginning of the Michaelmas Term, 1914, that number had dwindled to half, and it was still further diminished week by week as the Services took their toll. The atmosphere was very much that of the public school, and as I had never been to one it was all strange to me. It was very definitely the exception for a man to have his university career paid for by anyone save his parents, and the average undergraduate hardly gave a thought to what he was going to do when he went down; motor-cars were few – it is almost as easy today to get to London as it was then to go to Abingdon or Woodstock – so he rarely went a mile or two from the University during term, and in consequence the outside world meant little to him during the three or four years that he was in residence. This state of affairs was not of course peculiar to Oxford, for in April 1914 Stuart Donaldson, Master of Magdalene College, Cambridge, stated that of those who came up in 1909 a quarter had not taken a degree, and he 'ventured to think of that 25 per cent to whom he had alluded a very large number consisted of men who came up to have a good time, and did not care to read or work hard'.

The cost of living at Oxford and Cambridge was much the same, and it was estimated that a careful man need not spend more than £160 minimum a year, though this figure would not include his expenses in the vacations, or for clothes, or travelling. Again at both universities a good many undergraduates undoubtedly got into debt, but shopkeepers held their hands, and there was more than a little truth in Douglas Jerrold's toast, 'The tradesmen of Oxford – to whom we all owe so much'. It was generally considered satisfactory if a man paid his bills by the time his eldest son came into residence. Even in my time I remember a man going down owing £25 for shaving alone – quite a considerable sum of money in those days.

If there were no 'demos' or 'sit-ins' in those days ragging was rife, and some of it was reminiscent of *Tom Brown's Schooldays*. It was no uncommon thing for freshmen to be flogged round college with wet knotted towels, or turned out into the street without their nether garments. As for religion, it is difficult to resist the conclusion that at neither Oxford nor Cambridge did religion exercise much hold over the undergraduates at that time. Nor is this surprising, for the undergraduates came mostly from the public schools, where the religion taught was that Established by Law, and where enthusiasm of any sort – save for athletics – was sternly discouraged. It was not that there was much militant atheism at either university, but rather that the general attitude was one of indifference, though nineteenth-century rationalism had its followers. The senior members in the main made little or no effort to counteract this tendency, and since as often as not they professed agnostic views themselves their presence in chapel by virtue of their office was hardly calculated to stimulate piety in the young. In effect, most undergraduates would probably have declared that they belonged to the Church of England, without giving much thought to the matter, and certainly without doing anything about it.

All through that autumn of 1914 our numbers at Corpus continued to dwindle, until at one time we were reduced to seven undergraduates, though that was later in the war. A contemporary of mine got a commission in a very crack regiment, which some of us thought made him unduly pleased with himself. So as he was staying on in Oxford for a few days to collect his kit we arranged for three telegrams to be sent to him on successive evenings, and delivered when he was dining in hall where they had to be read aloud. The first ran, 'Congratulations on your commission, Kitchener'; the second 'Thank you for joining my army, George'; and the third, 'For God's sake remain neutral, Wilhelm'. The telegrams served the purpose we had in view.

Of course Corpus with its reduced numbers was only typical of the University as a whole, so that normal conditions of academic life were out of the question. The Union held no debates, so one by one the clubs closed down. The New Tory Club never opened at all, but the Junior Tory struggled on into 1915. Before the war Oxford had been defined, by no means inaccurately, as 'an oasis of university in a desert of clubs', but the clubs never recovered their popularity, and the Second World War dealt the death-blow to most of them. With purely college activities it was the same: only the Sundial Society kept up an appearance of life until 1917, though the *Pelican Record* appeared regularly throughout the war. For the rest, hardly a day went by without the Roll of Honour containing at least one Oxford name. We had two V.C.s at Corpus, one of them a man of the year above me, and the last person whom his contemporaries would have considered likely to win such a distinction. Admittedly I was away from Oxford during three and a half years of this period, but from time to time I went there on leave, and so kept in touch with the doings of those I knew.

Oxford after the First World War was something like what London must have been in the early days of the Restoration, that is to say in the desire of everyone to forget what had gone immediately before and to make up for lost time. The undergraduates were a curious mixture of several academic generations. Boys fresh from school rubbed shoulders with the veterans of Gallipoli a mere three or four years older than themselves but a decade apart in outlook and experience, and men who had been privates were once again on a footing of equality with those who had been their officers. All this led to some curious incidents which I believe would have been impossible in any other country save England. In company with another Corpus man I was 'progged' one night drinking in the bar of the George café by a proctor who had served under my companion in the Dardanelles. In due course we were apostrophized and fined, and it was only then that the proctor and my fellow-delinquent gave any indication that they had campaigned together. No praise can be too high for the University authorities of that time for their handling of an extremely difficult situation with the most consummate tact: they went out of their way to stretch a great many points, and in retrospect I do not think that we took undue advantage of their indulgence. Certainly there was not the friction between authority and the undergraduates of which one hears so much today, but then we were singularly lacking in the inferiority complex which distinguishes the modern student: the Dons went their way and we went ours, to each other's mutual satisfaction.

Had they not been so understanding things might have gone very differently, for those of us who came back from the forces had no idea of the difficulties of civilian life in the matter of rationing, shortages, etc.; also we thought ourselves the salt of the earth as the saviours of the country, and as such entitled to the best of everything. Furthermore, the atmosphere was one of violence and revolution, with which Oxford might so easily have become infected: in fact Soviets were formed in several colleges to safeguard undergraduate rights, the most powerful being that at St John's under the chairmanship of Leslie Hore-Belisha. But the discontent soon died down as the result of tactful handling on the part of authority, and my personal experience was that the older the Don the more understanding he was likely to be. Of the humanity of our own President, Thomas Case, one incident will suffice to tell. During the war there were cadets in part of the college, and one morning it was reported that one of them had had a girl in his room all night. Case was urged by the Dean to report the matter to the military authorities but he refused. 'He's a decent young man,' he said, and added with a twinkle in his eye, 'After all, we were young ourselves once.'

Had the war lasted much longer the old traditions would have been broken, for not enough of those who had been up before would have come back to enable them to be revived. At Corpus those of us who came in this capacity were a mere handful, but we were enough: we determined to have learnt nothing and forgotten nothing, and with the willing help of the mob of freshmen we got all the college activities going once more, that is to say the Owlets, the Pelican Essay Club, the Sundial Society, and the Wasps. The Dons helped us with all these clubs, with the possible exception of the Wasps. In sport there was a similar renaissance, and by the summer of 1919 the college was outwardly what it had been in the summer of 1914. Whether the atmosphere was the same at the close of the Second World War I cannot say from first-hand knowledge.

The President of Corpus as I have already said was Thomas Case, and words are quite inadequate to express the affection and respect which we all felt for him. He was an ideal Head of a House, for in addition to the prestige which he enjoyed as the leading authority of the day on Aristotle, and as having been a Cricket Blue, he took a close personal interest in every man in the college, and he was insistent that each undergraduate should do something for its honour. If I were asked to name his outstanding quality I should say it was his humanity. Although he was seventy when I first knew him he never seemed an old man: as Lord Curzon very well expressed it in a letter to him when he left Corpus at the age of eighty, 'The secret of your success, I suppose, has been that you have always *remained young*; perhaps too you have been more consistent than most, and have not made too many genuflections in the Temple of Rimmon.' The last statement was unquestionably true, but though Case could rarely be moved from a position which he had taken up even his opponents recognized that his disagreement was always good-natured and unselfish. He called himself a Palmerstonian Liberal, which gave him a good deal of scope in the early decades of the present century.

With Colin Coote,
Etretat, 1929

Rome, autumn 1932
Viscount Lymington, Sir Rennell Rodd, and the author (from left to right)

At the Hôtel de Ville, Rheims, October 1936. From left to right: A. R. Wise, M.P.; the Lord Chief Justice, Lord Hewart; M. Marchandeau; Sir Charles Petrie; Sir Patrick Hannon, M.P.

Lillington, 1938
The author with his wife and son Peter

Sir Charles and Comte Robert de Vogüé, 1

In effect, he was one of those comparatively rare individuals whom one will always feel a better man for having known.

Case was also a wit, and some of his sallies will long be remembered. One day when two undergraduates were following him up the High and one of them was heard saying to the other, 'Look at that old boy's trousers; they're far too long for him.' Case turned round: 'Yes,' he remarked, 'My trousers are like young puppies – they want strapping.' On another occasion, after a Bump Supper or a Wasps' Dinner the chaplain's oak had been screwed up, and when that worthy, the Revd Charles Plummer, wanted to take chapel the following morning he was unable to get out of his rooms. Looking from his window he saw the President walking in the Fellows' Garden and called out in his high falsetto, 'Mr President, Mr President, I'm screwed.' To which came the instantaneous reply, 'Sleep it off, Mr Plummer; sleep it off.'

After I had gone down Case asked me to stay a weekend with him, and on the Saturday afternoon we drove in a landau out to Boar's Hill to have tea with the then Poet Laureate, Dr Bridges. The conversation eventually got round to Flecker, concerning whose merits the two old men held diametrically opposed views to which they gave expression with no little warmth. 'I don't believe Case ever read a line of Flecker,' Bridges whispered to me when he got an opportunity, while on our way back to Corpus in the carriage Case said he failed to understand what any sensible person could admire in a poet who saw beauty in the Oxford gas-works. Although Bridges was a Corpus man and used to come into college a good deal I never knew him really well, though on one occasion I had the good fortune to be present at a verbal duel between him and G. K. Chesterton at a meeting of, I think, the Cardinal Society in Christ Church. On encountering the Poet Laureate in the quad next morning I referred to the incident, and was told that 'arguing with Chesterton is like trying to water a prickly shrub in the desert'. In his youth Bridges had been a remarkably good oar, and had rowed in the Corpus Eight in a regatta on the Seine in the 1860s, when legend has it that the whole crew were kissed by the Empress of the French.

My tutor was R. B. Mowat, who was to meet his death in an aeroplane accident during the Second World War: he was an admirable mentor for a young man such as myself who was a good deal of a theorist. It was not that Mowat was uninterested in theories, far from it, but he always insisted that his pupils should correlate theirs with the relevant facts. He was also a sworn foe to sensational writing. The only time I remember him to have been really annoyed with me was when in an essay I once referred to the death of Murat as 'the tragedy of Pizzo'; he told me that phraseology of this nature might be all right for a certain type of journalism, but that it would never do for the Schools. Years after I went down I saw a good deal of him at the Bonar Law College at Ashridge, and there I came to appreciate in him a quality which I had not observed in my undergraduate days, his intellectual honesty. In the twenties and thirties of the present century the trimming of sails had become so much a matter of course as hardly to occasion surprise, so that to change front without appearing to do so was the hall-mark of the real 'authority'. Not so with Mowat: he was not a great historian, but if he thought he had been wrong he said so, and even those who disagreed with him could not withhold their admiration for his courage.

Sir Richard Livingstone, later President, tutored me for a time in Classics for the History Prelim. In one respect at least he was like Case, and that was in his preservation of a fresh outlook on life. He once told the British Association that one of the great problems of the day was to keep the middle-aged mentally young, and he certainly solved it himself. 'Livers', as he was always called, was a rare compound of the scholar and the man of action, for in both Belfast and Oxford he displayed administrative ability of no mean order. As President of Corpus he was an unqualified success, and it is little short of a tragedy that he did not immediately succeed Case, for the regime which intervened did not act in the best interests of the college. It also fell to his lot as Vice-Chancellor to supervise the transition of the University from war to peace at the end of the Second World War, and most ably did he perform the task, though at great sacrifice to his health. Perhaps his greatest tribute is the fact that every Corpus man feels prouder of his college because Livingstone was once its President.

To pass from the college to the University was, as we have seen, to enter a very strange world, and one for which the year 1945 could alone supply a parallel; still, taking it all in all, 1919–20 was quite a good vintage. The Union was not revived in all its pre-war glory until the Trinity Term of 1919, the elections having been held at the end of the previous term when Hore-Belisha beat Reggie Harris for the Presidency. Hore-Belisha was an admirable President, and it was in no small measure due to his efforts that the Union so soon regained its old position in Oxford life; not even his most bitter enemy would deny him the credit for that. He was in due course succeeded by Earp, and an anonymous poet wrote of the Union under the new regime:

> *No more benign Belisha, set on high,*
> *Demos enthroned, controls democracy,*

Instead, amidst unprecedented cheers
He bears good tidings – Labour without tears.
The vacant throne the Muse doth now usurp,
(The Muse, I should explain, is dolorous Earp).
And thus our Ship of State once more afloat,
Eager to prove herself a decent boat,
By gas propelled, conveys the same old crew,
(I mingle metaphors) to 'pastures new',
Leaving on shore but Haldane, in his digs
Intent upon the cult of guinea-pigs.
Again with fluid eyes and quivering mouth
We list the empurpled rhetoric of Routh;
Still, rich with Transatlantic quip and pun,
The lubricated words of Nichols run;
Still beardless Harrod, prodigy of youth,
Proclaims himself a priest of Marxian Truth,
Which Sachs with weighty word and solemn mien
Denounces as fantastic – or obscene;
Still Andrews soars to loftier realms of thought
Than puzzled Patten thinks he really ought;
Still 'from the ranks of Tuscany' a cheer
Bursts at the sight of fervid Chevalier;
Still, pince-nez dangling, Gallop does his best
To pour light mockery on all the rest.

Those whom I have already mentioned were only a few of my contemporaries who subsequently achieved fame, for in addition there were
Richard Hughes, Robert Graves, and Clifford Kitchen in the ranks of
literature; David Maxwell Fyfe, N. A. Beechman, Edward Marjoribanks,
and Ralph Beaumont among the politicians; judges such as Edward Holroyd Pearce and John Maude; and the Indian governor Roger Lumley,
who was a prominent member of both the Canning and the Oxford
Carlton Clubs. In sport we could boast at golf Cyril Tolley and Roger
Wethered, as well as cricketers such as Miles Howell, R. H. Bettington,
and R. C. Robertson-Glasgow. There was one undergraduate who at the
University played no part in the field in which he was subsequently to
make his name, and that was Anthony Eden: he was, indeed, a member
of the Oxford Carlton, but he never spoke in the Union.

It is curious how little we knew of what was going on at contemporary
Cambridge, and of the newer universities we knew nothing at all save
their names. There was a great gulf set between Oxford and Cambridge

VARSITY CELEBRITIES.

No. 4.—"THE PRESIDENT."

President of the Oxford Carlton Club in 1920

whose name was Bletchley. Even after the First World War very few undergraduates possessed cars, though some had motor-bikes, and as the journey from one university to the other by train was hardly tempting we rarely saw one another save in connection with sporting events. During the whole time I was in residence I went over to Cambridge only once, and that was for a Conservative meeting organized by Victor Raikes, at which the other speaker was Henry Page Croft. Victor, as always, entertained us extremely well, so that on the following morning I had to have a whisky-and-soda before my hand was steady enough to shave, and Cambridge hospitality was more than a mere memory during the greater part of the next day.

I have never been any good at games, nor did I indulge in them at Oxford apart from the odd game of tennis, but I rode a good deal on horses hired from the Randolph. After the war I was not unduly pressed where work was concerned for I had passed the History Prelim in 1914, and to qualify for a war degree all that was required was a further period of residence. On looking up the record I find that I read widely during my last year at Oxford – some fifty books ranging from Duff's *History of the Mahrattas* and Keynes' *Economic Consequences of the Peace* to Hardy's *Moments of Vision* and Masefield's *Reynard the Fox*. The task to which I did devote my energies was the foundation of the Oxford Carlton Club, so some account of its activities since those days may not be out of place, though looking back over the years I find it distinctly odd that the club should have been founded by so unorthodox a Tory as myself.

It has already been mentioned that the two Conservative Clubs in Oxford, the New Tory and the Junior Tory, had closed down as a result of the First World War, so when we came up again some of us addressed ourselves to the problem of their revival. It was soon decided to let sleeping dogs lie so far as the New Tory was concerned, for its debts were numerous and heavy – it was said to have owed £70 to its fish-monger alone – and we had no desire to inherit them. As for the Junior Tory, the name seemed unsuitable if there was only going to be one Conservative Club. Then when someone suggested Oxford Carlton the designation was at once adopted. It was indeed a happy thought, for the Carlton Club in London had most generously paid storage on the furniture, linen, and plate of the Junior Tory throughout the war, and it now handed them over to the new institution. The first premises were at 72 The High, but after a year the club moved to more spacious quarters at the corner of George Street and the Corn, where it remained until another war caused the suspension of Conservative activities in Oxford.

The original committee consisted of myself as President, Sir Henry Penson as Senior Treasurer, J. W. Russell as Junior Treasurer, and A. C. C. Willway as Secretary. Mowat was the representative of the senior members of the University on the Committee, and the others on that body were Lord Ivor Churchill, H. J. Hope, David Maxwell Fyfe, and C. R. S. Harris. When Russell was elected President of the Union his place as Junior Treasurer was taken by R. B. Rathbone. There was also a House Committee which looked after the amenities of the clubhouse itself, and the secretary of this was Ralph Assheton. One can, I think, truthfully say that we worked hard to make the venture a success, and we had singularly few disagreements; though sometimes perhaps we took ourselves a trifle too seriously, as for example when after an exceptionally good dinner we chose in Corpus quad by the light of the moon a club tie of variegated hues, namely purple for Church and King, blue for Toryism, and white to show the purity of our principles. (A later and more realistic generation modified this.)

The committee was elected at a crowded meeting in one of the Corpus lecture rooms, and my only rival for the Presidency was Edward Marjoribanks, whom I defeated by a comfortable margin. For some reason or another Marjoribanks was not able to come to the meeting, but I was hardly out of bed the next morning before he was round to offer me his congratulations and support. That was characteristic of him. Yet his character was complex, for although as a rule he cared very little for the opinion of the outside world he was at times almost morbidly introspective. One evening when he was alone with me in my rooms at 7 Oriel Street there cropped up in conversation the name of his grandfather, the Lord Tweedmouth who had been First Lord of the Admiralty in the Campbell-Bannerman administration, and who had subsequently become insane, his first symptoms appearing during a speech in the House of Lords. 'If ever I thought I was going mad I would shoot myself,' Majoribanks declared. At the time I laughed and told him that we had probably had too much to drink, and at our age we should not be discussing such gloomy topics; but I remembered the remark when his own tragedy occurred, and I wondered. John Buchan took the view that Marjoribanks committed suicide because of an unhappy love affair with a lady who, being still alive, must be nameless. But Buchan was always a romantic, and I find it difficult to disagree with Rosalind in *As You Like It* that 'Men have died from time to time, and worms have eaten them but not for love.'

Marjoribanks was certainly the best all-round man of my time, for he got a First in Greats, was President of the Union, rowed for Christ

Church when that college won the Ladies' Plate, and got a Trial. However, such are the uncertainties of political life that, apart from a personal grief at the time of his death, it may be that he was *felix opportunitate mortis*; but the country could ill spare one who both spoke and wrote so well. One wonders whether, had he lived another twenty years, he would have been the Rosebery, the Wyndham, or the Oliver Stanley of his generation.

The Conservative Party certainly gave us full support, and its leaders came regularly to speak at our meetings. The Oxford Carlton Club was opened by the then Duke of Marlborough, but before that there had been a memorable meeting in Wadham Hall addressed by F. E. Smith, newly become Lord Birkenhead. His elevation to the Chancellorship gave rise to many stories, and one of the best rests, so far at any rate as I am concerned, on the authority of the late Lord Justice Greer. The night it became known that F.E. was going to the Woolsack he was accosted by Horatio Bottomley in the smoking-room of the House of Commons, and duly congratulated upon the appointment.

Bottomley added, 'Upon my soul, F.E., I shouldn't have been surprised to hear that you had been made Archbishop of Canterbury.'

'If I had,' replied the new Chancellor, 'I should have asked you to come to my installation.'

'That's damn nice of you,' said Bottomley.

'Not at all,' retorted F.E., 'I should have needed a crook.'

Stories about Bottomley were legion in those days, and one of the best concerned him and Darling. Bottomley had been conducting his own defence as usual, and the time had come for him to make his concluding speech to the jury. 'Make it short, Mr Bottomley,' said the judge. The other agreed, and began his address, 'What I want to ask you, gentlemen of the jury, is *quis custodiet ipsos custŏdes*,' emphasizing the last word '*custŏdes*'. 'Not too short, Mr Bottomley,' interjected Darling.

Like the best undergraduates down the ages we were far from being conformists, and many of us had little use for the Lloyd George Coalition which the Conservative Party was officially supporting. Walter Long, then First Lord of the Admiralty, came down and addressed us at a most successful meeting, but he wrote me a private letter afterwards expressing some concern at the heterodox views he had heard put forward in reference to the Coalition. Bonar Law himself, although leader of the Conservative Party, refused all invitations to speak in Oxford on the quixotic ground that it was Asquith's preserve, and that it would be improper for him to trespass on it. Incidentally, there were all sorts of conventions to be observed in those days: one was that no undergraduate should participate in parliamentary or municipal politics in the City of Oxford, though I cannot recollect that we wanted to do so.

One of our guests who deserves more than a passing mention is the Right Hon. J. S. Sandars. Today he is forgotten, but when Balfour was Prime Minister he was to Balfour what Sir Horace Wilson was to Neville Chamberlain – indeed he was even more so, for on one occasion he actually altered the date of the meeting of Parliament without consulting either the King or the Prime Minister. Yet in the end he quarrelled with his chief in a very peculiar manner. When Balfour became First Lord of the Admiralty in the Asquith Coalition Government he asked Sandars to come back in his old capacity of Private Secretary, and the other agreed. They had lunched together at Balfour's house in Carlton House Terrace and were walking across to Downing Street when Sandars said, at the top of the Duke of York's steps, that he presumed Balfour would live in Admiralty House. The new First Lord replied that he did not propose to do so, and that he had told his predecessor, Winston Churchill, that he could stay on there for the present if he liked. Sandars at once said that he entirely disagreed with the decision, which would give the impression that Churchill was still in control of Naval policy. Balfour denied this, but Sandars continued to argue the point, and when the two reached No. 10 he asked his chief if that was his final decision. Balfour said it was, whereupon Sandars declared in that case he could not work for him, turned his back on A.J.B., and refused ever to communicate with him again.

Sandars was over eighty when he died in 1934. A relatively adequate obituary appeared in *The Times*, but thereafter the man who had controlled the Prime Minister of Great Britain during several important years of the nation's history was confined to oblivion: *The Dictionary of National Biography* does not even mention his name. Perhaps, however, this is what he would have wished, for he gave orders that when he died all his papers were to be destroyed, and this was unfortunately done. There was one story Sandars told us about Disraeli which I do not recollect ever having seen in any biography of the statesman. After the 'Leap in the Dark' and the subsequent loss of the General Election in 1868 there was considerable dissatisfaction in the Conservative ranks, and a deputation of Back Benchers went to inform Disraeli officially of the fact. The ex-Prime Minister faced his critics alone, the only friend he took with him being one of the Rothschilds from whom Sandars later had the story of what happened. As soon as the rebels had stated their case Disraeli at once said that if such was the feeling he would call a party meeting and resign the leadership. The mutineers were already congratulating themselves on their success when one of their number, more experienced than his colleagues, asked Disraeli if he also proposed to give up his seat. At this point Rothschild noticed that his friend had produced his handkerchief from his sleeve in a way which to the initiated was evidence that the owner was in a dangerous mood. Disraeli said that he did not propose to give up his seat. So an old parliamentary hand, a Knightley of Fawsley, went on to ask where he proposed to sit when his successor had been elected. 'In the same place,' Disraeli replied, 'where I sat when I attacked Peel.' On these words the mutiny collapsed, for every one of the rebels knew that if such was Dizzy's attitude no new leader could have any hope of success.

In connection with the Oxford Carlton Club there was the *Oxford Review*, a fortnightly publication which gave some of us our first experience of journalism. The original editors were David Maxwell Fyfe and Neville Barclay, both of Balliol, and they were succeeded by C. R. N. Routh of Christ Church and C. R. S. Harris of Corpus Christi. Its object, to quote David's first leader, was to be 'a vehicle of communication between the minds that do not see evil in institutions merely because they made an empire great, and cannot condemn capitalism for giving sufficiency and prosperity to the world'. For an undergraduate publication the *Oxford Review* maintained a very high standard during its brief existence. From the outside world we had political articles by Sir Hubert Gough, Lord Eustace Percy, Lord Henry Cavendish-Bentinck, Colonel Lane-Fox, and Sir Samuel Hoare who argued in favour of making Constantinople rather than Geneva the headquarters of the League of Nations. Marie Lohr wrote on the theatre, and Masefield sent us some verses. Naturally most of our contributors were undergraduates, and by no means all of them were Tories. Among the politicians were Leslie Hore-Belisha on 'The Only True Education' and Ralph Assheton on 'The Younger Pitt'. The literary team was exceptionally strong, for it included Charles Morgan, C. H. B. Kitchen, V. de S. Pinto, and Paul Bloomfield. Many criticisms could doubtless be made of Oxford Toryism in those days, but no one could say that it was not catholic in its approach.

Of course the *Review* never paid. We made some successful efforts to obtain advertisements from the tradesmen of Oxford, but this source of revenue did not last long, and the sales were an uncertain factor. During one crisis a number of us guaranteed five pounds apiece, but when it appeared likely that the fulfilment of this guarantee and the end of term, when the undergraduate is always in desperate financial straits, were likely to coincide, there was universal despondency among the guarantors. Happily a fairy godmother in the shape of Sir George Younger, then Chairman of the Conservative Party, came to our aid and paid off the deficit. When, at a small luncheon in the club, he announced his intention of doing this, the cheers were deafening.

In addition to the names I have already mentioned there were a number of other outstanding figures in the Oxford of those days, if not so many as in the generation which knew Jowett, Mackail, and Liddell; and one of them was Herbert Warren, President of Magdalen, of whom the Duke of Windsor has written:

'The President was a man of learning; it was therefore disillusioning to discover that the thing he appeared to value most in the world was his connexion with a certain baronet, a fact he managed to insert into every conversation. It was generally suspected that he was obsessed with the idea of filling Magdalen with titled undergraduates; hence, whenever he beamed upon me, I was never quite certain whether it was with a teacher's benevolence or from a collector's secret satisfaction with a coveted trophy.'

Whether Warren was quite so much of a snob as has been alleged is open to doubt, but the stories depicting him in that light are innumerable. Perhaps the best is the one which purports to give an account of the interview between him and the late Prince Chichibu of Japan when the latter came into residence at Magdalen. After various matters had been discussed Warren asked the Prince what his name meant in his own language, and was told 'the Son of God'. At this the President beamed, and remarked, 'You will find that we have the sons of many other distinguished men at this college.' Probably a good many of these snob stories had originally been told about Oscar Browning by generations of Cambridge men, or about Mahaffy at Trinity College, Dublin.

Another Head of a House of whom many anecdotes were told was the Warden of New College, Spooner, but most if not all of the 'spoonerisms' attributed to him – certainly the bawdy ones – were not his. Of the respectable slips, 'I suppose you came by the town drain', and 'Two rags and a bug' are probably the best.

Of course the Oxford about which I have written above was not the normal university in any sense, for the great majority of undergraduates were several years older than is usually the case, and vastly more experienced. There can also be little doubt that those who returned from the First World War were far harder workers than were their predecessors. Perhaps I cannot do better than finish this chapter with a quotation from an article of mine which appeared in *The Globe*, of which I was then the Oxford Correspondent, on 27 November, 1919:

'Outwardly, the Oxford of today is the same as the Oxford that existed before the war, but inwardly there has been a change. Most of the old clubs, political, literary, or social have been revived, and the old activities are being pursued with their old-time vigour; but the spirit in which these things are being done has changed – and changed for the better. There is a keenness which was lacking and there is much more real enthusiasm . . . in politics this is particularly the case: Tory, Liberal, and Labour clubs have been founded, and are being organized in a manner wholly unknown in Oxford before; and it is perhaps only typical of the age that they should be broader in their outlook.'

After the lapse of more than half a century I see no reason to disagree with these conclusions.

PART TWO

Second Look
1920–1945

CHAPTER V

The Home Front in the Twenties

I CAME down from Oxford at the end of the Trinity Term 1920 to find that my father was dying of cancer, and within ten days he was dead. I knew that he was ill, but I had no idea how serious his illness was. Largely in consequence of this event I made a marriage which did not turn out a success: my first wife and I were totally unsuited to each other. Within five years the marriage was brought to an end, leaving only one satisfactory result, our son Dick, with whom my relations have always been very friendly, and of whom I am most proud. He was born in 1921, eleven years before my second boy, of whom more anon.

Against this personal background I dabbled in Conservative politics, though I have always been a Tory rather than a Conservative, and I have often criticized official Conservatism when it has seemed to me, under the influence of Whiggery and Big Business, to have departed from what I believe to be the basic principles of Toryism. On the other hand critical as I have been, not least in the days when I was collaborating with Douglas Jerrold on the *English* and *New English Review*, the Liberal and Labour alternatives have never appeared to me in the least attractive. In this connection I am reminded of a conversation between my father and the late Lord Rosebery at the turn of the century. After some discussion of the existing political situation Lord Rosebery said, 'But wouldn't you agree that one party is as bad as the other?' To which my father replied, 'Not quite.'

In the earlier decades of the present century Conservatism began to be affected by a funest influence, namely that of Big Business, which had in the main favoured Liberalism because of its *laissez-faire* beliefs. When it became obvious that the Liberal sun was setting, Big Business, terrified at the growth of Socialism, came across to the Conservative camp, where it soon acquired a dominant position. For a time this development was obscured from the electorate by the incompetence – on the home, not the international, front – of the first two Labour administrations, but in due course the working classes came to the conclusion that Conservatism was just a capitalist conspiracy, and the General Election of 1945 was the result. The Tories of the past, Shaftesbury, Richard Oastler, and J. R. Stephens, had championed the small man against Big Business, and the working classes had never identified their party with the 'bosses'; even in the great Conservative *débâcle* of 1906 such constituencies as Hoxton and Stepney returned Conservative members to Westminster. The influence of Big Business in the party during the leadership of Bonar Law, Stanley Baldwin, and Neville Chamberlain enormously facilitated the work of the Socialist propagandists.

This was bad enough, but Big Business is always at heart timid, and it infected Conservatism with its timidity; having no principles of its own it persuaded its new allies to compromise on theirs. Let us take two instances. The first is plural voting. It is an arguable proposition that an elector should be allowed to use as many votes as he possesses qualifications; it is an arguable, if revolutionary, proposition that the rule should be that an elector should only vote once; what is not logical is that he should be allowed to vote two or three times, but no more. By accepting this compromise in 1917 the Conservatives abandoned the safe ground of principle for the extremely unsafe one of expediency, with the result that in a generation we reached the position of one man (or woman) one vote.

My second instance is the female franchise, where the same fate befell the compromise by which women were given the vote at thirty. There is everything to be said for women voting on the same terms as men; there is even something to be said – though not by me – for not allowing them to vote at all; but there was nothing to be said for regarding them as unbalanced and irresponsible creatures who suddenly and automatically at the age of thirty acquired that sense of responsibility which their menfolk had achieved at twenty-one. Such a compromise was doomed to failure from the beginning, and it lasted exactly eleven years. In the light of these experiences the Conservative Party would be well advised to be a little more careful about such compromises in the future, or it will again be overtaken by events for which it has not allowed.

If one looks back over the years between the two wars one can hardly help being struck by Conservative respect for the *fait accompli*. Once a measure reached the statute book it was only on the rarest occasions that for some obscure reason it was not sacrosanct in Conservative eyes, even if it was based on principles the very reverse of Tory. This attitude continued after the Second World War, until in 1948 the electorate was edified by the spectacle of the House of Lords rallying with the greatest enthusiasm to the defence of the Parliament Act of 1911, which it had originally passed only under the most dire constraint.

In spite of all this I was not then so critical of official Conservatism as I was later to become, and not long after I came down from Oxford I was adopted as prospective candidate for West Bromwich. But I found that nursing a constituency so far from London was incompatible with earning a living so I withdrew my candidature. In the autumn of 1923 Baldwin suddenly decided to go to the country to seek a mandate for Tariff Reform, so I thought I would have another try to enter the House of Commons. Accordingly I asked Sir Reginald Hall, who was then Chairman of the Conservative Party, what he could do for me; North Cornwall was, I was told, in need of a candidate, so I was sent off down there with a totally inadequate cheque for £600 and the information, 'If that isn't enough you will either have to raise the balance locally or pay it out of your own pocket.' The official policy which I had to champion was a duty on manufactured articles combined with a bounty on arable land of £1 per acre, together with a minimum wage of 30s a week to labourers as a condition of the grant of the subsidy. Nothing was said about food taxes, though we were pressed on the point in the election campaign.

North Cornwall stretched from the Devonshire border North of Bude down to Newquay and inland almost to the outskirts of Plymouth; it was overwhelmingly agricultural except for one or two small country towns and a few seaside resorts. I had only twice set foot in the constituency, and that merely on holiday. Politically it was solidly Liberal, and at no time had it ever returned a Conservative candidate; the sitting member was Sir George Croydon Marks, who had been unopposed since the second General Election of 1910. In short, my prospects were nil, but I was young and enthusiastic and I thoroughly enjoyed what was a perfectly clean fight. When the figures were announced I did not feel that in the circumstances I had done too badly:

Sir G. Croydon Marks	L	12,434
Charles Petrie	C	9,853

Anyhow, I had broken the Liberal ice of North Cornwall for my party since the seat was won by a Tory at the General Election of the following year.

This reverse cured my parliamentary ambitions for the following twenty years, and the next time I made a move in the direction of the House of Commons was during the Second World War when the perfectly safe Conservative seat of South Dorset unexpectedly became vacant at a by-election. Here the omens appeared more favourable, since I not only lived in the county, but was Chairman of the Dorset Ashridge Circle. I was actually on the short list of three, but I met my Waterloo when I came before the selection committee. Had I been through the divorce court? My answer in the affirmative clearly shook them, but what sealed my fate was my reply in the negative to the question was I prepared to pay my own election expenses and contribute £300 a year to the funds of the local Conservative Association.

Finally in 1945 I toyed with the idea of letting my name go forward for Oxford University where I was given to understand that there was a good deal of support for my candidature. But when I heard that Sir Winston Churchill particularly wanted to see Sir Arthur Salter, who was standing as an Independent, in the House of Commons I took no further action.

In retrospect, I have never been more thankful for anything in my life than for the fact that none of my parliamentary yearnings came to anything.

At any rate until recently English politics have been characterized by a rough good humour, particularly at election times. One example has always struck me as typical of this. When the first Lord Gretton, of course before his elevation to the peerage, was contesting Burton-on-Trent at the General Election of 1935, his Labour opponent was a Mrs G. Paling. One of this lady's speakers remarked from the platform, 'John Gretton is a dirty dog.' At this a Gretton supporter shouted from the body of the hall, 'That's as may be; but we all know what dirty dogs does to palings.'

I once told this story to an American, who said it reminded him of an incident in the Presidential Election of 1908 when William Jennings Bryan was standing against Taft. The scene was a meeting in the Middle West, and Bryan was apologizing for the absence of his wife, who was worn out with her efforts in the election campaign, and was at that moment asleep in bed at the local hotel. 'But,' thundered the great orator, 'next March she'll be sleeping in the White House at Washington.' At once came a voice, 'Then she'll be sleeping with Bill Taft.'

If I failed to get into the House of Commons in the early 1920s I did, in 1921, achieve the distinction of being elected to the Carlton Club as its youngest member. One of the most frightening experiences in ordinary life is the first visit to a club of which one has just been elected a member.

The apologetic explanation of who you are to the hall porter; the haunting fear that you have unwittingly taken the chair of the outstanding figure of the club, a man renowned all over the world for his exploits in peace and war; and above all the suspicion that by your behaviour you are confirming the servants in their belief that the type of member now being elected is very different from the ones they used to have – all these are emotions which no clubman is ever likely to forget.

I have experienced them on several occasions, but never more strongly than when I was elected to the Carlton. Walter Long had proposed me, very kindly introducing me into the club himself although he was by no means well: he had, in fact, recently been compelled to relinquish the office of First Lord of the Admiralty owing to ill-health. The Carlton in those days was a much more formidable institution than it is now, and as visitors were not admitted the new member had little idea of what he would find when he first crossed the threshold. In my case all went well under Long's chaperonage, and in any event we went to the club about noon on a spring morning when it was practically empty. I was told where, as a new member, I should and should not sit; I was warned that if I wanted to wear a hat in the club it must be a silk one; and particularly was I told that in the coffee-room I must not occupy one of the tables near the fire until I was at least an Under-Secretary or a Privy Councillor. On looking round I espied a row of tables along the wall, so I asked hopefully if it would be all right to sit there. 'Good God, no,' replied Long, 'nobody knows the fellows who sit there. We call that Brook Street.'

Walter Long then gave me a glass of the most excellent sherry accompanied by a warning against cocktails to which his son Eric was unfortunately partial in preference to superior beverages. Then he took his departure, leaving me feeling particularly forlorn, so that as soon as the club began to fill up with members coming in for lunch, I slunk away.

My real agony took place some weeks later when, one particularly hot night of that very hot summer, I mustered up sufficient courage to go to the Carlton again to dine. As I put on my dinner-jacket I tried to remember all the instructions I had been given. I drank one glass of sherry, feeling that a second might give an impression of a partiality for the bottle unbecoming in a young man; I took care to read a paper of which there were several copies lying on the table in the morning-room in case I should be accused of monopolizing the one which my elders and betters might want to peruse; then I ordered my dinner to be served at an hour which I trusted would not be considered either too early or too late. On entering the coffee-room I chose a table which seemed to be neither too conspicuous nor too inconspicuous, and having seated myself I felt things had not gone too badly.

At the next table to mine there was an elderly member reading the evening paper. Half-way through dinner he suddenly said, 'Do you think this fine weather is going to continue?' I was so startled at being spoken to in such early days that I could only stammer out a few words in reply to the question. Whereupon my neighbour endeavoured to put me at my ease. 'I see,' he said, 'you are astonished at me speaking to you since you are a new member. Well, you'll find a lot of narrow-minded fellows in this club, but I'm very broad-minded myself: I hold the view that if a man is fit to be elected to the club, he is fit to be spoken to when he gets inside it.' Several months elapsed, and the fogs of November were shrouding Pall Mall in darkness, before I again ventured into the Carlton Club.

That was more than fifty years ago. Today the Carlton is one of the friendliest clubs in London. It certainly has its proportion of bores, though I doubt if this is any higher than in most other clubs, and occasionally they give rise to incidents which add to the gaiety of life for their fellow-members. During the Second World War, for instance, when two old men, both somewhat deaf, were discussing a mutual friend, this is what was heard of their conversation:

'What's George doing now?'
'What's who doing?'
'George.'
'He's living down in Herefordshire.'
'Living where?'
'In Herefordshire. He's married, you know.'
'He's what?'
'Married. Got six children.'
'Got what?'
'Six children.'
'Very unusual in these days.'
'Yes, but he doesn't do anything else, you know.'

On another occasion two equally elderly members were discussing their recent prostate operations at the top of their voices in the coffee-room at dinner, whereupon a certain M.P. who shall be nameless sent a waiter across to them with a request that they would discontinue their conversation at any rate until he had finished his savoury.

The outstanding eccentric of the Carlton Club between the wars was

Charles Agar, a very rich man who was for some years heir presumptive to the earldom of Normanton. He walked about the West End with a large green umbrella of the sort used by commissionaires, and in the club itself he was in the habit of betaking himself at mealtimes to the committee-room where he ate sandwiches and drank champagne out of quarter-bottles. The Night Porter always found considerable difficulty in getting him off the premises when the club closed. One evening when he thought Agar had gone he saw a light on the landing: on investigation he found Agar lying on his stomach on the floor reading an evening paper by the light of the little candles, used for sealing wax, from the writing tables which he had arranged round him in a sort of fairy circle. At one time Agar had a flat over Rumpelmeyers (now Prunier's) in St James's Street, and when the Second War came he refused to black it out, so the landlords cut off the electricity. However, he got over this difficulty by undressing in the lift and throwing his clothes on to the landing as he took them off, so that on one occasion when the occupants of an adjoining flat were coming home one evening they were surprised when they rang for the lift to find in it a naked Agar.

At this time, having been temporarily cured of my desire to enter the House of Commons, I began to write, and in 1925 I joined the staff of the *Outlook*. That paper, a weekly, which had been founded by George Wyndham for W. E. Henley, had included Garvin among its editors. The weeklies, which were a product of the latter half of the nineteenth century, have a distinguished place in the history of British journalism. They were originally published on a Saturday morning, to be read over the weekend by those who had either received them by post (there were Sunday deliveries of letters in those far-off days) or had bought them on their way home from their offices on Saturday afternoon. The Sunday newspaper was unknown in any respectable household, and in an age when the Victorian sabbath was still observed there was plenty of time to peruse a weekly from cover to cover before Monday morning. As they carried a great deal of weight both in political and literary fields, in these circumstances it is little wonder that men like Lord Robert Cecil, later third Marquess of Salisbury and Prime Minister, thought it worth his while to contribute to the *Saturday Review*.

When I became a member of the staff of the *Outlook* the paper was owned by the Duke of Westminster and was edited by A. Wyatt Tilby. The Duke had not, so far as I was aware, any great interest in journalism, in fact it was generally believed in the office that he bought the *Outlook* from that most eccentric character, Sir Charles Ross, only for sentimental reasons connected with his step-father, George Wyndham. Whether or not this is true I do not profess to know, but from the journalist's point of view he had as a proprietor, like Lord Thomson of Fleet in more recent times, the great merit of not interfering with what was written in the paper. The editor saw him from time to time, the rest of us never.

Fleet Street was already changing in the middle twenties, but it was still far from being as impersonal as it was subsequently to become. Northcliffe was but recently dead, and such newspaper proprietors as Lords Beaverbrook, Burnham, Riddell, and Rothermere, as well as Lady Bathurst, were powers in the land. Nor had the editors yet become nonentities, for in addition to the immortal Garvin there were R. D. Blumenfeld of the *Daily Express*, 'Taffy' Gwynne of the *Morning Post,* and Leonard Rees of *The Sunday Times*, to mention but a few names out of many. One man whom English journalism should never forget I knew well, and that was the prince of leader-writers, Ian Colvin, who combined greater courtesy and wider knowledge than are the possession of most mortals. He also commanded a felicity of phrase which has rarely been equalled and never excelled. Perhaps the most outstanding example of this was when the first Lord Birkenhead, in one of the crises which preceded the break-up of Lloyd-George's coalition, declared that he was captain of his soul; on which Colvin commented in a leader in the *Morning Post,* 'A small command, but we would imagine no sinecure'. Colvin had the bitterest pen, but the kindest heart, in Fleet Street.

Blumenfeld was always very kind to me, and when I first entered journalism he was at the height of his fame. No man ever better deserved his reputation, for in sober truth he made the *Daily Express*. In its early days the struggle was hard. He often used to have to go to the House of Commons on a Friday afternoon to raise the money from various guarantors with which to pay the week's wages. Gwynne I also knew well both in Fleet Street and in the Carlton Club, where for several years we served on the library committee together; and in its later days I did a good deal of work for the *Morning Post*. The demise of that paper was nothing short of a tragedy, for apart from its being extremely well written, it stood for something in the national life. No doubt the strong line which it adopted during the controversy over the Indian White Paper in the early thirties caused some decline in the circulation (it must be confessed that Gwynne was inclined to edit his news), but the situation was far from catastrophic, and had a few of the rich men in the Conservative Party put their hands in their pockets the paper could easily have been saved.[1]

1 There were plenty of rich men in the Conservative Party in those days. Sir George Younger told me that when as Chairman of the Party he wanted £100,000 he knew four men who could be relied upon to put up £25,000 apiece.

During some of this time I was also working for the *Observer*, and in all my somewhat extensive acquaintance with editors I have never come across one more helpful, generous, and courteous than Garvin. I was writing such a difficult column for him that the work might easily have led to considerable friction between us, but because he always knew exactly what he wanted this was avoided. When he was not satisfied my attention was called to the omission in a manner at which it was impossible to take offence, but which nevertheless admitted of no question. What was not always realized by the general public was the immense pains which Garvin took with his articles, for they were based upon an omnivorous reading of the foreign press. At one time they were the only British newspaper articles which were translated in full for Hitler to read.

Of course Garvin had his foibles, one of which seems to have been to go to his office as rarely as possible, another was to object to his proprietor entering it at all. During the years that I worked for him I never set foot in the *Observer* building; our discussions were invariably conducted over an excellent meal in the grill-room of the Hyde Park Hotel. He did his own writing entirely at his house at Beaconsfield. There were innumerable people who almost literally foamed at the mouth at the mention of Garvin's name, but, all the same, they read him Sunday after Sunday — a state of affairs which gives point to Northcliffe's observation that in the case of a writer, be he an author or a journalist, it does not much matter what people say about him so long as they say something.

There is something in the allegation that the fatal complacency of the British public between the wars was encouraged by the press in the desire not to antagonize advertisers by alarming its readers, for the advertiser does not as a rule care for a paper which adopts a disquieting tone. Anyhow, the British press, with the exception of a few papers, was an unreliable guide during the inter-war years in all that related to the international situation. It failed to draw attention to the fundamental weaknesses of the League of Nations; it assumed that the Italians would never conquer Abyssinia; and it was consistently wrong about the civil war in Spain; nor did it bring to its readers' notice the inherent rottenness of the Third Republic in France.

One weakness of the press, then and now, is the temptation first to think too much in terms of news, and secondly to give the reader what he is supposed to want, which means that the news is too often 'slanted'. When Northcliffe said that if a dog bites a man it is not news, but that if a man bites a dog it is news he was speaking the truth, but even so a lot depends on the way in which the story is presented. If for instance

John Smith takes Doris Brown home in his car after the annual dance of the Little Blankton Tennis Club and behaves properly, no one is in the least interested; but if he tries to take advantage of her and is charged with indecent assault then he and she at once become news; at the same time the facts can be told either objectively or in such a way as to create the impression that the men of Little Blankton are a lascivious lot, and that no woman's honour is safe there after nightfall. The maxim that the customer is always right may be admirable in the shop-keeping world, but it has its dangers for the journalist – and the politician.

As the days to which I am alluding are now nearly half-a-century ago it may not be without interest to the modern reader to hear about journalistic earnings at that time. When I was assistant editor of the *Outlook* I received £15 a week for a five-day week, and this sum was fixed, whatever I wrote. The serious monthlies paid at the rate of £1 a page for the most part, though in several cases this was reduced after the slump. Of course the popular dailies would pay very high prices for special articles by writers with well-known names, but the ordinary occasional contributor rarely got more than £10 10s – at any rate that was all I received from the *Daily Mirror*. Some editors were in receipt of salaries of £5,000 a year, but they were very few in number; it is therefore no exaggeration to say that considering the influence they wielded and the responsibilities they bore, journalists were very badly paid indeed. At the same time the cost of living was not high in comparison. In 1926 I married my present wife, and we rented a house in Horley in Surrey, then almost rural, at a figure of £100 a year. It contained three entertaining rooms, three bedrooms, the usual offices, and there was also a small garden.

Horley in those days had many advantages of which not the least was its proximity to Brighton. How or where I first met Sir Harry Preston I do not remember, but it was at about this time that my wife and I acquired the habit of going to the Royal Albion, and occasionally of staying there – once we even spent a memorable Christmas under his roof. Harry never seemed to have any fixed tariff: if you were a friend of his the charges were extremely reasonable, but for the ordinary public they could be extraordinarily steep. He believed, however, in giving value for money, so that if Mr and Mrs Jones of Bradford or Mr and Mrs Smith of Birmingham were paying through the nose, they would have the satisfaction of reading in the *Morning Post* that they had been staying at the Royal Albion in company with such notabilities as the Earl of Lonsdale and Senator Marconi, and sometimes even with the Prince of Wales. On Saturday night there was dancing: the carpet in the lounge was taken up and Sir Harry and Lady Preston opened the proceedings to the strains of 'The Blue Danube'.

Those were pleasant days. Not only had the failure of the General Strike removed the threat of revolution, it had, curiously enough, taken much of the bitterness out of industrial relations. At the Foreign Office there were in succession three of the best Foreign Secretaries of the century in Ramsay MacDonald, Austen Chamberlain, and Arthur Henderson. Inflation was unknown, and if the cost of living moved at all it was in a downward direction. We did not know that it was merely the lull before the storm. For a few blissful years, in fact, we seemed to have got back to the days before the First World War. If any of my younger readers query this statement let them look at a newspaper of 1927 and compare it with one of today.

As the twenties drew to a close two events took place which had a considerable influence upon my future career. In 1927 my elder brother died, leaving only two daughters. I therefore succeeded to the family baronetcy, but to nothing else, as neither a penny nor an acre went with it. As one who strongly approves of hereditary titles I had not the slight- est hesitation in using it when it came my way, and I have never regretted doing so.

The second event of this period was my first book, *The History of Government*, which I wrote in 1929. Published in Great Britain by Methuen and in the United States by Little, Brown, in the two countries it sold 1,319 copies. I have no exact record of what I made out of it, but if the sum was more than a hundred pounds I should be astonished. The public has always had an exaggerated idea of the money to be made out of the writing of books, for the vast majority of writers fare very indif- ferently; in some ways authorship is an even more uncertain profession than journalism. As Douglas Jerrold well put it in *Georgian Adventure*, 'Popular novelists apart, no man has ever lived out of the writing of books, except on a scale which satisfies only saints, scholars, heroes, and members of the writing classes.'

Very early in my literary career I was confronted with the question, do reviews sell books? Although I have now had many years' experience both as an author and a reviewer, and even a few as a publisher, I should not like to give a definite answer. Probably reviews have more effect in the case of fiction than in that of other classes of literature. Once the potential reader of a novel has been assured that it is a good story of the type he likes he will go for the book without more ado, because that is what he wants. On the other hand, the potential reader of a non-fictional work passes through two stages: first of all the subject has to interest him, and then he has to be satisfied that it is adequately treated, so he constitutes a more difficult problem. Northcliffe's dictum that it does not much matter what people say as long as they say something, which may or may not be true where individuals are concerned, certainly applies to serious books. Even a hostile review, so long as the work in question is not described as dull or inaccurate, is decidedly better than no review at all. If the reviewer describes the author as a bloody-minded and pestilent fellow with whom no reasonable human being is likely ever to agree, there are sure to be some bloody-minded and pestilent people among the readers of the review who will want to see what the book has to say. It is silence that kills.

One publisher, even more prosperous than his fellows, once remarked to me that books are largely sold by talk, and there is a good deal in this. 'My dear, you simply must put so-and-so down on your library list', and 'I've just finished a damn good book, you ought to read it', are the recommendations that help sales enormously, and particularly is this so in the larger centres of population.

It was fashionable in the twenties to talk of various interpretations of history but for my own part, as a historian, I have always held with Dionysius of Halicarnassus, that history is only philosophy teaching by example; I also fully concur with the statement that history is but past politics and that politics are but present history, the term 'politics' being, of course, interpreted in its widest sense. Yet it is not so long ago that history was studied in water-tight compartments, officially called periods, and that these were supposed to have relatively little to do with one another. The fall of the Western Empire, the discovery of America, and the French Revolution were regarded not so much as milestones but rather as boundary lines, and to suggest that one era merged into the next came very near to heresy.

One instance of this attitude is very clearly imprinted on my memory. When I was at Oxford modern history, in the eyes of the authorities, ceased with the Treaty of Berlin in 1878, and woe betide the unhappy undergraduate who let his imagination wander beyond that date. I well remember at the close of a lecture asking about the cession of Thessaly to Greece, an event which took place three years after the Berlin settlement, only to be told by the horrified and indignant lecturer, the late Sir John Marriott, that he was there to teach history, and not to talk politics.

Perhaps it is our misfortunes that have transformed our attitude, for in the seventies we are no longer as sure as we were in the twenties that progress must necessarily be uninterrupted, and that all changes are for the good. Yet that was the view that was almost universal in Britain fifty years ago. After all, our grandfathers travelled in coaches, while we ride in motor-cars, and they had neither wireless nor aeroplanes, so it is but natural that we should be superior to them in other ways. We have progressed from the ape in the forest to the robot in the suburb, and to suggest that there can be any looking back now is an insult to the dignity of man. From this it follows that when any survival from the past is discarded, it is a sign of progress. Because we can move over the ground more rapidly than our forefathers, therefore we are in advance of them, and when we overthrow the forms of government, especially monarchical ones, that they set up, we prove ourselves progressive. Such was the fashionable philosophy between the wars. It was a veritable *trahison des clercs*. Most of them are sadder and wiser now.

The fact is that for two decades we hailed too many 'new dawns', we began too many 'new eras', and we turned over too many 'new pages', and the end of it all was totalitarian war. In consequence there is today a welcome disposition to approach history in a far more humble spirit, and to receive its lessons with becoming humility. 'L'histoire,' wrote that great Swiss thinker, Gonzague de Reynold, 'est une allée de cercueils: dans chacun de ces cercueils se dessèche le cadavre d'une nation qui est morte pour avoir été infidèle a soi-même et à sa destiné.' We have had some light on that lesson of recent years.

CHAPTER VI

Some Figures of the Twenties

THE first Prime Minister of whom I remember anything was Arthur Balfour, whom I met in his later days at a reception at Lord Farquhar's.[1] His reputation in the eyes of his fellow-countrymen well illustrates one characteristic which is common to all the inhabitants of the British Isles, and that is their glorification of defeat and the defeated. Corunna, Mons, and Dunkirk all tell the same story, namely that of an ill-equipped force being landed on the Continent of Europe and then overwhelmed in circumstances which might easily have been foreseen; yet they arouse an enthusiasm among Englishmen never attained by Crécy, Poitiers, Agincourt, or even Waterloo. Whatever the Forty-Five may or may not have been, Culloden was a Scottish defeat at English hands; nevertheless, its bicentenary in April 1946 almost attained the proportions of a national celebration. As for the Irish, the hundred-and-fiftieth anniversary of the failure of the 1798 rising was the occasion for widespread demonstrations of an almost orgiastic character, though except for one celebration by the Military History Society no one in Ireland apparently ever thinks of commemorating the battle of Fontenoy which was one of the greatest achievements of Irish valour. Nor are the Welsh by any means exempt from this curious characteristic, for their national heroes are Llewelyn and Glendower, both of whom signally failed to achieve their object. Balfour, like Joe Beckett in another sphere, owed a great deal to this national foible: it was not until the Conservative Party had lost three General Elections in

[1] A curious character who, as Treasurer of the Conservative Party, swindled it out of its funds; according to tradition he performed the same service for the Royal Family, *cf.* Beaverbrook, Lord: *The Decline and Fall of Lloyd George*, London 1963, p. 203.

succession under his leadership that the feeling in favour of his replacement became more widespread.

Looking back on Balfour's career it is impossible to resist the conclusion that he was admirable as a second-in-command, but that he did not possess the gifts of a leader. As the lieutenant of his uncle, particularly during his tenure of office as Chief Secretary for Ireland, he was brilliant, but he was not the man to place at the head of affairs: in a crisis he either failed to make a decision at all or else he took the wrong one. As a leader he had, too, a frustrating effect on the rank and file of his party. Times innumerable he would address a meeting when it was confidently expected that he would give a lead in some moment of crisis, but no lead would be forthcoming. He was a master of the type of speech which sounds impressive but really says nothing. When I was very young I remember calling with my mother in the brougham for my father who had been at a meeting addressed by Balfour in the St George's Hall in Liverpool. When he got in the carriage Mother asked him what the great man's speech was like, and was told that it was wonderful. This, however, did not satisfy her, so she asked what he had said, only to receive the same answer. When she had repeated the question several times, Father said, 'Well since you press me he didn't say anything at all.'

The late Sir John Squire's parody of a speech by Balfour was not very far from the truth:

'But even allowing – which I am far from allowing, I shall come to that presently – that we have been superficially inconsistent, are honourable gentlemen opposite so ignorant of the most elementary forms of our constitutional practice, of that parliamentary custom which in the opinion of many of us has a higher sanction even than the laws of the land, as to think that the speeches of the Opposition ten years ago either are, or should be, or should be expected to be, valid criteria of the actions of a government today?'

Of recent years Mr Kenneth Young's masterly study of Balfour[1] has necessitated a drastic revision of many opinions previously held concerning him, for it is clear that the statesman was also a good deal of a lecher, though in a rather detached and superior way. Mr Young has noted in this connection that he was careful to 'spread his emotional interests over a wide field'. But the centre of his private life was Mary Wyndham, who early became the wife of the eleventh Earl of Wemyss, whom he

[1] *Arthur James Balfour*, London 1963.

originally met with her mother at Lord Leighton's studio: he helped the husband politically, and in the process he helped himself to the wife. The liaison was particularly active during Balfour's Chief Secretaryship, but it lasted for a number of years after that, for as late as 1898 the lady was corresponding with him about a self-induced abortion.

The truth is that Balfour is one of the most difficult characters in modern history to assess. A man of great charm, a philosopher and a scholar, he undoubtedly added to the lustre of the office of Prime Minister by having held it, and yet it is given to few men to rouse such different feelings as those expressed in the nicknames 'Prince Arthur' and 'Bloody Balfour'. But the fact is illustrative of his paradoxical nature. No man could be so far-sighted, yet on more than one occasion he proved unable to see what was close at hand. At the same time it must be admitted that as leader of the Conservative Party he had difficulties to face which might well have proved too much for one who possessed greater talents in that particular direction. The division of opinion among the ranks of his followers on the subject of Tariff Reform more than once threatened to disrupt the Conservative Party altogether, and he felt it to be his duty to prevent this at all costs. The not unnatural consequence was that he came to be mistrusted by both the Protectionists and the Free Traders. That he did prevent a split on the tariff issue must be conceded, but in doing so he was very often the despair of those who were called upon to collaborate with him. In the House of Commons his qualities showed to greater advantage than in the country, for he was brilliant in debate, whereas on the platform, as we have seen, he too often gave the impression of not having made up his own mind.

My recollections of Bonar Law, who was not a dominant figure in the political scene for long, I have given on an earlier page. Stanley Baldwin was very different. His influence in the twenties and thirties cannot be over-estimated. On the few occasions, purely formal, that I met him I found him somewhat unattractive, but we know now that he was very far from being what he wished to be considered, and the 'image' which he created for himself was false. He posed before his fellow-countrymen as the bluff, straightforward John Bull Englishman of tradition, who believed in a policy of live-and-let-live. Actually there was concealed under the good-natured exterior of this Worcestershire ironmaster, as Lord Rosebery wrote of Walpole, 'a jealousy of power, passing the jealousy of women, and the ruthless vindictiveness of a Red Indian'. Baldwin was also one of the most astute party leaders of the twentieth century, not excluding Harold Wilson, and whatever view may be taken of the morality of his proceedings in connection with the General Election of 1935 his conduct of it was masterly. The widespread depreciation, even vilification, of Baldwin during the Second World War, when he received an average of thirty abusive letters a day, cannot obscure the fact that for several years he was one of the most popular Prime Ministers his country has ever known. Particularly was this so with the women. There was a time when it was as dangerous to criticize S.B. in female society as it would have been to tell an improper story in a Victorian drawing-room. As an instance of this, Donald McI. Johnson, who fought Bury in the Liberal interest in 1935, has told me that he was warned not to criticize Baldwin personally or he would antagonize even his own Liberal supporters.

Baldwin also possessed the supreme merit of being able to learn from experience; indeed, it may be said to have been the only way in which he did learn. In this connection his astuteness in 1935 is in marked contrast with his bungling in 1923: he learnt his lesson on the first occasion, and he never rushed his fences again. His besetting weakness was laziness, though this was for several years concealed even from his colleagues by the devoted service of such Parliamentary Private Secretaries as Charles Rhys and Geoffrey Lloyd.

On the other hand he showed up very badly over the crisis of the Hoare-Laval Pact when he said to Austen Chamberlain, 'Austen, when Sam has gone, I shall want to talk to you about the Foreign Office', and then gave it to Anthony Eden. His weakness for chicanery of this sort must not be overlooked in any estimate of his character, while it took nothing less than King Edward's abdication to rehabilitate his position in the eyes of his fellow-countrymen after his mishandling of the Hoare-Laval crisis. In retrospect, Baldwin would appear to have been at his best on the occasion of the General Strike, in face of the violent press campaign conducted against him by Beaverbrook and Rothermere, and in his handling of the abdication. He was certainly at his worst when he plunged his party into the disastrous General Election of 1923, in the conclusion of a naval agreement with Germany in direct violation of the Treaty of Versailles behind the backs of France and Italy, and at the time of the Hoare-Laval Pact.

When all is said and done, however, Baldwin is surely not to be judged by any specific act of commission or of omission, but rather by the effects of what may be termed Baldwinism upon Britain and the world. By this word many of us who lived in the period preceding the Second World War understood the triumph of expediency over principle, a Conservative Party in which only the yes-men had any hope of promotion, and a policy which took little or no account of the progress of events on the mainland of Europe. In effect, the charge against Stanley Baldwin is that he anaesthetized British public opinion, and it is a charge that cannot be refuted.

Whether he had a sense of humour is a moot point, but he used to tell a story of how he was dining quietly one night at the Carlton Club with a well-known Scottish duke when there entered the coffee-room a tall man with tow hair, whiskers, and over-dressed in a fancy fashion. The duke at once remarked that the newcomer was an Irish earl. 'How do you recognize an Irish earl?' asked Baldwin. The duke replied, 'My father told me that when you saw a man come into the club with a velvet collar, two or three of his flies open, and looking as if he had forgotten to pull the plug, you could be sure he was an Irish earl.' Baldwin's wife, Lucy, had no sense of humour at all, and many of the stories told about her were worthy of Lady Hawkins in an earlier generation. One of the best was that when she was in the chair at a meeting in aid of unmarried mothers she besought all the men present to make themselves responsible for at least one unmarried mother during the ensuing twelve months.

Austen Chamberlain was a very different man in every way from Balfour, Bonar Law and Baldwin, and he was one of the few statesmen of my earlier years for whom I had a real regard. He had been trained to a public career, though in later life I sometimes fancy that he rather regretted the lack of any business experience. But in the eighties and nineties of the last century no one realized that the day would come when ex-Cabinet ministers would be driven to the City to repair fortunes shattered in the service of the State, yet that was to be Austen's own fate. If he was less lucky than Bonar Law in political matters he was much more fortunate in his domestic experiences, for whereas Bonar was left a widower at a comparatively early age, Austen possessed in his wife one whom to know was in itself a gift from the gods. She has been criticized in some quarters for her alleged pro-Italian attitude during the period immediately before the Second World War, but the fact is that her efforts were directed towards breaking the Rome-Berlin axis, a reason for her activities which her critics for various reasons are inclined to ignore.

Austen had an intense dislike of what he considered to be bombast or ostentation, and this sometimes led him to take an unjust view of dead statesmen whom he believed to have been guilty of these crimes. A case in point was George Canning. Austen was dining with me one evening, and we were discussing Canning whose biography I had recently written. He expressed himself in strong terms regarding Canning's love of the limelight, as it appeared to him. The next day I sent him a copy of my book, for which I received the following acknowledgement:

'It is very kind of you to send me your *Canning*, which I have indeed marked down for holiday reading. He always interests me. I am quite unable to deny his greatness or the mark he left on the world, but I must admit that he is to me a kind of Dr Fell. I will hope, however, that you will make me see him in a pleasanter light.

'In one of those books of questions of your loves and hates, likes and dislikes, which were at one time fashionable in country houses, I once came across the question, "name three books of undoubted merit which you have been unable to read", and I confessed to Gibbon's *Decline and Fall*, Plutarch's *Lives*, and *Paradise Lost*. I fear that, if I were asked to name three great statesmen of undoubted merit whom I nevertheless did not admire, Canning's name would be on my list.'

On the other hand he had a great respect for Castlereagh, who appeared to him to be endowed with those qualities in which he considered Canning to be deficient. At the time of the Locarno Pact he specially borrowed a portrait of Castlereagh from Lord Londonderry to be hung on the wall in the room in the Foreign Office where that document was to be signed.

Austen's own views of those who had preceded him at the Foreign Office are not without interest, and he gave expression to them when, in 1927, it was decided to hang portraits of the six greatest Foreign Secretaries since the post came into existence in 1806:

'My six Foreign Ministers are Castlereagh, Canning, Palmerston, Salisbury, Lansdowne, and Grey – Lansdowne as the minister of the Anglo-Japanese Alliance and the Anglo-French Entente. I rejected without hesitation Fox, for whatever his greatness (as to which I have my own opinion) it was not shown as Foreign Minister; Grenville because whatever claims he had were of an earlier date when he was Pitt's mouthpiece; Lord Aberdeen (Peel's ministry), Malmesbury, and Lord John Russell (whom I reserve with Granville for the Chamber of Horrors), Lord Dudley, Lord Stanley (of Dizzy's first ministry, the Derby of his second), Lord Rosebery, and Lord Clarendon. The last is the only one for whom a serious claim has been advanced to come in front of any of the six whom I have chosen. He had a considerable reputation, but I cannot, even after reading Herbert Maxwell's *Life* for that very purpose, find anything to justify it, so I stand by my six. They are not all favourites of mine. I don't care much for Palmerston; Canning inspires the same kind of mistrust in me that he did in his contemporaries; and Salisbury in his later years was, I think, weakly temporizing and without initiative to meet the new conditions of a rapidly changing world. But viewed objectively I don't think you could omit any of the six or prefer others to him.'

One incident, of possibly more than purely personal interest, connected with Austen is especially fresh in my mind. Lunching with him at the United University Club one day in November 1930, just after my wife and I had returned from Italy where I had had an interview with Mussolini, the conversation naturally turned on Italian colonial ambitions. At that time the Duce was seeking expansion in the Mediterranean area, and Austen was worried over the possibility of a conflict between France and Italy in respect of Tunis. 'The best solution for Europe', he said, 'would have been to let Italy expand into Asia Minor, as she was promised by the Treaty of London. No British interest would have been affected, and it would have provided a guarantee against the spread of Russian influence in the Eastern Mediterranean. But the Turks are a nation again, and it is too late to think of that now.' I asked him why the Greeks had been encouraged to invade Asia Minor to their ruin. 'That is a thing', he replied, 'I, too, have always wondered: I asked Curzon and Arthur Balfour several times, but could never get a satisfactory answer out of either of them.'

It was nothing short of a tragedy that Austen should have died only a few months before his brother became Prime Minister. Had he lived two or three years longer he could have given Neville invaluable advice on international problems, thus avoiding many a mistake; as it was that advice was sought, sometimes with fatal consequences, from other and less informed quarters.

Perhaps the finest thing in his career was the resignation of the Secretaryship of State for India in 1917. The campaign in Mesopotamia, which came under the India Office, was proved to have been grossly mismanaged. When a Commission inquired into it a very disquieting state of affairs was revealed, particularly where the medical services were concerned. There was never any suggestion that blame attached to Austen, but he was Secretary of State for India and it was his department that was involved; therefore he resigned. There was no need to have taken this course; his action has certainly not been allowed to constitute a precedent; it is hard in fact to imagine any modern politician, whatever his party, acting in a similar manner. Austen acted as he did because he was first and foremost a great parliamentarian, who believed that if the parliamentary system is to be worked successfully the rules must be observed, otherwise disaster will ensue. It would have been easy for him to have remained in office; there was a complacent majority in the House of Commons that would have accepted any reasonable explanation from a minister in the middle of a war, and there was a censored press. Nevertheless, Austen refused to take the line of least resistance, and his behaviour proved him at once a great constitutionalist and a great gentleman.

Like his father before him Austen had one notable characteristic, namely an encouragement of youth and a delight in its society. As A. P. Herbert once put it, there was nothing 'high-hat' about him. Self-important back benchers may have thought that he treated them too superciliously in the lobbies and smoke-room of the House of Commons, though in taking offence they forgot the fact that his eyesight was poor in later years, but the young men at Oxford and Cambridge found him a most delightful companion. On such occasions there was nothing in the least formal about him; he was always the centre of a group of eager, almost importunate, questioners, whose curiosity he was only too delighted to satisfy.

On one of these occasions Austen really excelled himself. He let us into a good many secrets, such as the story of how Lord Beaverbrook got his peerage, in the telling of which he proved a good many of the legends concerning this were inaccurate. One story about his own father I particularly remember. It appears that one cold winter night while Joe was a member of Gladstone's administration he was bidden to dine at Windsor, and Austen, then an undergraduate at Cambridge, lent his father an old pair of trousers to put on over his Privy Councillor's breeches in order to keep his legs warm in the train. It must be remembered that at this time Queen Victoria regarded Chamberlain's views with the greatest suspicion. On arriving at the castle Chamberlain was shown into a room, for the purpose, as he supposed, of removing the superfluous nether garments. He was, therefore, in the very act of divesting himself of them when the door opened, and in walked the Queen. She had, it transpired, given orders for him to be directed to that particular apartment because she had some official business to transact with him before dinner, so a great deal of explanation was necessary before Chamberlain was able to excuse himself for the occupation in which he had been discovered.

As a young man I was not brought much into contact with politicians other than those of the Conservative variety: Asquith, for instance, I met only once, and that was at a tennis party on Boar's Hill. Although I was far from sympathetic to his political views I have always had the greatest admiration for him as a scholar and a man. A most serious mistake, however, which was to cost his party dear, was the one he made in 1924. At the General Election in the previous autumn the Conservative administration of Stanley Baldwin had suffered a serious reverse, and although its supporters emerged with 258 seats – the strongest single party in the House of Commons – they were far from having a majority over Labour, who came second with 191, and the Liberals combined. Such being the case Asquith, who had a following of 159, decided to put the Conservatives out and Labour in, which he proceeded to do upon the Address, with the result that the first Labour Government under Ramsay MacDonald came into office in the early weeks of 1924. Acting in this way gave Asquith two advantages; first he could put MacDonald out whenever it suited him to do so, and secondly, as there had been two General Elections within little more than twelve months, King George V would refuse MacDonald a dissolution if he asked for one – in this case he (Asquith) would be sent for to form a government, which he would then do with the support of the Conservatives, who would prefer a Liberal to a Labour administration.

There was something to be said for this point of view, and when the results of the General Election had first become known at least one of the Conservative leaders, namely Austen Chamberlain, had been in favour of putting the Liberals into office on conditions. What, however, upset Asquith's calculations was the fact that he no longer had to deal with the united and disciplined Liberal Party of pre-war days. 'The Liberal Party,' Austen wrote at this time, 'is visibly bursting up. It holds constant meetings to decide its course; then 40 vote with the Govt., 20 vote with us, and the rest (including the leaders) walk out, or absent themselves.' This was bad enough, but when the Liberals did put the Government out in the autumn of that same year, 1924, the King allowed MacDonald to dissolve, and at the ensuing General Election not only did the Conservatives sweep the country but the Liberal strength was reduced to 44. It proved to be the end of Liberalism as a parliamentary force.

Before leaving Asquith I should like to tell one more story about him. It is peculiarly Edwardian in its flavour and well illustrates his relations with Lloyd George in the days before the First World War; it also reflects the contemporary suspicion of their respective weaknesses. A well-meaning but tactless supporter one day observed to the Prime Minister, 'Do you know what the Chancellor of the Exchequer calls you behind your back?' On receiving a reply in the negative, he continued, 'Well, he calls you old Veuve Clicquot.' 'Oh, does he?' said Asquith. 'Next time you meet your friend the Chancellor of the Exchequer you can tell him that behind his back I always call him old Pol Roger.'

In an earlier chapter I have mentioned that I first got to know John Buchan when I was at the War Cabinet Office, and during the twenties I saw quite a lot of him in various connections. Looking back on his career one can only conclude that he attempted to do too many things; at any one of them he would have excelled, but as there are only twenty-four hours in the day it was physically impossible for him to get through all the work he undertook. During the middle period of his life this became slightly obvious, before he was called to Canada to the task with which his career had begun in South Africa, namely that of Imperial consolidation. How well he did his work in Ottawa and how intimately he got to know the Canadian people are common knowledge; for there, as his biographer Janet Adam Smith has put it, he rediscovered 'a sense of purpose'. But the tragedy was that he returned to his real vocation so late. Had he lived he would almost certainly have been appointed ambassador to the United States.

As an author it is no disparagement to Buchan's memory to say that his writing was uneven, but when much more recent literature is forgotten *The Thirty-Nine Steps* and *Greenmantle* will still be remembered and the most recent figures for his sales which I have seen quoted demonstrate his continued popularity with a new generation of readers. On the other hand his purely historical works would seem unlikely to survive, for he was inclined to read more into his characters than the facts always justified.

Contrary to the generally accepted opinion Buchan had strong likes and dislikes in the matter of historical personages. Nothing would induce him to put pen to paper with regard to any character of whom he disapproved, as one instance will prove. One summer holiday when my wife and I were at Felixstowe, among the other guests at the Felix Hotel was Dr Archibald Fleming, the minister at St Columba's, Pont Street, the church which we then attended. In the course of conversation Fleming and I agreed that it would be a very good thing if Buchan would follow up his then recent biography of Montrose with one of Dundee, for the works of A. and H. Tayler and Miss Gordon Daviot had not at that time appeared. Accordingly I asked both Buchan and Fleming to lunch at the old Carlton annexe, and at what appeared to be a suitable moment the subject was duly broached. To our great surprise Buchan was almost indignant at the mere suggestion that he should write about Dundee, whom he dismissed as a *beau sabreur* and nothing more.

Yet when he did decide on a subject he took immense pains in matters of detail, for throughout his life Buchan was never for a moment idle. He was, too, one of those happy beings who can work as well in a train as at a desk, and such were his powers of concentration that the presence of other people in the room when he was writing did not disturb him.

One other aspect of Buchan's activities has rarely received the attention which it merits, and that was his interest in, and encouragement of, youth. At his house at Elsfield he was continually entertaining Oxford under-graduates, who were thus, to their great advantage, brought into contact with pro-consuls and men-of-letters, with statesmen and journalists. Many a young man found in Buchan the proverbial guide, philosopher, and friend. When the Bonar Law College at Ashridge was founded he took the keenest interest in its growth, so that its subsequent success was in no small measure due to his efforts during those early days. He possessed the great gift of always treating young men as his equals, and though he would not hesitate to give unpalatable advice if he thought the occa-sion demanded it he never adopted a superior manner. He was a very real inspiration not only to that heterogeneous collection of undergra-duates who were at Oxford immediately after the First World War, but to all those who centred round the Oxford Carlton Club, of which he succeeded Penson as Senior Treasurer. Buchan always seemed so sure of himself, and if, as D'Annunzio maintained, inward sovereignty is the chief mark of the aristocrat, then he was an aristocrat to his finger-tips.

Many of his friends were puzzled when he went into the House of Commons. He seems to have had only a spasmodic ambition to sit on a Front Bench, his interventions in parliamentary proceedings were infre-quent, and it must be confessed that he was not a parliamentary success: Baldwin went so far as to say that he 'would be no use in the Cabinet'. To tell the truth, as a speaker he was not in the same class as his eldest son: he had a tendency to drop his voice at the end of each sentence in a way that was very irritating to those who were listening to him. On the other hand, that he should have wanted to get into Parliament at all reflects great credit upon that establishment between the wars – he would hardly have desired to enter it today – for it proved that the separation between politics and letters, which is so unhappy a characteristic of the modern age, was not yet complete. (The later arrival of A. P. Herbert at Westminster was also reassuring in this way.)

Nevertheless in his failure to make much impression at Westminster he was far from unique in the world of letters. Gibbon, for instance might as well never have set foot there for all the contribution he made to the debates; Lecky was too academic – Balfour's congratulations to 'the honourable and learned member for Dublin University on his interesting lecture' was Lecky's undoing; and Belloc was never in his element at Westminster. Nevertheless, there have been men who have shone in both spheres, as the names of Disraeli, Balfour, Morley, and Macaulay abundantly testify.

Just as Buchan's public usefulness appeared to be approaching its end there came his appointment as Governor-General of Canada, making him in spirit one of Milner's 'young men' again. (Some of us felt that he would have done better to have remained John Buchan but King George V thought otherwise.) The truth is that he had never lost the imprint of his South African experiences, being always far more at home in the Empire overseas than he was in European matters. Europe at once bored and frightened him, and he was content to follow where others led; thus he was one of Neville Chamberlain's strongest supporters at the time of Munich, not because he had made a close study of the issues involved, but because of his innate horror of war, based on what he had himself seen of it. Where South Africa and Canada were concerned it was a different matter – he did not hestitate to rely on his own judgement.

Finally, a word about Ramsay MacDonald, who was very definitely one of the great figures of the twenties. Although I never knew him personally, I know much more about him than I do about many of my personal acquaintances, owing to my later friendship with Rose Rosenberg, his private secretary, when she was helping me with my study of *The Powers behind the Prime Ministers*. If Asquith is possibly the most misjudged of recent Premiers there can be little question but that Mac-Donald is the most misunderstood and probably today the least known: not even Winston Churchill was the victim of so many vicissitudes or so often the sport of fate. Like Gladstone and Baldwin, he remained in office a little too long for his reputation, and the events of 1931 left no political party or section of public opinion with any particular interest in seeing that justice was done to his memory. Then again, to no inconsiderable extent was his unpopularity during the First World War his own fault for his lack of lucidity in explaining his point-of-view. Mac-Donald believed that Great Britain was wrong to have entered the war, but having entered it she must do her best to win it, and he told his audience that 'those who can enlist ought to enlist'. At the same time he urged that tempers should not be allowed to become heated, that after victory there should be a peace based on moderation and restraint. This was a counsel of perfection. However, as the modern Englishman exhibits as insensate a hatred for his enemies in time of war as he displays a sentimental yearning to take them to his bosom in time of peace, Mac-Donald was soon a voice crying in the wilderness.

Though he was never a pacifist, he became in effect the personification of all that the average Englishman dislikes in wartime, and it was not long before he was the most hated man in the country. When in December 1914 he went to Belgium as a volunteer member of a British ambulance unit attached to the Belgian army, he was promptly ordered home on the instructions of the British Government. In the spring of 1917, when with others he was about to sail with official permission from Aberdeen to visit Kerensky in Russia, the crew of the ship refused to put to sea unless he and two of his colleagues were left on shore. Whatever his platform, every meeting at which he was billed to speak was a potential riot, and a section of the press did all in its power to provoke violence by attributing to him provocative statements which he had never made, and by encouraging the public to break up his meetings. Finally, in the General Election in December 1918 he was defeated at West Leicester by a majority of over fourteen thousand votes. Had anyone prophesied at that time that within a few years MacDonald would be Prime Minister the remark would have been regarded as just as stupid as if it had been made about Winston Churchill on the morrow of the abdication of King Edward VIII.

In politics, however, the unexpected generally happens. In 1922, when MacDonald re-entered the House of Commons, this time to represent the Aberavon division of Glamorganshire, he was at once elected Leader of the Labour Party, and in January 1924, after the defeat of the first Baldwin administration, he became Prime Minister without ever having held any previous office. No reversal of fortune could have been more complete.

One of his first acts in his new position was to break with tradition by appointing a woman, Rose Rosenberg, as his private secretary. She told me she had always found MacDonald – unlike many of his predecessors and successors at No. 10 – to be a man of the most equable temperament; during the whole of the fifteen years that she worked for him, though she often saw him unhappy, disappointed, or annoyed, he had never lost his temper. So far as she personally was concerned the worst that ever happened if she made a mistake was a plaintive, 'Why, Rose, how did you come to do that?' Life at 10 Downing Street was very different from what it had been in the days of Lloyd George and was to be again in those of Winston Churchill. When MacDonald was Leader of the Opposition he had had Clem Attlee as his P.P.S., of whom Miss Rosenberg had no very high opinion, for she once described him to me as 'surely one of the idlest P.P.S.s there ever was'. One of MacDonald's peculiarities was that he liked his secretaries to make an immediate note of anything he told them. He was always suspicious of the person who merely said, 'Yes, Mr Prime Minister', for he had little faith in the unaided human memory. This was a foible which he shared with King George V, who much appreciated the fact that Lord Stamfordham wrote shorthand, and was thus able to jot down at once any instructions that he received from his master.

As one who had himself been an outcast, and as the leader of a party which was viewed askance in many quarters, it was only natural that MacDonald should be a little doubtful of the loyalty of those about him. His position recalls that of Michael Collins who, when he first took office, was greeted by an old Civil Servant with the words, 'I am delighted to have the pleasure of welcoming you, Mr Collins'. His immediate reply was, 'Like Hell you are!' MacDonald was far too courteous to express himself in this way, but as the head of a government which was anathema to the Right he knew that many people regarded the Labour administration in the same way as the Irish bureaucracy looked on Sinn Fein. Naturally this made him suspicious, so in Miss Rosenberg's office leading out of the Cabinet Room he had a tall japan cupboard with a special lock put up, of which only he and Rose had keys, where all papers of a secret or confidential nature had to be kept. This put a considerable strain on her tact, for she was strictly forbidden to show even to her chief's ministerial colleagues, let alone the other secretaries, parliamentary or otherwise, any of the documents without his consent.

As a statesman it was in the field of foreign affairs that MacDonald's claim to distinction really lies. On coming into office in January 1924 he decided to combine the Foreign Secretaryship with the Premiership, thus following the example of Lord Salisbury in the closing decades of the previous century. It was not, perhaps, an ideal combination of offices, but in this instance if either of them suffered it was the Premiership. The change from Curzon was distinctly one for the better, for although that 'most superior person' generally knew the course which ought to be pursued, he nearly always failed to pursue it. MacDonald, on the other hand, was possessed of a judgement, or perhaps one should say an instinct, that was usually sound, and he certainly did not share his predecessor's illusion that an occasional admonition would suffice to bring about a general recovery in Europe.

Partly owing to the French occupation of the Ruhr, and partly owing to the personal antipathy that existed between Curzon and Poincaré, relations between Great Britain and France could hardly have been worse, and MacDonald fully realized that an improvement in them was an essential preliminary to any amelioration of the international situation as a whole. Fortune undoubtedly favoured him, for soon after he took office there was a General Election in France, and Poincaré and his *bloc national* was replaced by Herriot and the *cartel des gauches*. The two Prime Ministers had much in common in their tastes and outlook and appreciation of the difficulty of their task: for it was Herriot who said that 'to disarm' was an irregular verb since it had no first person singular and was only to be found in the future tense.

The two men worked hard throughout the summer of 1924 to bring their respective peoples together again, their labours resulting in the Protocol of Geneva. Although it is true that this had to be discarded and replaced by the Locarno Pact, chiefly because it was in advance of public opinion at the time, the fact that it had been concluded at all marked a welcome improvement in Anglo-French relations. Unfortunately while these events were taking place at Geneva events were happening elsewhere which were to have much greater influence upon the future of mankind, even if they passed unnoticed in the corridors of the League – in the Kremlin at Moscow the newly-elected General Secretary of the Central Committee of the Communist Party of the Soviet Union, Joseph Stalin, was settling down to his work, and far away in a Bavarian prison Adolf Hitler was putting the finishing touches to *Mein Kampf*.

CHAPTER VII

France and Spain in the Twenties

THE continental countries with which my wife and I were best acquainted during these years were France, where my wife had a cousin married to a Russian émigré, and Spain. We also paid the occasional visit to Belgium, where she had been at school.

France of those days was, like Britain, looking back to the pre-war era, quite unsuspecting of what lay ahead, and was trying to resume the course of her history where it had been broken off by the events of 1914. Once more, if for the last time, she was mistress of Europe, which she had not been since 1870, a position so strange to her after more than forty years of German domination that she was not quite certain what use to make of it. Above all she was suffering from a *manque des hommes*, for with the possible exception of Briand no real statesman made his appearance in France during this period.

Personally I met few of the transient and embarrassed phantoms, as Disraeli would have called them, who held office in the last years of the Third Republic, but there was a memorable occasion when I did meet, and proposed the health of, Clemenceau at an Anglo-American Press lunch. I forget the circumstances of the event, which must have taken place not long before Père la Victoire died, but I well remember the deathmask of a face and the lavender gloves he always wore, the purpose of which we were told was to conceal the effects of some skin disease he was suffering from. It was there that he told us that when the Germans asked for an armistice the first person he informed was the Empress Eugénie.

Being a man of the Right my own political connections in France were mostly with members of the Action Française, and however strange it

97

may seem today, royalism on the other side of the Channel was still an active force in the twenties; that it never came to fruition was due to the lack of competent leadership and to the tendencies of all parties of the Right everywhere to run after a dictator. While the star of Boulanger was in the ascendant the misguided royalists attempted to hitch their wagon to it, although there was never the least doubt that *le brave général* was playing solely for his own hand and never had any intention of restoring the Bourbons. The result was that monarchism became involved in the discredit that soon attached to Boulangism, and people were heard to declare that the support given to an adventurer like Boulanger was just what one would expect from the House of Orleans. Since that date the Third Republic had been shaken to its foundations by innumerable crises (the Panama and the Dreyfus *Affaires* were the worst, but there had been many others nearly as bad), but no advantage had been taken of them by the opponents of the regime. The Action Française had its opportunity at the time of the financial crisis in 1926, and again when the Stavisky riots took place in Paris in 1934, but it merely demonstrated, thus showing the lack of that driving force necessary to overthrow the republic – yet the rottenness of the regime was exposed to all the world in the spring and summer of 1940.

The explanation of this probably lies in two facts. The first is the universal distrust of the House of Orleans, the claimants to the throne, which goes back to the Revolution and beyond. One night I was asked to a small dinner party to meet the Comte de Paris. Before he appeared an elderly Frenchman said to me, 'I wonder which it will be this evening – the *Fils de St Louis* or the *Fils de L'Egalité.*' Nobody could have been more charming or more dignified than the prince, and when he had gone the elderly Frenchman remarked, '*Fils de St Louis ce soir*' – and the attitude was typical. The second reason for the failure of the royalists was that for many years they were led by eminent men of letters, and it is a melancholy fact that great writers are almost always found wanting when the moment for action arrives. Paul Déroulede, Maurice Barrès, Léon Daudet, and Charles Maurras are the glories of French literature, but they were not intended to lead political parties. So in spite of the brilliance of its leaders and the activity of its propaganda the Action Française achieved precisely nothing in the political field.

From the beginning, too, the movement was regarded with suspicion by the Church owing to the positivist views of Maurras, for the doctrines of the Comte have long been anathema to the Vatican. Pius X, though no friend of the Third Republic, actually condemned the Action Française at the beginning of 1914, but the condemnation was not made public, and it was left for his successor to put it into force. Then again, the leaders of the movement were on the worst possible terms with the Royal House of France, whose restoration they were supporting; indeed, to such lengths did the cleavage go that when the Comte de Paris succeeded his father, the Duc de Guise, as claimant to the throne he started a paper of his own, the *Courrier Royal*. There was also a narrow nationalism and a violent anti-Semitism in the movement which not only alienated many moderate people but was diametrically opposed to the true principles of kingship. Above all the Action Française never struck any real roots in the country, even among those who possessed monarchist sympathies. It always remained a gathering of intellectuals, and though hundreds of thousands of people read their articles and books with relish they never translated what they read into political action.

I met both Maurras and Daudet on several occasions. The former was as deaf as a post, making conversation impossible; his writing, too, was almost illegible. All one could do was to listen to this French Garvin, but that was well worth while. I was present in the offices of the *Action Française* one night when, in the absence of Maurice Pujo, the editor, he was putting the paper to bed. It was a memorable experience: confusion reigned everywhere, everybody was talking at once as Maurras went to work with a will armed with a large pair of scissors and an enormous blue pencil, but the number came out on time with its accustomed brilliance. Daudet was another of the most brilliant talkers I have ever met, though his genius did not lie in the field of everyday politics: he sat in the Chamber for a Paris constituency for one Parliament, but he achieved no great success there. His pen was his real weapon, and his articles in the *Action Française* were a delight to read. Since the death of Labouchère there has been nobody in the British press, with the possible exception of Ian Colvin, who could write like Daudet. There was also a great sense of fun about him, and for a time his escape from the Santé prison by the famous *coup de téléphone* made him almost a legendary figure.[1]

Daudet had another claim to distinction in that like Fernando Maria Castiella, the late Spanish Foreign Minister, he was one of the few modern politicians to be a *gourmet*. It was therefore all the more fitting that immediately under the offices of the *Action Française* should have been situated the restaurant Scossa, where my wife and I had several admirable meals. It was much frequented by the Camelots du Roi, and

1 One of his supporters got hold of the private telephone of the Minister of the Interior and instructed the governor of the Santé prison to release Daudet at once, which was, surprising to relate, done. He took refuge in England, and told me the story of his escape while we were waiting for a bus in Trafalgar Square.

it was amusing to watch the suspicion with which they and the *agents*, of whom there were always several on the other side of the street, eyed one another. Jacques Bainville, the historian, was another member of the group, and I have always been told that the military articles, initialled C. de G., were written by de Gaulle.

Another French royalist friend of those days, though not, I think, a member of the *Action Française*, was the historian Charles Benoist, Minister to the Netherlands and the Holy See, and for a time tutor to the Comte de Paris. In his earlier years he had been a *deputé*, as we see from his *Souvenirs*, where he gives an account of his electioneering methods which might repay the study of aspirants to parliamentary honours today. At his first election Benoist's opponent was formidable on many grounds, not least because his uncle was Minister of the Interior. But he had his weaknesses, for *'avec sa figure sinistre et sa voix de bois, c'est un orateur abondant, coulant, mais térriblement monotone, et, en deux mots qui n'en font qu'un, mortellement ennuyeux'*. Benoist and his supporters determined to take advantage of this characteristic:

> 'By a simple trick we enhanced the unfortunate effect which he produced upon his audience. A hundred of our people attended each of his meetings. A quarter of an hour after he had begun to speak a dozen of them left, without the least disorder or noise; ten minutes later another twenty went out, one at a time from different parts of the hall, as if they could stand the speech no longer. Soon his own supporters became infected, and M. Berthelot finished his harangue before half-empty rows of chairs.'

The strategem succeeded, and Benoist won the seat, a Paris one, which he then held for many years.

Politics apart, life in France was easy in those days, as it was in England. One of the most pleasant holidays my wife and I ever spent was at Etretat, where, incidentally, we made the acquaintance of Colin and Denise Coote. Tourism being in its infancy, and the visitor not catered for to the extent that is the case today, one morning when we were coming in from bathing we were startled to see all our possessions being trundled along the front in a wheelbarrow. On investigation we discovered that some authority had decided that it was *fin de saison* and that the hotel at which we were staying was to be closed, so our things were being transferred to another one; no one, however, had thought to inform us of what was in the wind. We were not the only sufferers, and as the second hotel proved to be more expensive than the first, there were some acrimonious discussions, in which my wife played a prominent part, when the various bills were presented.

We spent our honeymoon in the spring of 1926 in Mallorca, which was far from having attained its present popularity. In those days our only means of access was by a steamer from Barcelona, which made the journey three times a week. The few British residents congregated at the club El Terreno were a curious assortment: some had come to the island because of its cheapness, others were there in order to practise their pet vices in relative privacy, while a third section had been prominent in the more notorious *causes célèbres* of the previous decade. Then there were the eccentrics. At Alcudia Puerto there lived two English ornithologists who had not spoken to one another for years, and who quarrelled in scientific journals and reviews all over the world: as a result the village was divided, not into monarchists and republicans, but into partisans of one ornithologist or the other. The local inhabitants, it may be added, considered every Englishman to be mad, and they had much to justify them in their belief.

Tourism in anything approaching its modern dimensions was unknown. The foreign visitor, usually elderly and often infirm, generally confined his attention to Granada, Seville, and Toledo among the larger towns, and to such seaside resorts as San Sebastian, Santander, and Malaga. Elsewhere he was rarely to be encountered – my wife and I went right down the east coast of Spain from Valencia to Murcia without meeting a single fellow-countryman. The Balearic Islands, now the playground of Europe, were then completely unspoilt; the drawback, however, was that it was not too easy to make oneself understood there, as most of the natives had only a rudimentary knowledge of Spanish and they most vilely mispronounced what little they did know. On the other hand living was extremely cheap, if somewhat primitive, so that it was possible to stay at a reasonable hotel for the equivalent of £3 a week *en pension*. For some £5 a month it was easy to secure an unfurnished house of half a dozen rooms, with a broad open *galeria* and an unobstructed view of the sea, most of the mountains, and the islands, together with a garden full of oranges and lemons and palms, apricots and olives, almonds, banana plants, and a perfect riot of flowers.

Despite King Alfonso's efforts to popularize the motor-car, this new method of conveyance was still in its infancy outside the larger centres of population and although there were a few cars, with an occasional motor-bus, to be met on the roads, the most prominent features were the herds of goats and the large two-wheeled carts, drawn by two or three horses, or a team of mules, with the inevitable *burro de carga* at their head. The normal method of getting about Spain was by train, which the younger generation of today may think of as a soulless affair – they can, however, be assured that a Spanish one in those days was a centre of social activity, particularly in Andalusia. The express steamed gaily along at an average speed of eighteen miles an hour, and when a station was reached the passengers almost without exception swarmed down to the platform and round the tiny *cantina*. After ten minutes or so the whistle would shriek piercingly, but this happened several times before any notice was taken of it. It was only after repeated official shouts of '*Señores viajeros al tren*' that the passengers regained their seats, and the train dragged itself out of the station. One might have been travelling in contemporary Connacht.

Punctuality was no more an outstanding feature of the Spanish railway system than it was of the Irish, and travellers had to draw heavily on their resourcefulness as well as on their patience. Once when I was on the Andaluces Railway between Bobadilla and Ronda the train was seven hours late. I was nearly famished, while Ronda seemed as far off as ever, so it was clear that desperate remedies were necessary. Accordingly, at the first likely station I went along to the engine and asked the driver if he would like a drink; the proposition was readily accepted, and an agreement was reached whereby I was to pay for the engine-driver's brandy while he kept the train waiting until I had taken the edge off my appetite at the station buffet. The compact, faithfully observed on both sides, had one unexpected but very acceptable consequence, for when the driver resumed his place on the engine he drove much faster, actually making up two hours of the lost time before reaching Ronda – much to the alarm of an elderly English lady in my compartment who, accompanied by a canary in a cage, was on her way to spend the winter at Algeciras.

Austen Chamberlain used to tell of a similar incident which in his youth happened to his father and himself on the same line. Although the train was hours late by Joe Chamberlain's watch, it arrived at each station at the scheduled time according to the clock on the platform. The Chamberlain party were mystified, until the future Foreign Secretary looked out of the carriage-window and saw a porter setting, with the aid of a broom-handle, the hands of the station clock to the nominal time of arrival. With typical national courtesy the Spanish authorities were determined to leave nothing undone that might impress their distinguished visitor, even to inculcating the belief that their trains ran to time.

In these circumstances a good deal of time was necessarily spent at the larger junctions, pre-eminent among which was Bobadilla, in Andalusia. In the twenties there was an admirable refreshment room there presided over by an Irishman of the name of Dyer, who had never forgotten the land of his birth, as his fellow-countrymen would discover if they happened to find themselves on his premises on St Patrick's Day. At that time there were a number of deserters from the British regiments at Gibraltar to be found wandering about that part of Spain, and Dyer may originally have been one of them.

Mention of Irishmen in Andalusia recalls the story of Richard Chenevix-Trench, who was afterwards Archbishop of Dublin. It would appear that when he and another undergraduate from Trinity College, Dublin, were cruising in a small yacht in the Mediterranean at the time of the First Carlist War, with their tiny crew they assisted, in the true Charles Lever style, the local Carlists to seize, I think, Malaga; in due course the government forces recaptured the town, and the two Irishmen were sentenced to be shot. When the time came to face the firing-party Chenevix-Trench kept his eye on the Spanish officer in charge of the proceedings, and as soon as he saw that he was about to lower his arm, he himself dropped to the ground. The ensuing volley thus passed harmlessly over his head, though it killed his companion, who had failed to display the same presence of mind. At that moment the British consul, whom Chenevix-Trench had been expecting, made his appearance to cover the two apparently inanimate forms with the Union Jack. When the future Archbishop felt the folds of the flag round him he rose from the ground none the worse for his experience. Nor does the story end there, for the relation of it in Ireland had much to do with his appointment to the see of Dublin in 1863. Nineteen years later Tait died, leaving the see of Canterbury vacant. Chenevix-Trench was very desirous of being translated to it, but the tale of his youthful escapade had reached Queen Victoria, and what had enhanced the Archbishop's popularity in Dublin completely ruined his chances at Windsor.

To return, however, to the twenties of the present century: the splendid roads, the paradors, and the first-class hotels of today were still in the future, and provincial Spain, at any rate, was very much what it had been in the days of King Alfonso's grandmother. These were the days when the *sereno*, or night-watchman, still went his rounds, when at most hotels separate tables were as yet unknown. It would nevertheless be wrong to suggest that the Spanish scene was static during the reign of Don Alfonso XIII, for this was certainly not the case; a revolution was in progress in many of the habits of the people, and the Spain of 1930 was not by any means the Spain of 1920, still less was it that of 1902. One reason for this was that the advent of the Directory in 1923 meant the end of the *cacique*,[1] or local political 'boss', around whom the social life of the smaller towns and of the countryside had for many years been centred. It has even been stated that the greatest change in Spain during the present century, not excepting the Civil War, took place when the women began to wear short skirts. However this may be it is undeniable that another contemporaneous event, namely the arrival of the aeroplane and the motor-car, has had consequences of the very first importance. They have annihilated distance. In the earlier years of the reign there was, for example, nothing like that exodus from Madrid on a Sunday that in summer makes the roads from the capital resemble a motor-racing track, or, as the pessimists would have it, a battlefield: there was no means of getting anywhere, so people had to be content with sauntering in the Retiro or pacing the streets.

What was not changing was the character of the average Spaniard, so misunderstood abroad, where the prevailing conception of him as a romantic has no foundation in fact. An open country where nature seems omnipotent, with everything on a large scale, not unnaturally produces a nation of realists. The soil of Spain has not the richness of France; the landscape is by no means so varied as the Italian; and so the Spaniard differs very considerably from his fellow Latins. His prevailing characteristic is not love of his country like the Frenchman, and although he has plenty of provincial pride he does not carry it to the lengths of the Italian. He is, as the record of his history abundantly proves, a realist, an individualist, and, as is natural with one possessed of so much Moorish blood, a good deal of a fatalist. He is capable of extraordinary energy – some of the greatest feats in the annals of mankind have been performed by Spaniards – but he has not the taste for continuous effort, and until General Franco took charge of the country he has rarely found the leader who can persuade him to undertake it. Yet, with all its shortcomings, the Spanish race has imposed Latin civilization (in more than just the material sense) upon the greater part of the American continent.

Such was the Spain and such were the Spanish in the early years of the present century. There can be little doubt that no monarch could have

---

1 It also meant the end of other things. From time immemorial the subway at Bobadilla Junction had been used as a urinal, and when, soon after the Directory came into office, I was about to employ it for this purpose, a policeman came up with a sorrowful expression on his face and said, 'You will have to go to the proper lavatory. We have a dictator now.'

done more to keep in touch with the life of his subjects than did Don Alfonso XIII, indeed, down to the establishment of the Directory in 1923 it can be claimed that he was successful. At no time could he be accused of a lack of sympathy for the common people, and he always retained a keen sense of humour. He made a special point in the middle years of his reign of going about incognito, but his appearance was so distinctive that it is permissible to wonder how many people were really deceived.

The sentries outside the Palace received careful instructions not to notice the King when he went out unofficially, but these orders were not always obeyed. On one occasion when the King drove out in a sports car a soldier, who had never been on guard before, duly presented arms. Don Alfonso stopped his car, went up to the man, and asked, 'Why did you do that?' 'Your Majesty...' came the stammering reply which the King cut short with a smile, and the words, 'Tomorrow at the guard-mounting you will see the King, and then you will not mistake me for him again.' Next morning at the parade, the Sovereign, this time in uniform, went up to the sentry of the previous day and said, 'You see the King always wears a uniform or has a guard. When you see someone who looks like him, in ordinary clothes, you will remember that he is an ordinary Spaniard, and you will accord him as much respect as any other Spaniard. That is as much as even the King can deserve.'

Much of the strength of the Directory in its early days was derived from Primo de Rivera himself, for his character appealed to his fellow-countrymen. The wits might sing,

> *Naipes, mujeres, y la botella*
> *Son el blasón del Marques de Estella ...*

but the Spaniards liked him for his failings as much as for his virtues. There was less ostentation about him than about most men in high places. He was the despair of those who were responsible for his safety, and, like Don Alfonso himself, he had no idea of the meaning of fear. When he went to the theatre, which was frequently, he sat in the stalls like anybody else; at his club he always occupied the table at the window where he had taken his meals as an ordinary general. A true aristocrat, he hated display, and when he returned to Madrid after his victorious campaign in Africa, he entered it as a private individual. There was also about him the unfailing courtesy of the *andaluz*, as was shown, for instance, at a critical moment in the Moroccan War, when he found time to write a personal letter of thanks to an elderly English lady, previously unknown to him, who had sent him a message of congratulation.

Unfortunately there was another side to the picture, his defects, which proved to be the undoing both of himself and of Spain. I had several interviews with Primo during the course of a number of visits to Madrid while he was in power. The chief impression he made upon me was one of honesty and patriotism, but at the same time he was a soldier above all else, and that was at once his strength and his weakness. He saw things clearly along a certain line, but he could look neither to the right nor to the left. I felt this very much in conversation with him: so long as the subject was of his own choosing all was well, but he soon got out of his depth. In this respect I found him in marked contrast with Mussolini, with whom he has so often been compared, who talked well on any subject. Like so many soldiers, Primo de Rivera recognized only two colours, black and white, but in politics the distinction is rarely as clear as that. With the passage of time and the emergence of fresh problems, social and economic, with which his early training had not equipped him to deal, he got out of his depth, and therein lies the explanation of the blunders which marked the later years of his tenure of office. Only a genius, which Primo neither was nor claimed to be, can afford to stand alone. But he estranged all the old politicians, the best of whom would otherwise have helped him, with the result that he became increasingly more and more isolated. At the same time there can be no shadow of doubt that the *pronunciamiento*, and the closing of the Cortes which followed it, were extremely popular; had a plebiscite been taken the Directory would have obtained an overwhelming majority. Primo de Rivera never lost his popularity with the masses, however much the middle classes and the intellectuals might have sneered at him.

The tragedy of recent Spanish history is that the King was not the complement of the dictator. Don Alfonso never had any other end in view but what he believed to be the best interests of his country, but he was by no means easy to deal with; his long experience of shady and second-rate politicians had made him a cynic whose confidence it was not at all easy to win – he was liable to *idées fixes* of which it was very difficult to disabuse him. Primo, as we have seen, had serious limitations, one of which, not uncommon with dictators, was his failure to appreciate the force of tradition. He thus tended to ignore the Crown, though it is impossible to say what truth there is in the story that he was prepared to replace the King by one of his sons if he opposed his wishes. With the passage of time the relations of the two men improved somewhat, though they were never cordial. But the damage had already been done. Not only did Primo's off-hand treatment of the monarch weaken the prestige of the throne; on the other hand the King became identified with the dictator's policy in the eyes of every enemy of the Directory.

Although this is not the place for an examination of the political state of Spain under the Directory, a quotation from my diary, written in Madrid on 14 May 1926, may be of some interest:

'Everything is being done by the Government, and, outside Catalonia and Valencia, nothing by the people. In Madrid, especially, there is no desire to get out of the old rut, and although King Alfonso and Primo de Rivera have done wonders, they have not captured the imagination of the people in the way that Mussolini has done. There is certainly no wish for a return to Parliamentary Government; it is sheer apathy and nothing more.'

Madrid in those days was already a changing city, although its transformation had not long begun. The older streets and buildings were being ruthlessly pulled down to make way for the new arterial roads such as the Gran Via, the Calle de Alcalá was already flanked along almost its entire length by palatial buildings, and in the suburbs a perfect frenzy of development was to be observed everywhere. The old hotels, in one of which Pigott of the forgeries had so dramatically put an end to his contemptible life, had given place to the Ritz and the Palace, in both of which the King took a keen personal interest, while *Thés Dansants*, American bars, and all the other appurtenances of modern civilization were already in existence to delude the unsuspecting foreigner that the Spanish capital was much the same as any other European or Latin American city. At the same time, those who preferred the old Madrid of Lope de Vega and Velasquez could still leave the twentieth century behind them by turning into the Plaza Mayor or by walking along the Calle de Toledo. Above all there was the eternal Puerta del Sol, which had not yet been displaced as the centre of the city. Today with its flower-beds it may look prettier, but owing to the expansion of Madrid it no longer has its old pre-eminence as the focus of the capital's activity.

The real life of Madrid was still centred in the cafés, and the *tertulia* was in its heyday. The cafés, each of which had its own particular class of client, recalled the coffee-houses of London in the reign of Anne. In one a group of Legitimists would talk of Don Jaime de Borbón as His Catholic Majesty, while in another a few doors away the theories of Bakunin and Marx would be vehemently canvassed. The poets congregated in one café, the dramatists in another, so that in each there was a small circle which formed a nucleus. They were the places where opinion could best be sounded, and the shrewdest foreign diplomatists were often to be found in the old café Molinero, now, alas, no more, in what was then the Gran Via. To attract the attention of the waiter you clapped your hands or made a hissing sound between your closed teeth.

In spite of the appearance of the new hotels, cosmopolitanism in Madrid was still a thing apart, for although very many Spaniards were to be found in them they went there for the same reason that the contemporary Londoner took his dinner in Soho, namely for a change. To see the real life of Madrid one still had to do as the *madrileño* did. This involved a daily *paseo* between 1 and 2 p.m., and 7 and 8 p.m. along the Carrera de San Jerónimo, through the Puerta del Sol, and back by the Calle de Alcalá. One had to lunch not earlier than two o'clock and dine not earlier than half-past nine – at the seaside resorts you could sit down to dinner at midnight – and on Sunday after Mass one had to walk in the Paseo de la Castellana. In spite, however, of this apparent devotion to pleasure, and of the custom of an afternoon *siesta*, the *madrileño* was no slacker, for the shops never closed before eight o'clock, and the English feast of Saturday afternoon had no place in the Spanish calendar. During the months of August and September all who could afford it went to San Sebastian, or sent their wives and children there, leaving the capital deserted for eight weeks; then at the beginning of October came the rush back, and by the end of the month Madrid was normal once more.

My wife and I were in Madrid at the time of the British General Strike in 1926, where it was believed for a day or two that we were going the way of Russia; so much so in fact that there was a general reluctance to change English money, which gave one a very uncomfortable feeling indeed. It must be remembered, however, that whenever there is unrest in a foreign country, particularly in Spain, the British press always makes the most of it, so the Spanish newspapers can hardly be blamed for taking full advantage of the opportunity to retaliate that May. The wildest rumours were in circulation: Winston Churchill had been mobbed in Whitehall and forced to take refuge in the Home Office; one paper even went so far as to inform its readers that Baldwin had announced his intention of abolishing the parliamentary system. It was all rather amusing, a little disturbing, and extremely instructive.

CHAPTER VIII

The Gathering of the Storm

As the twenties passed into the thirties the international horizon, which for a brief space seemed to have cleared, clouded over for the last time on the 'glad confident morning', though at the time none of us appreciated the fact. In 1929 the depression struck. 'Everything nailed down is comin' loose', as the Angel Gabriel said in *Green Pastures*, and so it soon proved, for like some fell disease the slump was descending on the world. It had begun on the New York Stock Exchange towards the end of October, and before long American banks were closing by the hundred while the number of U.S. unemployed was in the neighbourhood of eight millions. It cannot be denied that the first reaction produced in Europe was a sardonic satisfaction that the boasted American prosperity was not eternal. The general mood was well reflected in an Italian newspaper which depicted a very miserable Uncle Sam spewing out dollars, beneath which was the caption, 'He'll feel better when he's got it all up.' Soon, however, it came to be realized that in this modern world when one house catches fire the whole community is in danger. The next two years witnessed a crash almost without precedent, by the end of which the finances of Central Europe were once more in chaos, and Great Britain was off the Gold Standard to which she had become tethered by Winston Churchill during his tenure of the Chancellorship of the Exchequer.

The repercussions of these events in the field of politics were serious, for the catastrophe came at a more than usually unfortunate moment. The men who had given Europe what it was hoped would prove to be new life, but which now turned out to be a mere breathing-space, were no longer there to ride the storm, and their successors could not bend the bow of Odysseus. Stresemann was dead, Briand was dying, and

Austen Chamberlain was out of office. A General Election in the spring of 1929 had put Labour in (but again without an overall majority) chiefly because Baldwin thought he could win on the slogan of 'Safety First' backed by innumerable pictures of himself smugly smoking his eternal pipe.

Elsewhere parliamentary government itself was beginning to rock on its foundations. This was notably the case in Germany, where events were really ominous. In September 1930 there was a General Election, bringing to the new Reichstag 107 Nazis and 77 Communists. This result was quite unexpected in British official circles, where the Nazi strength had not been put higher than 30, so that once more the Foreign Office would seem to have been badly served in the matter of information. Considering that only three months earlier the last Allied soldiers had been withdrawn from Germany – that is to say four and a half years earlier than was stipulated in the Treaty of Versailles – this Nazi success was an interesting commentary upon the German mentality. Nevertheless Britain, official and unofficial, anaesthetized by its belief in the efficacy of the League of Nations, did not stir in its sleep. So a mere eight months before the Second World War began the late Lord Lloyd was perfectly justified in telling an audience at St Andrews that 'for nearly twenty years the English people have been living in a fool's paradise, taught that the world was moving at an ever-increasing pace towards the millennium, when it was clearly rushing to disaster'.

In these circumstances, and in view of the fact that United Nations has unhappily inherited more than one of the League's weaknesses, it may not be out of place to examine briefly its position during some of the most momentous years of the present century. It started with two severe handicaps, namely its close association with the peace treaties and the defection of the United States, but other weaknesses developed with the years.

Let it be said at once that on its non-political side the League unquestionably did a great deal of good, and the United Nations has done well to see that its activities in this direction were not abandoned. Under its auspices much valuable information of a sociological and hygienic nature was collected and sifted, with the result that the various governments of the world were then induced to enact legislation based on this data. Indeed, it is here that one must sympathize with those who maintain that the League should have done more. There are many matters, perhaps trivial in comparison with the great political issues, but which nevertheless affect the ordinary citizen just as closely, which it might have taken up, and so impressed with its usefulness millions of people all over the world who were not in the least interested in politics. Its magnificent work in connection with notorious abuses is beyond praise, but the man-in-the-street is not usually either a drug-addict or a consumer of the merchandise handled in the white slave traffic; he is, however, the victim of varying currency systems, weights and measures, and rules of the road, while he has long cried out for a fixed Easter. It may be said that these are trifles unworthy of the notice of an international organization, but they do affect the life of the individual; and from the beginning it was clear that if the League was to establish itself in the hearts as well as in the heads of mankind it would have to do its work, not from the top downwards but from the bottom upwards.

All this is not to say that from the political point of view the League was always a failure. In 1921 it prevented war when the Yugoslavs invaded Albania, and again four years later when Bulgaria attacked Greece. By arbitration it settled such disputes as those between Finland and Sweden over the Aland Islands, and between Turkey and Iraq with regard to their common frontier. In the matter of refugees, too, much valuable work was done.

On the other hand, the League was successfully defied by Mussolini as early as 1923 on the occasion of the murder of General Tellini. Besides this, it had too often turned a deaf ear to the complaints of the minorities with the exception of the Hungarians in Transylvania, whose spokesman, the patriarchal Count Apponyi, was allowed to discourse at any length at Geneva on the subject. (Possibly this was because he was an expert, since in earlier days he had been responsible for the harshest of the laws passed against the Romanians in Hungary.) This rebuff and these shortcomings in the heyday of the League were ominous, for if this was possible in the green wood what would happen in the dry? Another one of its basic weaknesses was that the promise of the statesmen when they were assembled at Geneva bore too little resemblance to their performance when they got back to their respective capitals. The atmosphere by the Swiss lake was favourable to the growth of illusions which had a short life when the stern facts of the chancelleries were produced, with the result that time after time hopes were raised only to be subsequently dashed, so that on each occasion the League lost something of its prestige owing to its apparent failure. Nor did the attempts which were made to pretend that this had not happened do anything to help matters, for the League had always more to fear from its friends than from its enemies.

Another weakness of the League on its political side was the absence of any positive moral basis, a weakness which became more marked with the passing of the years. The fact that it made peace rather than justice its goal was the cause of much of its ineffectiveness. War is clearly not a thing to be lightly undertaken, and it should be the very last resort of a civilized people; but it would be idle to pretend that there are not injustices which drive men to take up arms sooner than submit to them. The record of humanity is the nobler for many a struggle in which the advantages of peace have been deliberately sacrificed in the pursuit of justice. Moreover, the League was established to vindicate the right. Sight of this was lost by the sentimentalists, who thought peace was an end in itself, and by the politicians, who were guided by an overmastering desire to leave well alone. The result was one which no supporter of the League could have desired, namely that for fear peace should be broken it showed itself afraid in the name of justice to call to account the more powerful miscreants. ʻχαλεπωτάτη γαρ ἀδικία ἐχουσα ὅπλα ('Injustice is at its worst when it is armed') wrote Aristotle, and it was precisely with that type of offender that the League was most unwilling to deal.

Inevitably such an attitude led to the consolidation of the *status quo*, and thus to a repudiation of one of the very objects of the League, for Article 19 of the Covenant expressly stated that 'the Assembly may from time to time advise the reconsideration by Members of the League of treaties which have become inapplicable and the consideration of international conditions whose continuance might endanger the peace of the world'. No action was ever taken under this clause, the consequence of this neglect being to give a very definite fillip to that unilateral denunciation of treaties which was to be so prominent a feature of the thirties. Yet to suggest that the League was not perfect was almost to the end considered the rankest heresy in political circles in Great Britain, and it was the same whether they were Conservative, Liberal, or Labour.

As early as the summer of 1931 the international horizon was everywhere overcast. With the second Labour government tottering to its fall, overwhelmed by difficulties by no means all of its own creation, events were taking place which were to change the face of the world. In the Far East, where the Japanese militarists were in the saddle, it was only a question of weeks when the attack on China would begin. In Southern Europe with the rise of the Second Republic, Spain had taken the first steps in the direction of one of the bitterest civil wars in recent history, and in Germany the pocket-battleship *Deutschland* had been launched, pointing the way to the revival of that navy which had as much as anything else precipitated the previous war. It was the parting of the ways: behind lay the now unfulfilled promise which had seemed so fair on the morrow of Locarno less than six years before, while ahead was the gathering storm.

A great deal of nonsense is written and talked at the present time about the allegedly idealistic attitude of youth in the thirties, but as the clouds gathered the disillusionment grew. After a visit to the Coningsby Club, a Conservative organization of young Oxford and Cambridge men, Austen Chamberlain wrote, 'The discussion which followed was interesting for the great diversity of view which it disclosed from something indistinguishable from Fascism on the one hand to extreme Pacifism and Socialism on the other. They gave me the impression of extreme *malaise* and uncertainty, a groping after something which eluded their grasp. They need a very clear call and bold leadership. I don't see any sign of their getting it at present.' That was in the heyday of Baldwinism.

It was also the heyday of paradoxes. Throughout the decade the Labour Party was clamouring for a strong line to be taken against foreign countries of which it disapproved on ideological grounds, but it regularly voted against the provision of such armaments as might be necessary to carry these policies into effect: as late as the summer of 1935, that is to say nine months after the Nazis had obtained control of Germany, the mere suggestion that it might be necessary to rearm was sufficient to convert a Conservative majority of 14,521 in East Fulham into a minority of 4,480. Then we had the young men of Oxford who voted in the Union that they would never again fight for King and Country, but hardly had they come down than they were crowding into the Armed Forces of the Crown to do that very thing. Of course we must admit that the politically-minded in Britain did not push matters to the same extreme and absurd lengths as the French Right which, having fulminated against the Third Republic for years on the score of its neglect of the national defences in the face of a resurgent Germany, proceeded to collaborate with Hitler when war came.

A by-product of all this in Britain was the temporary upsurge of Fascism. It is true that very few people of note actually joined Oswald Mosley, but a considerable number were sympathetically inclined towards him, as the membership of the January Club clearly proved. They were not enamoured of Fascism as such, but they were so weary of the drabness of the Baldwin regime that they were prepared to embrace almost any alternative. Whether, had Mosley succeeded, they would have liked what they would then have got is another matter. Then there were others, among whom I include myself, who were attracted by the doctrine of the Corporate State in the hope that it might provide a solution to the uneasy relations between Capital and Labour: there was even a group at Chatham House where the possibilities of the Corporate State were examined.

How seriously Mosley should have been taken it is not easy to say. At the time many people dismissed him and his movement with the comment that they were not of any real importance since the English would never tolerate the authoritarianism of Fascism or Communism, and forty years ago it was possible to make this claim without fear of serious opposition, but that is not so today; it is to be feared now that a dictatorship either of the Right or of the Left would meet with a much less hostile reception. The Englishman of the seventies is a very different man from his father, and his grandfather would not recognize him at all. He has now for so long been accustomed to look to the State to regulate his life for him that he has come to take it for granted that the State is an end in itself. This attitude is not confined to those on the Left who, brought up on the theories of Karl Marx, might anyhow have been expected to embrace it, but nowadays hardly a week goes by without the self-styled supporters of private enterprise in commerce and industry beseeching the Government to shore them up when their business affairs run into trouble.

In retrospect it is difficult to avoid the conclusion that Mosley really failed because of his methods, which were obvious, not because of his ends, which were concealed. His continued flirtation with Hitler and Mussolini caused his movement to be regarded as something not far removed from a foreign conspiracy: had he put his followers into blue pullovers instead of black shirts much would have been forgiven him – he has admitted this mistake in his autobiography. Then again there was grave mistrust among the more sober-minded regarding the implications of his anti-Semitic policy. It is true that the Jewish problem in those days loomed very large, and it was assuredly not to be solved – any more than is the coloured problem today – by ignoring it, but Mosley's intransigent attitude did him much more harm than good. Finally, when the Second World War came and Fascism was felt to be unpatriotic its fate was sealed.

Whatever view one may take of Mosley's policy there can be no question that he excelled in the exposition of it, though it must be admitted that the thirties did not constitute a period of great oratory in the main, at any rate in Great Britain. At his best the late Lord Lloyd of Dolobran was very good, but he could not be depended upon; Mosley would be in the first flight for half-an-hour but after that he tended to repeat himself (yet it must always be remembered that he once held the Oxford Union enthralled); Mosley's early colleague, John

Strachey, admittedly ran him close, but the intellectual content of Strachey's effervescence was apt to prove too thin for the Albert Hall on a Sunday afternoon. I speak with some authority in these matters for in May, 1934, I did a debate with Mosley at the Savoy when Jack Squire was in the chair, and among our audience was William Joyce, later to attain notoriety as 'Lord Haw-Haw', complete with black shirt.

What militated against Mosley and his movement from the very beginning was the impression he created that he wanted followers, not colleagues. Only those who were prepared to accept his lead unquestioningly were really welcomed. More than one man prominent in contemporary public life would have joined him could they have done so on a basis of equality, but they were not willing to enroll merely as Fascist yes-men. The late Lord Lloyd, for example, was at that time one of the outstanding figures in the Conservative Party, with an immense following; he was attracted by much that Mosley advocated, and he was not uninfluenced by the example of Lord Rothermere who for a time backed Mosley in his newspapers. I remember one day lunching with Lloyd at his house in Portman Square, the only other person present being his wife, Blanche. When the servants were out of the room he asked us for our candid opinion as to whether he should or should not join Mosley. Blanche argued strongly against him doing so, and I concurred with this. Whether her advocacy swayed the balance I would not like to say, but Lloyd was certainly not the man to play second fiddle to one who had yet, in his opinion, to win his political spurs. It had been the same earlier with the New Party, when the first-class brains who joined it soon fell away.

In particular Mosley never made any appeal to the intellectual classes. The January Club, which was founded for the purpose of attracting them, for a time looked like being a success, but one of its most prominent members, Francis Yeats-Brown, author of *Bengal Lancer*, was soon writing, 'The January Club will probably collapse: anyway I'm not going to the next meeting. Mosley is not human enough.' Jack Squire was another man of letters who was attracted at first, but found the atmosphere uncongenial before long. Probably Mosley's fundamental mistake was in ever leaving the Labour Party. In his difficulties with J. H. Thomas, of whom he paints the most unflattering picture in *My Life*, it is impossible not to sympathize with him; but he was too much of a young man in a hurry, quite apart from the question whether he was really as popular with the Labour rank-and-file as he clearly thought he was. Cavour never forgot that 'the shouts in the *piazza* cannot be taken as manifestations of public opinion'; Mosley never remembered. Yet had he remained with the Labour Party he would almost certainly not have been expelled, and could hardly have failed to become Prime Minister, for he was head and shoulders above the rump that was left in 1931 after the schism.

The thirties were a great decade for movements, both on the Right and on the Left, though it is those connected with the latter that have received the greater publicity, at any rate in retrospect; needless to say it was with the former that I was associated. In the spring of 1931 I was asked by Douglas Jerrold to take on the foreign editorship of the *English Review*, of which his firm, Eyre and Spottiswoode, had just acquired control, and of which he had become editor-in-chief. His character and outlook are difficult to describe, for he was very much a mixture of opposites. He was not an easy man with whom to work, for he was liable to change his opinions, not on fundamental principles but on their practical application, at very short notice. By nature I think he was kindly disposed towards his fellow-men, but he had a tongue like an asp, and he could be ruder than any man I have ever known with the possible exception of P. J. Grigg. Much, however, must be forgiven him on the score of temper, for he was rarely out of pain, having been badly wounded in the First World War while serving with the Royal Naval Division on the Somme. His approach to a problem, I always thought, was rather French than English, and he had a great affection for France.

Jerrold's idea was to use the *Review* as a platform for real Toryism as opposed to the plutocratic Conservatism represented by the official party then under Baldwin's uninspiring leadership. With its backing of a real galaxy of talent, both literary and political, the *English Review* of those days was as good value for a shilling as ever appeared on the market. Before long a luncheon club was founded in connection with it which used to meet at Gatti's, where only one speech was made, namely that of the principal guest. The committee, apart from Jerrold and myself, consisted of Arnold Lunn, Gerald Lymington (now Earl of Portsmouth), and Arnold Wilson, with Stephen Bull as Honorary Secretary. The luncheons, which were confined to the male sex, proved popular, and the speeches made at them were not without influence, though there was always a tendency towards an excessive representation in the audience of South Kensington colonels in which the Royal Borough in those days was prolific.

The *English Review* Movement, as it soon came to be called, stood for realism in the treatment of international problems and for the abandonment of unilateral disarmament. We had considerable backing in both

Houses of Parliament, notably from Lord Lloyd, and I do not think that in retrospect it will be denied that we were working along the right lines. What brought our plans to naught was the controversy about the Indian reforms into which the Conservative Party threw itself with a zest that left it no time or energy to spare for the problems of foreign policy or national defence. The opponents of the reforms were a decided minority, for the greater part of the party rallied to Baldwin, refusing to hear any criticism of his statesmanship either at home or abroad. Every other consideration was forgotten in the struggle between the India Defence League and the Union of Britain and India, and no holds were barred by the combatants on either side. I may well be wrong, but looking back on the scene after forty years it seems to me that if Winston, George Lloyd, and their supporters had refused to follow the Indian will-o'-the-wisp and had concentrated on the problems of national defence, they might well have received such support as to compel the government to put the country's armed forces in a state of readiness that might have changed the course of history.

My own opinion, which Jerrold generally shared, was that in view of the growing strength of the Third Reich the Indian problem was of secondary importance, though I agreed with the India Defence League to the extent that self-government should be given a trial in the provinces before the principle was applied to the central administration. Furthermore, it seemed to me to be a curious method of procedure to go to so much trouble to produce the Simon Report and then to ignore it altogether. In holding these opinions, however, Jerrold and I were in a minority even among our associates in the *English Review* group, though Lloyd always gave us a sympathetic hearing. I think he shared our views to some extent – his wife certainly did – but this intense loyalty to Churchill prevented him from openly proclaiming his concurrence with them. This loyalty dated from the time when Lloyd came back from Egypt in 1929 and Churchill alone among the Conservative leaders espoused his cause. When Winston became Prime Minister he gave ample proof of his gratitude, and it is one of the major tragedies of recent British history that death removed Lloyd at the very moment when at long last he had the ball at his feet.

That the *English Review* served a very useful purpose I shall always maintain, but it could have done more had it not been for the Indian controversy, for the resulting differences of opinion on that issue distracted attention from the attempt we were making to evolve a social policy, based on status rather than contract, which should attract the moderate men of all parties. Writing in the *North American Review*

Daniel Webster declared that 'there is not a more dangerous experiment than to place property in the hands of one class, and political power in those of another. . . . If property cannot retain the political power, the political power will draw after it the property', and his theory is as applicable today as when he wrote. In the pages of the *English Review* we stressed the fact that in a Socialist community, where the means of production, distribution, and exchange are in the hands of the State, it is the State that will ultimately exercise the predominant political power; we therefore urged that the creation of a property-owning democracy was the only sure guarantee of freedom. At the end of 1935 the *Review* was sold by Eyre and Spottiswoode, and Jerrold ceased to be its editor. It continued to exist under two different proprietorships for about eighteen months before it was amalgamated with the *National Review* under the editorship of Lady Milner.

By this time my wife and I had left Horley and settled in Kensington, where our son Peter was born in 1932. In our world there was still a good deal of social activity, which centred round the embassies, for members of the diplomatic corps attached to the Court of St James's were not the same types, in general, as they are today. Cocktail-parties were coming in, but evening receptions, at which the men wore white waistcoats and ties, were still the vogue. As there was no shortage of servants people still largely entertained at home, though there was already a certain amount of entertaining by the members of the Carlton Club at its recently-opened annexe. The large dinner-party had by no means died out, and the most prominent dispenser of this sort of entertainment was Mrs Ronnie Greville. At one of her dinner-parties, when she noticed that the butler was swaying ominously at the other end of the room, she wrote on a scrap of paper, 'You are drunk; leave the room at once', and gave the note to a footman to pass to the offender. When the butler had read the message he put the piece of paper on a salver, and then handed it to Austen Chamberlain. I have this story on the authority of the late Lord Dynevor and Osbert Sitwell, both of whom were present on the occasion in question.

Of course in those days there was much more space in the national press devoted to social events than is now the case: the *Morning Post* was pre-eminently the paper for the chronicling of them, with *The Times* not far behind. There are far fewer parties now, but I still find reading the accounts of them, and noting by whom they were attended etc., a relief after a surfeit of 'demos', sit-ins and unofficial strikes, varied only from time to time by the failure of some industrial concern. The national press today seems to be almost exclusively devoted to crime, sex, and business.

In 1930 some of us had the happy idea of founding the Eighteen Club in order to keep the various post-war Oxford generations, which were interested in politics on the Conservative side, in touch with one another. I was its chairman during the whole of its life, and among its office-bearers at one time or another were George Whitehead, Gresham Cooke, Stephen Bull, William Forster, Stormont Mancroft, and Roger Gray. The club consisted of forty members who, apart from the fact that they had to be in agreement with the principles of the Conservative Party, required only one qualification: that they should have been *in statu pupillari* at Oxford since the Armistice in 1918. We dined in full evening-dress once a month, except in August and September, at the Carlton Club annexe. Members were encouraged to bring guests, and once a year there was a mixed dinner when the guests had to be women.

There were no formalities and no speeches, and the consequence was that invitations to come as a guest were rarely refused by the great, who have few chances of dining out without having to sing for their dinner. Austen and Neville Chamberlain, the late Lords Salisbury and Lloyd, Grandi, the Duke of Alba, and the then Greek minister, Simopoulos, were among those who dined as our guests. As may be supposed, many a good story went the rounds on these occasions, one of the best in my opinion concerning the Marqués de Merry del Val, for so long Spanish ambassador at the Court of St James's. It appears that he was once at a public dinner where the worst type of jingo was making a speech, who, as the saying goes, was putting his foot in it every time he opened his mouth; ending with the announcement that 'playing the game' was an exclusively English characteristic for which there was no word in any foreign language. Whereupon Merry del Val remarked to a neighbour, 'And I know two words in French which apparently cannot be translated into English – *"de trop"*.'

One night there was a discussion as to the best recorded repartee, and so far as I can remember the following specimens were awarded the prize. The first was the retort of Wilkes to Sandwich after their quarrel. Sandwich said to Wilkes in some public place where all could hear, ' 'Pon my soul, Wilkes, I don't know whether you'll die upon the gallows or of the pox,' to which the other replied, 'That depends, my lord, whether I first embrace your lordship's principles or your lordship's mistresses.' The second example concerned Henry IV and Cardenas, the Spanish ambassa-dor. The French King was threatening to invade Italy unless Spain gave way over some question at issue: 'I will breakfast in Milan, and I will lunch in Naples', the monarch declared, at which the Spaniard observed with a profound reverence, 'And doubtless Your Majesty will arrive in

Sicily in time for Vespers.' The third dealt with Clemenceau and Barrère, who was for so long French ambassador in Rome, but who had been a *communard* in his youth. During the First World War he was summoned to Paris by Clemenceau for some purpose, but when he got there it was to find that the Tiger was at Compiègne, whither Barrère followed him. When the ambassador eventually found Clemenceau the following conversation ensued:

'*Vous êtes en retard, Monsieur l'Ambassadeur.*'
'*Malheureusement, M. le Président, mais j'ai brulé tout Paris pour arriver ici.*'
'*Vous avez brulé tout Paris?*'
'*Mais oui.*'
'*Pour la deuxième fois.*'

Another specimen of French wit that I have always liked, though it hardly comes in the category of repartee, is Fouché's remark when he heard that Napoleon had made Talleyrand Vice-Grand Elector of the Empire: 'It is the only vice that he has hitherto lacked.'

Neville Chamberlain came to the Eighteen Club in the autumn of 1937; that is to say while he was still accessible, and before the *camarilla* had succeeded in isolating him. Naturally the dinner was well attended, and no man could have been more charming or affable than was the Prime Minister that evening. Although he was just recovering from an attack of gout, he stayed until a late hour, the centre of an eager group of young men, whose questions he answered with the most disarming frankness. He had readily accepted the invitation, whereas on a previous occasion his predecessor, Stanley Baldwin, had coldly refused, and from this we augured well for his Premiership, but unfortunately he soon became as distant and unappreciative of his followers' loyalty as had been the former Prime Minister. All the same, that evening at the Eighteen Club will long live in the memory of those who were present, if only because it showed what might have been.

One evening somebody, Quintin Hogg I think, asked the late Lord Salisbury who was the greatest orator he had ever heard, and without hesitation the reply was 'Gladstone'. Lord Salisbury went on to say that the G.O.M. had the knack of making even his opponents almost feel that it was morally wrong to vote against him. One wonders whether his oratory would have the same effect today. Rhetoric in the grand manner is out of date, but all the same, as we have seen, there is a lack of good speakers even in the modern style, while since the death of Rennell Rodd there has been no outstanding British exponent of the *discours d'occasion*. Of foreigners before the Second World War I was most impressed by Hanotaux, although Antonio Maura and Antonio Goicoechea were both very good. Those who regularly attended the sessions of the League Assembly at Geneva set Herriot above Briand. Probably the microphone has ruined oratory. It effectively prevents gesture, and seriously limits the use of those inflections of the voice upon which the great speakers of the past depended so much for their effect. That oratory has declined can hardly be denied, but whether this matters is quite another question.

For many of us the Eighteen Club was the *alpenglük* of our Oxford careers. It was not, as Hore-Belisha once said of Philip Guedalla, that we carried the Union manner with us in later life, but that conversation flowed in the same easy manner that it did when we were undergraduates. How, indeed, could it be otherwise, in company that included John Boyd-Carpenter, Quintin Hogg, Alan Lennox-Boyd, Maurice Macmillan, Stormont Mancroft, Toby O'Brien, John Tweedsmuir, and Derek Walker-Smith? It was not to be expected that the Second World War would leave the Eighteen Club unscathed, and we lost five members whom we could ill spare.[1]

Like its more actively political contemporary, the Coningsby, of which the membership consisted of both Oxford and Cambridge men, the Eighteen Club represented the desire on the part of the younger Conservatives to keep together in spite of the diversity of their views. If these young men had received the sort of encouragement which Disraeli gave to the rising generation in his day they might have exercised a real influence upon their party: the material was there had any leader known how to make use of it. But a few soft words at a dinner – and the chance of fighting a hopeless seat – were all that ever came their way.

The gradual approach of war in 1939, as compared with its suddenness in 1914, was very marked in the way in which it affected the Eighteen and Coningsby Clubs. Before the Munich crisis only a small proportion of the members were in the Territorials, and many held that there would never be another war between Great Britain and Germany. By Christmas 1938 the younger generation, in marked contrast with no inconsiderable proportion of its elders, was holding that a clash was inevitable, and was crowding into the Armed Forces of the Crown. After Easter 1939 the monthly dinners of the Eighteen Club had to be abandoned, as all the members who were of military age were drilling every night. In this way the two clubs were a microcosm of the larger world.

1 Lord Arundell of Wardour, Sir Stephen Bull, Bt, P. C. Heathcoat-Amory, Lord Shuttleworth, and the Hon. F. Stewart-Mackenzie.

CHAPTER IX

The Lighter Side

IN 1934 my wife and I bought with a modest legacy an equally modest house with seven acres of garden and paddock at Lillington, a small village three miles from Sherborne in the county of Dorset. We sold it ten years later when the predilection of the modern world for total war, as evidenced twice in a generation, convinced us that at the end of the conflict then in progress we should not be able to afford two houses, and the nature of my work made it essential that I should spend by far the greater part of my time in London. It was a memorable interlude in a life largely spent in towns, which taught me a great deal about many things I should never otherwise have discovered.

I had originally fallen for Dorset when I went on walking tours there with the late A. D. Burnett-Brown in undergraduate days, also because at that time I was a great Hardy 'fan'. Lillington itself is typical of innumerable Wessex villages, which have diminished in size and population within the last couple of centuries as the larger centres have proved increasingly powerful magnets. Once upon a time it possessed a manor house of what would appear to have been considerable size, but in the early years of last century it was taken down, and all that remains to recall its existence are the terraces and fishponds to the south of the churchyard. From my study window there was a view over the Blackmore Vale, with High Stoy in the distance, which for sheer delight could not be surpassed in the whole west of England: the beauty of this view, at any time of the year, often seriously interfered with my concentration upon what I was supposed to be reading or writing. Nothing would have given us greater pleasure than to have stayed on at Lillington, but even if we had been able to overcome the difficulties of the war and its aftermath the inflation of the last decade would have rendered it financially impossible.

The charm of Dorset lies in its infinite variety. In the case of so many other counties one particular feature, however attractive, seems to dominate the whole area. Dartmoor and Exmoor at once come to mind when Devon is mentioned; Hampshire conjures up a vision where the warmth of red brick villages predominates; and it is impossible to think of Wiltshire without the mind dwelling upon the majestic splendour of Salisbury Plain with the spire of Salisbury Cathedral as a lodestar for the weary traveller. Dorset is different – in the space of a few short miles there are probably greater varieties of scenery there than in a similar compass anywhere else in the British Isles. The reed-encirled flats round Poole Harbour, where the heath meets the sea; the essentially farming country of the Blackmore Vale, with its green meadows and mingled oaks and elms; and little winding lanes which wander from village to village; the embattled coast, so dangerous to yachtsmen and so attractive to the eye, which begins to the east of the estuary of Poole and extends past dreaded Chesil Beach till it meets the coloured cliffs by West Bay, Charmouth, and Lyme Regis, where commence that line of headlands which are so characteristic of the Devon littoral; the grim heaths which are grimmer than all the heaths in England – all these may be seen by a motorist in an afternoon's run in his car.

As in the case of Lillington itself, the best of Dorset often lies off the main road, and is accessible only to the more adventurous. To turn down a side lane, and then to take a turning off that, is frequently to be rewarded by the sight of a hamlet clustering round its church in some 'bottom' with a background of meadow or heath. The hills are never far away, and those who have spent their lives in sight of them can find fresh beauty every day in their rapid changes of colour.

The physical configuration of Dorset has an important effect upon its social life, for the little valleys tend, even in the twentieth century, to the development of isolated communities which have no very close ties with their neighbours on the other side of the hill – the same state of affairs prevails in County Wicklow in Ireland and for the same reason. We were greatly impressed with this during the time we were at Lillington. There seemed to be hardly any county life as a whole, in marked contrast, for example, to East Anglia. It may be that the Second World War did something to produce a change (we left at the beginning of 1942, although our house was not sold until two years later), though I doubt this very much. Then again, of the two main roads both running from east to west, one of them, namely that which links Salisbury with Exeter by way of Shaftesbury and Sherborne, is only on the fringe of Dorset. There is, it is true, a road from north to south which connects Sherborne through Dorchester with Weymouth, but at the time of which I am writing it was in places little more than a lane, while during several months in the year public transport along it was practically non-existent. All this tended to render Dorset society at all levels more self-contained than is usually the case elsewhere. When my wife and I visited at friends' houses it was very rare to meet people other than those of the immediate locality, unless the occasion was a political one. We did not have the same experience when our social activities took us, say, into Somerset or Wiltshire, although both those counties are infinitely larger than Dorset.

This prompts a further reflection. Since the two World Wars a great many professional people have gone to live in the country (I am not referring to the weekend cottage section of the community) either on retirement or, as in the case of writers and painters, to work there. It would be interesting to know how many of them have really found the experiment a success. It clearly works all right where a number of people with similar tastes have congregated in the same places, but these are usually on the coast, such as Weymouth, Sidmouth, and Dawlish, or in North Wales, and the centre of interest is the golf course; equally there are a number of villages, again generally at the seaside, where artists gather.

This, however, is not what I have in mind, and I find it difficult to resist the conclusion that to get full value out of living in the country one has got to live a country life, which means that one must farm to a greater or lesser degree. The one common tie is the land; unless you are in some way concerned with its cultivation you are cut off from your fellows. A man living in the heart of the country may be a scholar with an international reputation, he may write best-sellers, or on his visits to London he may prove a most successful manipulator of the Stock Exchange, but he will never be completely *d'accord* with his neighbours, though he will be respected by them for his triumphs in fields of which they know nothing.

It may be objected that surely the man who takes up his residence in the country to shoot, hunt, or fish is an exception. I doubt it, for field-sports are not popular (in the etymological sense of the word) in England as they are in Ireland. One afternoon my son Peter and I went into a shop in Ballina, County Mayo, to buy some handkerchiefs, on the morning of which Peter had walked up Knox Street with a gun under his arm to shoot snipe. The shopkeeper's first question was about the day's sport; it was not until this had been discussed in all its aspects that we got to the lesser problem of my handkerchiefs. That could hardly have happened in England – at any rate in the south.

One thing my experiences in Dorset did impress upon me, was that nothing could be more absurd than the townsman's theory that the countryman is stupid. During the Second World War this point was discussed at an Army Brains Trust in Salisbury, at which A. G. Street was on the panel, and I shall not readily forget his vigorous defence of those who lived in the country. He cited as an example the use of escalators on the London underground railways, explaining that as a sensible countryman he let them take him up or down as the case might be. 'But,' he asked, 'what do you find Londoners doing? Why, running up and down the damned things.'

Mention of A. G. Street not unnaturally takes the mind to Shaftesbury, one of my favourites among Dorset towns, which I first visited as long ago as 1909. It is true that its past was more notable than is its present, among the more memorable incidents of its earlier days being the death of Canute there in 1035, whereby hangs a tale. One wet Saturday in the late summer of 1935 when Toby O'Brien, who was then in charge of the Peterborough column in the *Daily Telegraph*, was staying with us at Lillington, we decided to break the monotony of the day by going over to Shaftesbury to lunch at the Grosvenor, which at that time was run by the excellent Bert Eley. Before we set out Toby asked me quite casually if anything had ever happened at Shaftesbury; I referred to the encyclopaedia, and informed him of the demise of Canute. From that moment I dismissed the matter from my mind, but not so Toby, for we had not been long at the Grosvenor before he was asking what preparations were being made to celebrate the nine hundredth anniversary of Canute's death. Eley wisely hedged, for the fact was that very few people in Shaftesbury had ever heard of Canute, and fewer still knew – or cared – that he had died in their town. It so happened that our visit coincided with a period when there was no general news at all, for it was the lull before the storm of the Italian invasion of Abyssinia. Toby duly returned to London, and being short of copy for his column started ringing up Eley for the latest news of the Canute celebrations. Eley began to feel that something should be done, so he consulted the Mayor of Shaftesbury. The upshot of the whole matter was that on the anniversary of Canute's death special coaches were attached to the nine o'clock train from Waterloo in which travelled the members of the Viking Society, the representatives of the Kings of Denmark, Norway, and Sweden (also of the Latvian Republic which someone had mistaken for a Scandinavian Power), and an attractive young woman who was stated to be the senior living descendant of Canute. We had a sumptuous lunch at the Grosvenor with the Lord-Lieutenant, the Earl of Shaftesbury, in the chair: he most generously provided the pheasants for the repast, though he was forced to admit to my wife, 'Until today I hadn't heard of Canute since I was at Eton, and I wouldn't recognize the fellow if he walked in through the door.' Endless speeches were made extolling Canute as the precursor of the League of Nations, which was then much in fashion, and portraying him as a sort of Lord Robert Cecil born nine hundred years before his time. It was all a great tribute to the organizing ability of Toby O'Brien, and an excellent example of the power of the press in certain directions.

Another amusing incident connecting a King of England with a Dorset inn is concerned with George III. When that monarch was in the habit of paying regular visits to Weymouth, one of the stopping places of the mail-coaches was a little village of which the principal inn was known as the Ass's Head. Having heard of its good reputation for the food it provided, on one occasion the King had a meal there. This pleased the landlord so much that he changed the name of the inn to the Royal George, exhibiting on the signboard a full-length portrait of the reigning monarch. However, the old discarded signboard found its way into the possession of the host of the rival hostelry in the village, who bought it for a few shillings and then displayed it outside his premises. Then a day or two later it so happened that the driver and guard of the mail-coach had been changed, and the new driver, being strange to the district but having been told to stop at the Ass's Head, pulled up not at the Royal George but at the rival establishment. To prevent a recurrence of such a mistake the landlord of the Royal George nailed to the bottom of the painting of George III a board bearing the inscription 'This is the Original Ass'.

It has always seemed to me that the country inn is the one unbroken link that connects the present with the remote past, for its life is the same as it was in the Middle Ages, in spite of all the social changes that have taken place in the interval. The tavern scene in *Piers Plowman*, the conversation in the inn-yard in *Henry IV*, and the meeting of the Penny Club in Ben Jonson's *New Inn*, all might take place today. As a modern writer has put it, 'To the inn time is static. In one breath it has seen all English history, and we of today are only late arrivals among its guests.' To quote William Combe:

> Along the varying road of Life,
> In calm content, in toil or strife;

At morn or noon, by night and day,
As time conducts him on his way,
How oft doth man, by Care oppress'd
Find in an inn a place of rest?
Where'er his fancy bids him roam,
In every inn he finds a home.

We had not been long at Lillington before we discovered that we had
very little in common with our country neighbours. This was neither
their fault nor ours, but it meant that we tended to import friends from
elsewhere, and we very often had guests for the weekend. On referring
to the Visitors' Book I find that among those who stayed with us more
than once were Toby O'Brien, John Boyd-Carpenter, Victor Raikes,
Stephen Bull, Alan Lennox-Boyd, Derek Walker-Smith, Roy Wise, and
Francis Yeats-Brown: Ivy Chamberlain was with us during the Munich
crisis, and there was a never-to-be-forgotten visit by Jack Squire when
he set out at the New Inn at Cerne Abbas to show the men of Dorset
how a Devonian could drink cider. A few of our guests came by car, but
most arrived by the evening train from Waterloo on Friday and returned
by the breakfast train from Sherborne on the Monday. They were happy
days, when for some sixty hours we managed to forget the deepening
gloom in the world outside.

Both by ourselves and with our house-guests we much frequented the
pubs of the district, which were numerous and attractive and to our
great advantage, for darts were just becoming popular, and we were
much addicted to the game (though very bad performers), which brought
us in touch with another section of the Dorset community which was
definitely to our liking. One great centre was the aforementioned New
Inn at Cerne Abbas, then kept by one Bown, a retired policeman from
the Dorset constabulary, and we were among its most regular frequenters.
Another haunt of ours was the Mermaid in Yeovil of which a Mr Croft
was the landlord; though at times he could be something of an autocrat
he was the most kindly and hospitable of hosts. When once in 1944 I
stayed under his roof, I was much intrigued to read a notice in my bedroom which said, 'In the event of incendiary bombs falling in this room,
guests are requested to extinguish them with the sand provided for the
purpose, and then to inform Mr Croft.' There was no suggestion that at
any stage of the proceedings Croft would assist in the operation.

One friend of ours in particular who used the Mermaid a good deal
was Major H. Charlewood Turner, a real eccentric if ever there was one
– also almost the only man I have met who could get excessively, but

never objectionably drunk, and then drink himself sober again. I first met him in the early thirties at the Bonar Law College, Ashridge, and when we started a Dorset Ashridge Circle, of which I was Chairman, he became the Honorary Secretary. Turner had had a more varied career than many men I have ever known; had any publisher been enterprising enough to persuade him to write his reminiscences it could hardly have failed to prove a best-seller. The son of a bishop, and himself no mean classical scholar, Turner had been the correspondent of the *Morning Post* in Vienna and comptroller of the household to the Duke of Teck, while he was with Lenin in the abortive Russian Revolution in 1905 as a special correspondent. So much for truth: fiction went even further, making his exploits almost legendary. It was confidently stated among his friends that when serving with the Bulgarian *comitadjis* he had taken a Turkish pasha's head off with his own scimitar.

In his day Turner must have been a first-class newsman. He told me once that when he was in Vienna the Editor of the *Morning Post* telegraphed him to go to Belgrade to report on an abortive rising which had taken place there. When he got to the Serbian capital he found that the leader of the revolt was in prison, and inaccessible. This would have baulked most people, but not Turner, who realized that the only way to get a story out of his man was to be imprisoned with him. He therefore took his clothes off and proceeded to bathe in the Danube in a state of nudity, for which act of indecent exposure he was duly incarcerated. While in prison – there was apparently only one in Belgrade in those days – he found out all he wanted, and the *Morning Post* had a scoop. Turner told me that his real difficulty was to stay in prison long enough to get all the information he wanted, so active was the British legation in endeavouring to secure his release.

Not long after we settled at Lillington two of our closest friends, Vyvyan and Sybil Pope, took up their abode at Salisbury, and until the Second World War broke out we saw a good deal of one another. Vyvyan was B.G.S. Southern Command, with Alec (now Major-General) Lee, as G1. One of the tragedies of the war was Vyvyan's death in an aeroplane accident in Egypt just after he had been promoted Lieutenant-General. What he did not know about tanks and the best way to use them was not knowledge; it is no disparagement to his successors to say that had his life been spared Rommel would have met his match earlier than was actually the case. It was through Vyvyan that I first met, and got to know, Wavell, of whom I saw a good deal off and on until his death.

More than that of most soldiers Wavell's career has always seemed to me to have been influenced by his character and outlook, which was assuredly not that of an ordinary Wykehamist. His biographer, John Connell, has written of him:

'Wavell was a conscientious, dutiful man. He had in him a strong streak of humility, which led him all his life to rate some of his own finest qualities lower than others did. He early discovered that he had an excellent brain, but he thought always that he was lazy. Recalling his own boyhood and young manhood, he accused himself more than once of taking the easier course; few who knew him in his maturity would have agreed with this self-criticism. He had great powers of concentration, and his intelligence moved very quickly. He had no particular patience with bores, fools, or shallow show-offs; and of this characteristic his famous and formidable silences were a manifestation.'

All this is undoubtedly true, though one cannot help wondering whether his failure to exercise a stricter control over Perceval at Singapore was not a case of taking the easiest course. Early in his service life the Curragh Mutiny in the spring of 1914 had a profound influence upon him. Believing that it is a soldier's duty to obey orders, Wavell had no sympathy with Gough and the other officers who refused to act against Ulster if called upon to do so; equally he had no use for the politicians who put the Army in an almost impossible position, foremost among whom he blamed Winston Churchill. 'What a muddle we've got into over this wretched business', he wrote to his father, 'All due to the professional politicians – both sides equally bad.' From this opinion he never wavered, and there can be little doubt that the seeds of suspicion of Churchill were sown in his mind long before the two men were called upon to collaborate in the Second World War.

Wavell was never 'a man of the world' in the ordinarily accepted sense of the term, as I once had personal proof. When he was writing his biography of Allenby it required a considerable effort on my part to explain to him why 'The Bull' in his last days at Cairo roused the wrath of King George V and irritated Austen Chamberlain, but it is extremely doubtful whether he learnt, and still less whether he applied, the lesson. Churchill clearly found it impossible to like Wavell, but the blame cannot be apportioned – it was just an incompatibility of temperaments.

Yet one point on which the two men were agreed was that Britain would have done better to have accepted the challenge of the Third Reich in 1938 rather than wait until the following year. 'I always held that we should have fought at Munich time', was his considered opinion, and he believed that better use was made by Germany of the twelve months' delay than by Britain. That is a moot point even today, but there can be no question that as G.O.C. Southern Command he took full advantage of it himself. When he arrived at Salisbury in the spring of 1938 he was appalled to find that in spite of the threatening international situation the Tidworth Tattoo was to take place as usual, and he had to stand idly by while a battalion of regular infantry spent its time not in preparing to resist tanks, but in practising the drill of its forebears in the reign of James II. He saw to it that although there was a Tattoo at Aldershot in 1939, there was not one at Tidworth.

When war came the Greek diversion was probably the worst cross that Wavell had to bear, not least because of its unfortunate repercussions upon the situation in North Africa. He had, in fact, always been sceptical about the value of the guarantees which the Chamberlain government had handed out so generously. As will be shown in its place in the autumn of 1938 I did a lecturing tour of the Balkans on behalf of the British Council, and on my return Wavell asked me to give my impressions to the officers of the 3rd Division at Tidworth – in summing up at the end he told them that he could think of a dozen ways of getting a British army into the Balkans but none of getting one out again without heavy loss. All the same he did not go so far as Boney Fuller who wrote that the campaign 'should never have been fought', for Wavell's verdict was that 'it was not really such a forlorn hope from the military point of view as it may seem from its results'. In retrospect it can be seen as one of those episodes in which political necessity overrides the dictates of sound strategy.

Sherborne, our nearest town, with its Abbey and School, was marked by an academic air reminiscent of Oxford in the days before the university city became an industrial centre. The ruins of the old castle, and the presence of the new, across the River Yeo, recall feudal times. Once a year, on the occasion of St Michael's Fair, locally known as Pack Fair, which took place on the first Monday after October 10th, Sherborne presented a very different sight. In the early hours of the morning the townsmen paraded the streets beating upon tin trays and frying-pans, and blowing bugles and whistles. This custom was supposed to have had its origin when, after the Abbey was repaired in 1504, the masons celebrated the end of their labours in this noisy manner. At one time horns used to be sold in the shops, though for what purpose is not clear. There was a Horn Fair at Charlton in Kent, of which Defoe gives an account in his *Tour through England and Wales*, and it may be that the same idea lay behind the two festivals.

Leland wrote of Sherborne in Tudor times, 'It standeth by making of clothe but most by all manner of crafts.' In the eighteenth century it pleased Defoe, who noted, 'I came to Shireburn, a large and populous town, and may properly claim to have more inhabitants in it than any other town in Dorsetshire, tho' it is neither the county town, nor does it send members to Parliament; the church is still a reverend pile, and shows the face of great antiquity. Here begins the Wiltshire medley cloathing, tho' this town be in Dorsetshire.' At the present time Sherborne is probably best known to the outside world on account of its famous school.

A volume could be filled with accounts of old customs connected with the seasons of the year which still survived in Dorset when we lived there, or which had been observed in the memory of people still alive. Shrovetide, for instance, was never allowed to pass unnoticed. At Dorchester every year the children came a'shroving, singing this little song:

We be come a'shroving,
For a piece of pancake,
Or a bit of bacon,
Or a little truckle cheese
Of your own making.
Blow the fire and het the pot –
For we've come a'shroving.

This observance may well date from pre-Reformation times, when every Shrove Tuesday the band of children visited houses and cottages, to be rewarded with oranges and cakes. A local resident some years ago left a bequest of fifty pounds, vested in the Rector and Churchwardens of Durweston, the interest on which was to be divided annually among such school-children as went a'shroving to at least three houses. At Sherborne there was, until nearly the close of the nineteenth century, a similar celebration. Children used to take some old crockery, and go to neighbours' houses, singing:

Here I come, I never came before.
If you don't give me a pancake
I'll break down your door.

At the conclusion of the verse the crockery was thrown against the door and smashed, whereupon the occupant came out and tossed a pancake for the children to catch. It was not a little reminiscent of the activities of the Wren Boys in Ireland on St Stephen's Day.

May Day was also generally celebrated, especially at Shillingstone, where there is still a Maypole. It is said to have been at one time the tallest in England; it was garlanded with flowers, and danced round for the greater part of the night. In addition there were booths, coconut shies, and cheap jacks. The decoration of the Maypole still took place when we lived in Dorset, but the other festivities had fallen into desuetude. There was another famous Maypole at Cerne Abbas, and at Shaftesbury the children used to carry round 'Jacks-in-the-Green'. Incidentally, this latter custom still obtained at Oxford when I was an undergraduate.

Harvest was another occasion for rejoicing, and also for the making of that 'firmity' so familiar to readers of Hardy. It was made of wheat, raisins, or currants with a little flour to thicken it; the mixture was slowly boiled and sweetened with sugar, after which it was eaten like porridge with a spoon. Guy Fawkes Day was publicly celebrated in a number of places: at Marnhull there was every year until 1908 a torchlight procession headed by a band. Between the wars there was in Dorset, as elsewhere, a revival of the Fifth of November jollifications, but they tended to be more private affairs than of yore.

At Christmas the old mumming play of *St George and the Turkish Knight* was acted in many parts of the county – a custom which unfortunately seems to have been abandoned during the First World War – which destroyed so many things, both great and small, well worth preserving. It has however been revived at Evershot at least once since then. Mumming at Shillingstone died out in the seventies of last century – the mid-Victorian era, too, was not particularly favourable to the perpetuation of old traditions – but the men and boys of that village kept up the custom of the Bull until a later date. The procedure seems to have been for the bull, shaggy head with horns complete, shaggy coat and eyes of glass, to appear uninvited at any Christmas festivity, and no one knew when he might, or might not, appear. He was given the freedom of every house, and allowed to penetrate into any room escorted by his keeper. The whole company would flee before his formidable horns, which was not unnatural because as the evening went on neither the Bull nor his keeper could be certified as strictly sober.

One wonders whether this peculiar observance had its origin in Mithraism, indeed I have often wondered whether the Cerne Abbas Giant was Mithraic in origin, more particularly since when I was in Cluj, in Transylvania, I found in the museum there a statuette which was an exact replica of the Giant; on enquiry I was told that it had been dug up with some other Roman remains, and dated from the time when Dacia was a Roman province. Until very recently there was a very definitely phallic atmosphere about the Cerne Abbas Giant: loving

couples with a sense of tradition were wont even to have sexual intercourse in his phallus. But I doubt if the young people of today confine
their procreative activities to any one place, however hallowed by time.

There is one last Dorset story which must be told, but whether it should
be classed as history or tradition is quite another matter. One dark night
in 1804 or 1805 a young girl was waiting for her lover on the cliffs near
Lulworth Cove, when a small boat put in, and from it there landed two
men. Not only did the girl know something of the outside world, she was
also acquainted with French, for her father was not above a bit of smug-
gling when the opportunity served. She was, therefore, soon able to
recognize the men as Napoleon and Berthier, and to understand their
conversation which finished with a remark from the Emperor, clearly in
reference to a proposed landing, 'impossible ici', after which the two men
returned to their boat. If it be asked why the young woman did not give
the alarm the answer is that she was married and did not want her
husband to know that she was deceiving him. She is said to have been
born in 1784, and to have lived to the age of a hundred-and-four.

As befits a district with historic associations, the northern portion of
Dorset is not without its ghosts. If the traveller approaches Blandford
by the main road from Salisbury, some miles from the former town he
will find on his right Eastbury Park, once the seat of that prince of
trimmers, George Bubb Dodington. After Dodington's death, Earl
Temple offered an income of £200 a year to anyone who would reside
in the place and keep it in repair, but the bait was unsuccessful, and part
of the house was demolished. Eastbury is now haunted by a headless
coachman and a ghostly four-in-hand, which may, it is said, be seen
entering and leaving the park gates. Indeed, the neighbourhood seems
particularly favoured by the disembodied, for at Pimperne, a mile or
two down the Blandford road, is a dog that dashes out at the foot of
Letton Hill with much rattling of chains, but those who try to stop it will
find it is only an apparition. Blandford itself can boast a ghostly sheep
which runs, for no apparent reason, from the gas works corner into the
old burial ground in Damory Street.

The ghost of Sir Walter Raleigh (whether smoking or not is unstated)
is reputed to walk round the grounds of Sherborne Castle on Michaelmas
Eve. A little further away, between Poyntington and Oborne, where
there was fierce fighting between Cavaliers and Roundheads in the Civil
War, the dead soldiers of Charles and the Parliament are believed to
visit the scene of the engagement in which they lost their lives. Not far
from Sherborne is Trent Barrow, beside which is a deep pit always full
of water, into which one stormy night a coach, horses, driver, and pas-

sengers disappeared, leaving no trace behind; the catastrophe is said to be re-enacted from time to time. It must be confessed that none of these North Dorset stories is the equal of the West Lulworth legend of the phantom Roman army that marches along Bindon Hill to its camp on King's Hill, and even in this sceptical twentieth century the tramp of Roman feet and the blare of Roman trumpets have been heard.

Though in many ways they are alike, Dorset and Devon differ in some respects, possibly owing to the latter's proximity to Celtic Cornwall. Dorset does not have the Piskies, Pixies or 'little people', the legends of whom have a marked affinity to those current in Ireland. There are as many explanations as there are experts to put them forward, and though I am definitely not one of these I have always been attracted by the theory that the traditions of little people who make mysterious appearances and disappearances, chiefly at night, represent the dim recollection on the part of a conqueror of an earlier race which his ancestors displaced. It may well have been that for several generations the survivors of such earlier races lived on in remote places, and that at times they did pay fleeting visits to their former habitations. They may also have been of lesser stature than those who supplanted them, while nothing would be more natural than that a child or two of theirs should get lost and stray into the village from which its forebears had been driven.

Not the least of the difficulties in the way of reconstructing the distant past is the irritating habit in early civilized man of making myths out of historical facts; the Greeks were probably the worst offenders in this respect, but they were closely followed by the Irish. The reason is almost certainly that the deeds of heroes were handed down orally, and they lost nothing in the telling; it was not until the legends were reduced to writing that they could be subjected to investigation, and by then the age had often become too sceptical to bother to enquire what was fact and what was fiction. Yet modern research has often vindicated the veracity, at any rate in essentials, of writers who were scoffed at by their contemporaries as mere spinners of yarns if not as downright liars.

All this has taken me a long way from Lillington and its delights, and only the monetary considerations mentioned on an earlier page would have torn my wife and me from Dorset, but we left our hearts there when we had to go.

CHAPTER X

Europe in the Thirties

ONE of the most interesting times of my life was in the autumn of 1932 when I attended in Rome the Convegno Volta which was held under the auspices of the Reale Accademia d'Italia, whose president at that time was Marconi. We met in the extremely beautiful Farnesina Palace, originally built for the first member of the famous banking family of Chigi to come to Rome. The subject set for discussion was 'Europe', in all its aspects, and we were a very mixed collection of participants. My British colleagues were the first Lord Rennell (then Sir Rennell Rodd), Gerald Lymington (now Earl of Portsmouth), Paul Einzig, and Christopher Dawson. Most of the other Powers were much more extensively represented. From Germany there came, among others, Goering, Rosenberg, and Schacht; France sent of her best, including Bertrand, Gaxotte, Halévy, and old Hanotaux; and from their respective countries came the Duke of Aosta, Charles de Rohan, de Reynold, and Count Apponyi. I fear that our discussions, although many of them were learned enough, did not take us very far, but as we were all housed at the same hotel we saw a good deal of each other, which was particularly interesting in view of what the future held in store for some of us.

The sessions of the conference were presided over in turn by the leading representatives of the different countries. One afternoon when it was Goering's turn to preside he made an announcement regarding the wearing of decorations at an official reception that evening, but his French was so execrable that no one could make out whether they were to be worn or not; we accordingly consulted our French colleagues, who were equally in doubt, so at last we all decided to go decorated. We proved to be wrong, and the only person without decoration was Goering himself.

On another occasion a long-winded German was getting well into his stride when Rodd suggested that he and I should retire for a drink. When we had done so he remarked, 'Let me give you a word of advice as an old man to a young one. When Germans talk about things that end in "*-ismus*", and Frenchmen about things that end in "*-ologie*", it is wisest for an Englishman to retire to the bar.' This recalls another piece of advice I once received in my youth from an even greater diplomatist, Cardinal Merry del Val, who had been Secretary of State under Pius X. I was about to visit Spain for the first time; the Cardinal asked me if I spoke Spanish. When I replied that I did, he said, 'It may help you abroad to bear in mind what I always used to tell my *nonces* when I was Secretary of State: you cannot know a foreign language too well, but never let it appear how well you know it; in this way you will enjoy all the advantages of a native together with all the allowances that are made for a foreigner.' When I repeated this to the Cardinal's brother, then Spanish ambassador in London, he murmured, '*muy vaticano*'.

The meeting of the Convegno Volta was the first occasion on which I had met Schacht or Goering. The former I never saw again, but I – literally – ran into Goering the following year in the hall of the Hotel Flora, when we exchanged a few words, and he was very friendly. The impression I formed in those days, and subsequent events have not caused me to alter it, was that Goering should have lived in the Italy of the Renaissance, for he was also the typical *faux bonhomme*. As for Rosenberg, he had lunched with my wife and myself at our house in Tregunter Road, South Kensington, before I met him at the Convegno Volta, and we both found him extremely unattractive. He could speak neither French nor English, and as I have no German a most unenlightening conversation was carried on by means of a Baron de Ropp who accompanied him.

This, of course, was before Hitler came into power, and Rosenberg was a director of the *Völkische Beobachter*. Presumably he came to London to find out the state of public opinion, but in view of his personal limitations he could not have discovered much. He certainly did not strike either my wife or me as a man of any ability. One thing he made a point of impressing upon me, and that was the determination of his party to crush both the Jews and the Roman Catholic Church. At the time I thought he was talking nonsense, but unhappily he was not.

That visit of Rosenberg to lunch will always be memorable in my family. I had informed the Foreign Office that he was coming, but the Special Branch, or whoever keeps an eye on foreign politicians of doubtful antecedents, was determined not to let him out of its sight. We were having coffee in the drawing-room when my wife happened to glance out of the window; there, in a peaceful Kensington road on a Saturday afternoon, were two or three pseudo-working-men lounging against walls and lamp-posts, looking exactly like what they were, namely detectives. This incident has always seemed to me to argue a lack of imagination on the part of those responsible; at any rate they did not know the Kensington of those days, or if they wanted their men to escape notice they would have disguised them as retired lieutenant-colonels – today it would have been as hippies who lived in bed-sitters.

I was in Rome a good deal in the thirties, and I came to be very fond of the city and its life. On my visits I was very kindly made a temporary member of the Scacchi Club, which, as its name implies, was originally concerned with chess; it was one of the very few clubs allowed by the police in Papal times. One day I was about to have a drink at the bar when a man I did not know came up, greeted me by name, and asked me to have a drink with him. I accepted with my usual alacrity on such occasions, whereupon he said to the barman, 'Mix Sir Charles one of my specials.' At a suitable moment, when I had about emptied my glass, I asked the member his name. 'Borgia,' was the reply.

Of the outstanding figures of the thirties the one whom I knew best was Mussolini. I first met him in October 1930, and for several years after that I saw him regularly, so that I can probably claim to have known him as well as most foreigners, with the exception perhaps of Sir Ronald Graham. Now that he has been so long in his grave, I feel that the time has come to view him objectively as a historical figure rather than merely as a bad man who opposed British interests. The impression which he used to make on me personally as I crossed the floor of that vast room in the Palazzo Venezia was not that of the dictator with forbidding manner and beetling brows (though he could assume both when the circumstances required), but of the cultured man-of-the-world quite ready to indulge in the give-and-take of ordinary conversation. In particular, I recollect that he had a winning smile reminiscent of both de Valera and Neville Chamberlain. I never found that he made any attempt to 'lay down the law', though whenever I spoke with him I was always conscious of his wide knowledge. In this, as I have already stated, he was in marked contrast with Primo de Rivera, whose field was much more limited.

Perhaps Mussolini's greatest gift, just as his eyes were his most marked physical characteristic, was his extraordinary ability to dissociate in any question the important from the trivial. He went to the heart of a problem in a way that had the effect of clearing the brains of those with

whom he was conversing, and of reducing apparently insuperable difficulties to their right proportions. Marshal Balbo, in his *Diario*, alluded
to this quality more than once, showing how it had been of immense
assistance to the Fascists during the critical months that preceded the
March on Rome. If one were asked another of Mussolini's intellectual
attributes, the answer must be his encyclopaedic knowledge – knowledge
of affairs, of books, and, until his last years, of his own fellow-countrymen. At the height of his power he is reputed to have said that the
difference between the Fuehrer and himself was that whereas he was
the first-class head of a second-rate nation, Hitler was the second-rate
head of a first-class nation. Had Mussolini kept this distinction clearly
in his mind, many things might have been different.

It was never very easy to get him to talk of his early days, but I did ask
him once what truth there was in the story that during his exile in
Switzerland he had often been in the company of Lenin, Trotsky, and
Stalin. His reply was that it might well have been so, for he met a large
number of Russian exiles at Lausanne and Zurich, who had talked
interminably, but he could not remember any of them by name. On the
other hand, both Lenin and Trotsky have left it on record that they met
Mussolini.

Undoubtedly the most important discussion I ever had with the Duce
was in June 1936, at the end of the Abyssinian war and a week or two
before Neville Chamberlain announced the abandonment of Sanctions at
the 1900 Club Dinner. On our way back to England from Greece, my
wife and I were staying a few days in Rome with Luigi Villari at his
flat in the Via Antonio Bosio. When talking to Mussolini I made no
secret of my opinions: I had always been opposed to sanctions, and there
could be no doubt that British prestige had suffered a serious rebuff in
consequence of the Italian victory. I freely granted him that, but, I told
him, as Britain was an infinitely greater Power than Italy, Mussolini
could only have access to his new conquest by leave of the British Navy;
therefore, I went on, the prudent course for him to adopt was to let
bygones be bygones and not to 'rub it in' where Great Britain was concerned. It was, I pointed out, the tradition of British diplomacy to accept
the *fait accompli*, and if he played his cards properly he would find that
the Italian conquest of Abyssinia would prove no exception. Otherwise,
I argued, he would see himself compelled to go in with Hitler and on
Hitler's terms, for Italy was not strong enough to stand alone. Mussolini
listened most attentively, making no serious criticism. When the discussion was over he walked from his desk across the great length of the

room to the door with his arm round my shoulders, and our leave-taking could not have been more cordial.

In these circumstances I hoped that I had achieved something, and my optimism was enhanced when I heard that Victor Gordon-Lennox, then on the staff of the *Daily Telegraph*, had also seen Mussolini, and had talked to him in much the same vein. The British ambassador in Rome at that time was Sir Eric Drummond, later the Sixteenth Earl of Perth, a man who should never have been appointed to the post. He had previously been Secretary-General to the League of Nations, an organization which Mussolini, rightly or wrongly, regarded with considerable suspicion, he was naturally identified with its activities in Italian eyes. However this may be my wife and I were given a most frigid reception at the British embassy, and Lady Drummond came as near to being definitely rude as she could be without compelling us to ring for a taxi. This behaviour on the part of the Drummonds, combined with the complete silence of the Foreign Office, convinced me that neither Gordon-Lennox nor I would receive any support in official circles. Ere long the old bickering between London and Rome was renewed, and events took the course that I had predicted in the Palazzo Venezia.

Perhaps at this point it may be as well to stress the fact that I was not influenced by any special regard for the *beaux yeux* of Mussolini – though I confess to a personal liking for the man – or any special affection for Italy. What I was concerned with was the establishment of a situation in which Italy did not come in on the side of Germany in the event of war. Had Sir Edward Grey mishandled the Italian invasion of Tripoli in 1911 in the same way in which his successors at the Foreign Office mishandled the Italian invasion of Abyssinia in 1935 the Triple Alliance would have held together in August 1914 and the Kaiser might easily have eaten his Christmas dinner that year in Buckingham Palace. I further believed – and I am still of the opinion – that if Great Britain, France, and Italy in the late twenties and early thirties could have pursued a common policy towards Germany, and compelled the Little Entente to agree to a Habsburg restoration in Vienna and Budapest, a second world war might have been prevented; it would certainly have been shortened by the two years it took Great Britain and the United States to regain control of the Mediterranean.

Several organizations in Rome and London with which I was connected aimed to improve Anglo-Italian relations. Among those with whom I was associated in this work were Rennell Rodd and Hugh Molson, who never lacks courage in any cause which he espouses. The late Mrs Emile Mond was another tower of strength, while we also received the full support of two successive Italian ambassadors, Bordonaro and Grandi. While official relations between the two countries grew steadily worse we laboured on, though all save the most enthusiastic fell away. My own position was not unnaturally subject to a good deal of misconception, some of it deliberate, and, as we shall see, when war came the Establishment was careful to keep me out of any position of responsibility, though in actual fact while advocating a more tolerant policy towards Italy I was continually impressing upon my friends in Rome the dangers attendant upon their ever-closer collaboration with the Third Reich. Finally, the task became hopeless, and I abandoned it in despair: when Italy attacked Albania in the spring of 1939 I severed all connection with the various Anglo-Italian societies, though some time before this I had ceased to take any active part in their work.

As I naturally never saw Mussolini during his last years his decline and fall are rather beyond my terms of reference in this present work, and such evidence as has been published mostly proceeds from interested or ill-informed sources. For what it is worth my own interpretation is that events got beyond his control; sexual excess – apparently – undermined his mental powers just at the time when they required to be at their best; and he relapsed into the demagogue that he had been at the beginning of his public life. I have always felt that if a parallel be required in Italian history for the career of Mussolini it is to be found in that of Rienzi. Yet, if he had shown the wisdom of Franco and kept his country out of the war, at the end of it he would have been in such a commanding position that the Allies would have been obliged to give him practically anything for which he asked. For the rest, it is unfair to blame the Italians as a nation for not putting up a better show in a conflict in which they had no heart.

Like most dictators in history Mussolini was a great builder, but Futurism in art and Fascism in politics were so closely connected that the result of some of the Duce's architectural activities left a good deal to be desired. On the other hand the making of such avenues as the Via del Impero and the Via Imperiale undoubtedly improved Rome, though they displaced many streets, some of them picturesque, and all dear to those who had known them since childhood. Yet it is often the foreigner, returned to Rome after a long absence, who most deplores the changes, for aliens have a habit of becoming more Roman than the Romans in their love of the city.

When one passes from the buildings to the people who lived in them it is necessary to remember that in the middle of the period we are considering came the Lateran Treaty, in 1929, which effected a reconciliation between Church and State. From the unification of Italy in 1870 until that date Roman society was in the main divided between Blacks and Whites, though it is probably now too late to discover the name of the British diplomat who said that neither appealed to him, as the one was too dull and the other too disreputable. After the Austrians had been expelled from Lombardy, and the dynasties in Central and Southern Italy had been driven from their thrones, many of their supporters took refuge in Rome, which became for a brief space a veritable home of lost causes. What the city was like in those days, when the streets were dotted with the soldiers of the Second Empire in their blue tunics and red trousers, and the cardinals still drove about in their coaches, is well described by Disraeli in *Lothair*. I was lucky enough to get a description of it all first-hand from Rennell Rodd, whose experience of Rome dated from 1867, the year of the battle of Mentana.

These exiles and those who thought with them had naturally no desire to mix with the triumphant supporters of the new King, and so the Blacks held themselves aloof. It must be confessed that the Whites deserved a good deal of the criticism levelled against them. Revolutions always bring the scum to the surface, and the *Risorgimento* was no exception: indeed, in retrospect I often feel that the twentieth-century Italian would probably have been far better off if there had never been a *Risorgimento* at all. When one thinks of the innumerable great men and women Italy produced before she was united it comes as something of a shock to realize that one would be hard put to it to mention half-a-dozen whom she has produced during the past hundred years.

However this may be loyalty to the old order lasted very much longer than is commonly supposed. My Corpus contemporary, C. R. S. Harris, once told me that during the Second World War he entered a village in Sicily to find that for '*Viva il Fascismo*' or '*Viva il Duce*' on the walls there had been hastily substituted on the approach of the British troops the words '*Viva il Borbone*'. The memory of the dubious methods by which the House of Savoy achieved the Italian throne must have influenced many an elector of Black antecedents to vote against it in the plebiscite which converted Italy into a republic.

The only members of Mussolini's family with whom I came into contact were his daughter, Edda, and his son-in-law, Count Ciano. Whereas Edda was very good company indeed, with her diverting stories of Shanghai, where she and her husband had lived for a time, Count Ciano seemed to me to be one of those people of whom it could be said that if one bought him at one's own price and sold him at his there would be a considerable profit on the transaction. He met his match, however,

on one occasion at the hands of Lady Chamberlain, when he had asked
her how old Anthony Eden was when he became Foreign Secretary. On
being told he exclaimed, 'I was a year younger when I became Foreign
Minister here.' 'No doubt,' Ivy Chamberlain replied, 'but then Anthony's
father-in-law isn't a dictator.'

One more story before we leave the Duce: it is not well-known, and it
illustrates the difficulty which he sometimes had in dealing with the
British Government. Just before the Stresa Conference in the spring of
1935 the Italian ambassador in London, Dino Grandi, told Mussolini that
there would be opposition on the part of Great Britain to any aggression
where Abyssinia was concerned. Accordingly the Duce took his African
experts with him to Stresa in the expectation that either the Prime Minister, Ramsay MacDonald, or the Foreign Secretary, Sir John Simon –
surely the worst of modern times – would raise the matter. In the upshot
neither of them as much as mentioned it, from which Mussolini concluded
that he had been misinformed, for he could not believe that a problem
was of importance to a country when two of its leading ministers refrained
from even alluding to it when they had the opportunity. Henceforth he
paid little attention to the advice given him by Grandi, who, incidentally,
was always well informed in respect of British public opinion, and the
unfortunate ambassador was kept so short of news that more than once
he was driven to seek information from the British Foreign Office.

There was, however, a sequel. Hardly had Simon returned to London
than he asked Austen Chamberlain, who was not even in office, to see
Grandi, and to impress upon him the serious view which the British
Government took of Italian policy in East Africa. Austen did what was
requested of him, but although the ambassador displayed a keen percep-
tion of what lay ahead, Mussolini paid no heed to an informal warning
of this nature. Why the Foreign Secretary had to resort to this peculiar
procedure, when he could have raised the matter direct with the Duce
himself in Italy, has never been explained.

The Italian Royal Family was not much in evidence during the Fascist
regime, indeed, in the days of which I am writing the Crown Prince
Humbert was definitely unpopular. Later he lived down a great deal of
this unpopularity, but not in time to prevent the defeat of the monarchy
at the plebiscite, and since then he has cut no great figure in the world.
I once had an audience of King Victor Emmanuel III, who impressed
me as a very charming old gentleman, of encyclopaedic knowledge and
the shrewdest judgement, and whose manner would have put the most
nervous at their ease. In the course of our discussion, which was about
history rather than politics, the one thing that struck me very much was

his perfect pronunciation of English, even to the extent of referring to Italian towns by their English names. His own attitude was revealed on one occasion when he referred to a certain document as being 'at home in Turin'. I have no special claim to express an opinion on the King's attitude after the overthrow of Fascism, but it has always seemed to me that if he had abdicated earlier, or if some members of the Royal Family had joined the Resistance, the monarchy might have been saved.

During what I will term the Twenty Years' Armistice I came in touch with the monarchist parties in several European countries, offering my services to all of them, but only once was the offer taken up. On this occasion I was acting for the supporters of the Archduke Otto, having promised to deliver a packet of letters in Vienna which could not be entrusted to the ordinary post. I first of all obtained a *laissez-passer* from the Austrian minister in London, who may or may not have suspected my purpose, though I rather think that he did. This pass got me across the Austrian frontier all right, but when the time came for a meal I could not make up my mind whether to take the incriminating packet into the dining-car with me, where it might attract attention, or to leave it in my compartment, where it might be stolen. Having finally decided to leave it in the compartment, on returning from my meal I found that an officer in uniform had got in while I was away. Of course I jumped to the con-clusion that his presence could be no mere coincidence, and I was in a cold sweat until he left the carriage a few stations further on. Owing to a snowstorm I did not reach Vienna until the early hours of the morning, but tired as I was, by 9 a.m. I had delivered my packet. A few days later when I was dining with the British minister, Walford Selby, I had considerable difficulty in keeping my face straight when he told me, 'There is renewed activity among the royalists here. I think they must have received some instructions from their leaders abroad.'

My wife once had a similar experience, when she had been asked to take a woman's dressing-gown from one country to another. On opening the parcel in order to pack the garment she discovered to her dismay that the paper in which it was wrapped was covered with figures which were obviously a cypher. Fortunately, however, the customs officers were not interested in politics, and they let the dressing-gown through without a murmur.

Kings and princes are at a discount these days, and the world seems to think that it can get on better without them, just as it seems to think that it can get on better without God. Time will show whether it is right in either of these assumptions. In my opinion the real tragedy of this reaction against hereditary monarchy is that it has taken place at a time when the various Royal Families are distinguished for the ability of their members. After the overthrow of Napoleon I the world was made safe for kingship, but the contemporary exponents of that art were, with the exception of Louis XVIII, a pretty poor lot. Had there been a similar restoration of monarchs to their thrones after the overthrow of Hitler, I can vouch from personal knowledge that several European countries would have been decidedly fortunate in their rulers; for I can say without prejudice that the average level of intelligence of the members of Royal Families whom I have met has been much higher than that of the democratic politicians of my acquaintance.

Some of my most pleasant memories of the mainland of Europe in the thirties centre round the visits to Champagne which Lawrence Venn used to organize. He always proved himself the most charming and competent organizer, and there was never a hitch when he was in control. One did not habitually go anywhere by air in those far-off days, so we used to leave Victoria on Friday afternoon, spend two nights at the Lion d'Or in Rheims, and return to London on the Sunday night in the highest of spirits awash with champagne.

In October 1936 there was a party which was in the main parliamentary, but which included Lord Hewart, then Lord Chief Justice. Two years later, in July 1938, there was a more solemn occasion, when a number of us were invited to Rheims for the reconsecration of the cathedral, which was a most impressive ceremony. The President of the Republic was present, although owing to the usual political intrigue it was not decided until the last moment that he should come; in consequence, the only other head of state who could be obtained at short notice was the late Prince of Monaco, Louis II. As we were leaving the cathedral there was a delay while the Prince's A.D.C. engaged him in earnest conversation at the door. I was standing by Venn at the time, and asked him what he thought was the matter. 'I should imagine,' was the reply, 'that zero has come up twice running.'

After the ceremony in the cathedral we were all entertained to a most sumptuous lunch at the Hotel de Ville where Marchandeau, later Minister of Finance, but then Mayor of Rheims, presided. As there were to be innumerable speeches we of the British delegation persuaded Jock McEwen, at that time M.P. for Berwick and Haddington, to be our spokesman owing to his proficiency in the French language. Needless to say, he fulfilled all our expectations, expressing very adequately the opinion of his colleagues in his references to the damage done by the Germans to the cathedral in the First World War; indeed, his speech was forceful enough to occasion a protest by the German ambassador to the Foreign Office.

Finally, the more I travelled about Europe between the wars the more convinced I became that the real cause of its unsettled condition was the Treaty of Versailles. As I have said previously the victorious Allies, in opposition to their own interests, instead of reversing the work of Bismarck had carried it to its logical conclusion and completed the unification of Germany. This, however, is not to say that Germany should have been forcibly disrupted as was done in 1945, but rather that every encouragement should have been given to the centrifugal forces in the Reich, whose development would not have been difficult to set in motion, had a more judicious policy been pursued by the victors. In this connection a good deal of the blame must rest with the purblind democrats both in the Old World and in the New to whom the very idea of a hereditary monarch was anathema, and who welcomed what appeared to them to be a golden opportunity to get rid of the accursed thing. They little knew what a rod they were preparing for their backs before many years had passed.

Another result of the First World War which helped to bring about the Second was the overthrow of the Habsburg monarchy. In the earlier years of the century King Edward VII made strenuous efforts to persuade the ruler and statesmen of the Austro-Hungarian Empire to collaborate more closely with Great Britain in the maintenance of peace, and when I was in Budapest in December 1938 the Archduke Francis Joseph told me that there were still to be found at Ischl a number of documents relating to King Edward's visit thirty years before. In my *Diplomatic History, 1713–1933* I have related the sad story of the relations between the Allies and the Emperor Charles during the First World War, so it may be interesting here to quote a letter on this subject, which I received from Prince Sixte of Bourbon-Parma, who was the intermediary between the two parties:

'So far as England is concerned, I have nothing but praise for Mr Lloyd George. Your Prime Minister of those days understood the situation without any mental reservation of a political nature, and he saw in the possibility of peace the true interest of his country. When, in 1918, Clemenceau, in spite of the promise of Ribot, which was equally binding upon him, divulged the contents of the letters of the Emperor Charles, Lloyd George kept his word, and in spite of pressure from Clemenceau, refused to testify to the authenticity of this correspondence.'

All the same, it was not long before the British Government began to direct its extremely efficient propaganda towards the dissolution of the Habsburg dominions by encouraging the component nationalities to demand self-determination; in this it was supremely successful, and Austria-Hungary disappeared in the process. Unfortunately, however, it soon became apparent that self-determination was not a tap which could be turned on and off at will, so that the doctrine which British statesmen had to their own satisfaction applied to the Dual Monarchy was found before long to be disrupting the British Empire itself. If it was meritorious for the Czechs to break away from Vienna it was equally so for the Irish and Indians to sever their connections with London, and if Masaryk and Benes were patriots, then so were de Valera and Michael Collins, Gandhi and Jinnah, and for precisely the same reason; but it was some time before Whitehall saw it like that. If ever there was a weapon turned against those who first used it, that weapon is the doctrine of self-determination.

Whatever view may be taken of the Austro-Hungarian Empire on political grounds subsequent events have proved that it was an economic necessity, and for this reason repeated attempts were made between the wars to create some form of Danubian Federation. These attempts, however, were all shipwrecked on the rock of that extravagant nationalism which the Allies had encouraged in the First World War. Since 1945 power in Central Europe has passed to the Russians who have been very careful to avoid this particular mistake in their dealings with their satellites. On the previous occasion there must also be taken into account the vested interests which rapidly grew up in the Succession States. If there was to be a Danubian Federation its centre had to be Vienna, and once Vienna had again become the capital of a supra-national state the restoration of the Habsburgs would automatically follow, particularly since their heir was a young man of the calibre of the Archduke Otto.

So argued the statesmen of Prague, Belgrade, and Bucharest, and they were not far wrong. I remember one day in the early thirties talking to a Yugoslav general in the dining-car of the Arlberg Orient Express; he commanded a garrison in some provincial town, and to all outward appearances he had little cause to be discontented with his lot. He was actually telling me what a pleasant life he led, when, after a long pause, he suddenly blurted out, 'I'd give it all up tomorrow to be a subaltern again in Vienna in the old days.' It was this attitude that sent a shiver down the spine of the leaders of the Little Entente whenever they thought of the two-headed eagle of the House of Habsburg-Lorraine.

To sum up my impressions of Central Europe between the wars: the dominating factors were the Allied encouragement of the centripetal forces in the Reich, and of the centrifugal forces on the Danube.

CHAPTER XI

Some Balkan Reminiscences

THE history of the Balkans, like that of Ireland, can be described as a series of new beginnings, each claiming historical continuity, and each pretending that its predecessor never really happened. The period between the two wars was just such an era, in some ways the most hopeful that South-East Europe has known in modern times. Had the countries concerned been left alone for another twenty years to work out their own destiny the last evil effects of Turkish rule might have been eradicated, and the Balkan States, possibly working together in some form of confederation, might have played an increasingly important part in the counsels of Christendom. Unhappily, this was not to be. The thirties witnessed a revival, if in a slightly different form, of those intrigues by the Great Powers which were the dominant note in Balkan politics before 1914, and this led, through the bloodbath of the Second World War, to a state of affairs far worse than anything that South-East Europe had known under the most ferocious of the Ottoman Sultans.

It was between the wars that I made my visits to the Balkans, and as I saw a good deal of what was taking place, both on stage and behind the scenes, my impressions may serve as a footnote to history in spite of the fact that the situation there has since changed out of all recognition. Let us, therefore, enter the Balkans by way of Greece.

Curiously enough, it was no less a person than King George II of the Hellenes himself who first aroused my interest in his country. I met him at a luncheon party at Locker-Lampson's house in North Street on 13 February 1934, and from that day until his death I got to know him very well. As evidence of this, perhaps I may be forgiven for putting it upon record that when he returned to his throne on the collapse of the

Greek republic he asked me to write his farewell message to the British nation. Both during his lifetime and in retrospect he has been misjudged. Unlike his father, King Constantine, and his brother, King Paul, he was reserved; to him the first approach of a stranger was generally difficult, which mattered a great deal more in Greece than it did in England; he was not one of those who found conversation easy when he did not have anything to say. He learnt his lesson of kingship in a very hard school, and the tragic events which had marked his earlier years undoubtedly did much to drive him in on himself. Had he made a happy marriage, or had children, things might have been different, but to the end of his life King George remained a lonely man.

No monarch was ever more devoted to his subjects or their interests, nor, as the Second World War showed, has such faith been so well repaid. The loyalty of the Greek peasants to him was unshakable: twice was he voted to the throne by a plebiscite, which must be almost unique in the history of monarchies. With the society and politicians of Athens it was different; there was no link between them and him. Yet he was possessed of a keen sense of humour, and in spite of all that he suffered he never betrayed a trace of bitterness. To his friends no man could be more loyal. When it was known that the first restoration was about to take place I received the following holograph letter from him from Brown's Hotel dated 12 October 1935:

'Many grateful thanks for your letter and kind congratulations. I do hope I will be able to prove worthy, as much as possible, of the new responsibilities. The future has great difficulties in store for me.

'I am most touched and grateful for your support in the past and your kind suggestion of help in the future.'

King George II was never so happy as when he was in England, and Great Britain has never had a more sincere friend, even when she was treating him with that unconcern which she reserves for her real friends. 'We have got an English agent coming here next week,' Ciano once remarked to the Albanian minister in reference to an impending visit of the King of the Hellenes to Rome. For this reason I was particularly pleased to have been instrumental, through the good offices of Leo Amery, in securing for the King the award of the D.S.O., which made him the only foreign monarch in history to be decorated for valour while serving with British forces in the field, in this case in Crete. For his namesake, the fifth George, he had a respect almost amounting to reverence. The English way of life, too, appealed to him, particularly in its informality:

he liked to act with the minimum amount of ostentation. One afternoon he invited my wife and me to tea at the Royal Palace at Athens, the only other guests being Prince Paul, later King, and the late Prince Andrew, father of the Duke of Edinburgh. Just as we were leaving a servant handed him a box, which he gave to me with the remark, 'Here is a small present. Thank you for all you have done for me.' It was the insignia of one of his Orders.

The King's one great asset was his *Fidus Achates*, Dimitri Levidis, a master of resource who kept the coolest head in a crisis of any man I have ever known. He and I, with a few others, worked closely together to bring about the first restoration, and it was a proud moment when, on 14 November 1935, the King, seen off by the members of the British Royal Family, left Victoria for Athens. Certainly no monarchy was ever restored more cheaply. About twelve months before this event took place, and before Venizelos had played into royalist hands by his ill-considered rising, the maximum amount that the King and his friends could have raised was fifteen hundred pounds. At one moment there seemed a possibility that Zaharoff might put up some money, but the King was rightly reluctant to accept anything from that source, and after some very complicated negotiations with a man who claimed to be acting for Zaharoff the project was abandoned. In the end no money was required at all.

Soon after the monarchy was restored my wife and I paid our first visit to Athens. At that time one of the charms of Greece was that one passed so soon from Europe of the twentieth century to Asia of the eighteenth, from the bar of the Grande Bretagne to the villages of Attica where life was primitive in the extreme. Particularly was this the case in all that concerned the relations of the sexes. A woman of position would, in the most approved style of London or Paris, enter a bar and call for a drink without anyone thinking the worse of her for it, but less than an hour's motor-run away, in the hills, nothing would induce an unmarried girl even to speak to a member of the opposite sex unless some male of her family was present. Old customs were everywhere dying hard, especially in all that related to death. The funeral of a prominent politician, for example, was the occasion for a half-holiday, with social life largely suspended between the times of his death and burial. It was as if the big stores in Oxford Street had closed for the funeral of Stanley Baldwin or Clem Attlee.

As befitted the descendants of those who won Salamis, the sea was a magnet to all Athenians. The shore, which was within easy reach of the city, was thronged in summer, its attractive restaurants catering for all tastes and pockets. For those who could afford it there was excellent yachting, for the islands were close at hand, and the Yacht Club, new at the time of which I am writing, was one of the most comfortable of its kind. It stood on a promontory above the Bay of Munychia, where the triremes lay at anchor when Athens was mistress of the seas, and the narrow street by which one ascended the hill was that in which Critias met his death at the head of the Thirty Tyrants. As one sat on the terrace of the Yacht Club at one's feet were the ruins of the Long Walls, built at the height of Athenian power by Pericles and destroyed by the Spartans in the hour of the city's humiliation at the close of the Peloponnesian War.

In those relatively happy days before the Second World War it was not only the wealthy who had opportunities of enjoying themselves, for life was cheap in Athens and amusements were no exception. Even the *de luxe* hotels were not expensive by comparison with those elsewhere, and the cost of living for the resident was very low when judged by British standards. In any event the Greek, with his ancestors' zest for life, does not demand elaborate amusements. He finds delight in much that the sophisticated Western European would vote a bore, and he is the happier for it. Politically speaking, there may be something in the argument that the Greek is too much of an individualist to adapt himself easily to the modern world. But politics are not everything. Socially he is the better from this peculiarity, having the ability to amuse himself as an individual, and not in the mass or as a machine. And as the climate in normal conditions renders it easy to do this at very little cost, between the wars there were few cities where so many people knew the art of real enjoyment as in Athens.

The Athenian is today very much what he was two thousand and more years ago. An English historian has written of Pericles that 'his relationship to Cleisthenes, and the enmity which existed between his house and that of Cimon, urged him to espouse the cause of democracy'. Personal and family prejudices and affinities are still the basis of political divisions, one of the difficulties which will have to be overcome if the parliamentary system is ever to take root in Greece. For the rest, the Attic wit enables the Athenian to mock his leaders as in the days of Aristophanes, for within a few hours of the death of Venizelos, immediately after that of his enemy Condylis, the newspaper-boys were shouting through the streets, 'Meeting of Condylis and Venizelos'. The shade of Lucian must have smiled that day.

That was in the summer of 1936 when the Spanish Civil War was beginning and the conflict in Abyssinia coming to an end. Not many people in Britain realized what lay only three short years ahead. When I next visited the Balkans in November 1938 the position was very different: with Munich but a few weeks behind, outside the British Isles the one topic of conversation was not whether war would come again, but when and how. This being the case when the British Council, of which the late Lord Lloyd was then the head, asked me to go on a lecture-tour to Yugoslavia, Romania, and Hungary, I gladly agreed. It was a decision I never regretted. Unfortunately, however, the Yugoslav part of the trip had to be abandoned, as the Belgrade authorities, in spite of the kind offices of the King of the Hellenes, would not allow me to open my mouth in Yugoslavia in view of some aspersions I had made in a book upon the manner in which the Karageorgevitch dynasty had obtained the Serbian throne.

I left Victoria at 2 p.m. on 22 November 1938, travelling by the Simplon-Orient Express. The whole of the following day was spent in the train, and on the morning of the 24th I got up just as we were leaving Belgrade. So far the journey had been without incident, though I noticed that in Yugoslavia all the bridges were heavily guarded, presumably against Croat terrorists. Old Serbia I did not find very interesting as seen through the window of my compartment, and when the train reached Nish about noon on the 24th I was glad of the opportunity to stretch my legs on the platform. Then occurred an incident which clearly proved to me that I was back in the Balkans.

Just as I was about to get down from the coach one of the Wagons-Lits officials warned me not to go far from the carriage, because the train would be whistled out of the station very suddenly. I complied with his advice, fortunately for me as it turned out, for his prophecy was fulfilled to the letter; indeed, I only just had time to scramble aboard. When I was safely back in the train I asked my kind official how he had known what was going to happen. He replied, 'It is like this. The Simplon-Orient, as you know, only runs on alternate days. Now the station-master at Nish owns the only good hotel in the town, so that what he tries to do is to beguile foreign travellers to the end of the platform, and then send off the train, which means that they will have to spend two nights at his hotel.' One wonders how that station-master fared in the war.

At Nish we left the Greek carriages, and it was with a definite feeling of nostalgia that I saw them made ready for their journey South to Athens while we rumbled off to the East. We went on through the Dragoman Pass where in the previous winter the Simplon-Orient had been snowed up for two days, with the wolves howling under the carriage windows and the passengers eyeing one another askance. Then just before half-past four, a little over forty-eight hours after leaving Victoria, we pulled into Sofia, into what was then probably the least attractive station in Europe, with the possible exception of Cambridge.

After a week in Sofia I liked neither the place nor the people any better. I stayed at the Hotel Bulgarie which was the best in the town and really quite comfortable, but it swarmed with German agents, and I am perfectly certain that all my effects were thoroughly searched at least once a day. Although I was in the Balkans strictly as a lecturer for the British Council, and had no political mission whatever, it was everywhere assumed that I was doing some important work for the Foreign Office. At any rate, I was treated as if this were the case, that is to say with considerable respect combined with unbounded suspicion. As for Sofia itself, there can be few capitals in which there is less for the visitor to see. The background of Witoscha lends it a certain dignity, but the cathedral of St Alexander Nevski struck me as new and garish, the square of the Tsar Liberator – it is probably called something else now – was undistinguished, and the palace was ugly. On the other hand there were one or two places worth seeing outside the town, such as the old church at Bayona with its attractive paintings, and the monastery of Dragalevtsi, though the mural paintings there were not so well lit as those of Bayona.

What made life pleasant for me in Sofia was the kindness of Sir George Rendel, then British minister, and his wife. Their knowledge of Bulgaria was very wide, for Sir George belongs to that somewhat rare class of diplomatist who does not consider it beneath his dignity to find out all he can about the country to which he is accredited. He was, I always feel, particularly fitted to occupy the legation at Sofia, since while an undergraduate at Oxford he had written a prize essay on the *condottiere* of the Middle Ages.

During my stay in Sofia the Bulgarian Press Bureau attached one of its officials to me, nominally as a guide and interpreter, but in reality to ensure that I did not see more than was good for me. He was doubtless an excellent fellow in his way – with most of the fingers off his right hand which he said was due to having gripped a cluster of Turkish bayonets – but he had the disconcerting habit of arriving at the Hotel Bulgarie sharp at nine every morning. He clearly received a sum of money each day from the Press Bureau on account of expenses, and his one object was to spend it on drink at the earliest possible moment, but he could only spend it if I were with him, hence his early calls. The result was that by ten o'clock we were usually to be found in a café drinking that much over-rated beverage *slivovitza*. However, this weakness of my would-be guide, philosopher, and friend had its compensations so far as I was concerned, for by noon he was usually so much under the influence that I was able to leave him and go my way in peace.

In spite of her blunder in the First World War the country was clearly inclining once more towards Berlin, and German pressure was very strong. There was a certain amount of rioting during my visit; one night while I was at dinner at my hotel the troops opened fire in the street below the window, taking care, it may be added, to fire well over the heads of the crowd, a manoeuvre not wholly conducive to the quiet enjoyment of one's dinner in a glass-enclosed balcony on the first floor. The official explanation was that the trouble was due to students demonstrating for the annexation of the Dobrudja from Romania, of which the government strongly disapproved. The truth was that the riots were inspired by the Nazis, with the full knowledge of the authorities, to embarrass the Western Powers. My personal popularity in official circles markedly declined when I observed that it seemed to me odd that Bulgarian students clamouring for the cession of the Dobrudja by Romania should express themselves by chalking swastikas on the walls of the French legation.

Nevertheless after two days and nights of disturbances in the streets the situation was beginning to get out of hand, and with alarming rumours flying round Europe the Government had to do something. Accordingly more reliable troops were called in from the provincial garrisons to establish martial law for twenty-four hours, which meant that no one was allowed to leave his house or to use the telephone during that period. As only about half a dozen of the employees of the Hotel Bulgarie slept in, and none of the kitchen staff, the prospects for the day looked pretty grim. However, by a judicious mixture of threats and cajolery I persuaded the telephone operator to put me through to the British legation, and Sir George Rendel sent his car to get me out of the hotel. After that I spent an extremely pleasant day with the Rendels far away from Bulgarian political strife, motoring out to Kremekovtsi, enjoying a glorious walk in the hills, and ending with a visit to the convent there.

I had not been long in Sofia before the British legation was notified from the palace that the King, Boris III, would grant me an audience if I applied for one. Probably, like his subjects, the King was under the impression that I was in Bulgaria on some sinister mission for Mr Chamberlain and Lord Halifax. The following is a note of the audience on 28 November 1938, which I wrote immediately on my return to the hotel:

'His Majesty began the conversation in English, but soon relapsed into French, which he used for the rest of the audience, and this lasted an hour. He discussed my lecture with me, and was obviously desirous that I should stress to my audience the importance of tradition.

'He then mentioned his recent visit to Balmoral, and said how much he had enjoyed it. This led to mention of Ireland, and he asked me the exact implication of Mr de Valera's latest proposals. From this the King turned to general politics, and expressed himself most enthusiastically over the Munich Agreement and the Prime Minister personally. In his view there is room in the world for both Great Britain and Germany, provided that both Powers recognize their true interests. He does not think that Herr Hitler has any aggressive designs against the Low Countries.

'When I said that the recent speeches of the Fuehrer and the anti-Jewish campaign were an embarrassment to the British Government, he agreed, but said that when dealing with Germans such blunders were only to be expected. As for the colonies, His Majesty agreed that we could not surrender Tanganyika, and said that if Germany wanted any overseas possessions, Great Britain would obviously require them to be such that the line of communication with them could easily be cut. He expressed great satisfaction when I pointed out that there was constitutionally no need for a General Election until 1940, and he thinks 1939 will be a critical year.

'Of his own problems he said little except that he was trying to secure unity without too violent a change in the constitution, and that any settlement with his neighbours must, to be lasting, be peaceful and equitable. He was scornful about those who sought the limelight in which to talk politics.

'For the rest, His Majesty was very concerned about the state of France, expressed warm approval of the ratification of the Anglo-Italian Agreement, said he thought Japan would in the end be seriously weakened by her victories in China, and agreed that Russia would only become dangerous if war broke out in Western and Central Europe.

'He dismissed me with a request that I would remember him very kindly to the Prime Minister.'

So much water, and blood, has flowed under the bridges in Bulgaria and elsewhere since this conversation took place that it has long been *vieux jeu,* but it may serve to illustrate to some slight extent the outlook of European statesmen in the months preceding the outbreak of the Second World War.

King Boris himself impressed me as much more Bourbon than Coburg, but I didn't feel that distrust for him which others describe as their reaction. I think he knew that if war came again Bulgaria would once more be drawn in, on the wrong side, this time to her final undoing; he was therefore prepared to support any man or any scheme that appeared likely to prevent war. Unlike his father, King Ferdinand, he was not an intriguer, for he was too conscious of what was at stake both for his country and his dynasty to embark upon any adventure that could be avoided. I never saw him again; all the evidence goes to show that he was murdered by the Nazis when they realized that he was making preparations to avoid the worst consequences to the Balkans of Hitler's follies. King Boris was an able man, but as the ruler of a small country he could never in the last resort control events even in his own area when the Great Powers came to blows: it was not the will he lacked, but the resources.

My other activities in Sofia were my lecture (what it was about I have not the least idea, but there is an entry in my diary to the effect that 'it was not a success, as I felt completely out of touch with my audience'); going with the Rendels to *Thais,* which was surprisingly well done; and a number of luncheons, dinners, and receptions of varying interest.

My journey to Bucharest was not as eventful as it had once promised to be, especially when the frontier between Bulgaria and Romania had been closed due to the riots in Sofia to travellers unprovided with a diplomatic passport. At that time the wildest stories of atrocities were being passed round in the train. In particular tears were brought to the eyes of all save the most sophisticated by the statement that the crew of a Romanian vessel on the Danube had seized a couple of Bulgarian peasants who were working on the Bulgarian bank of the river, and had then burnt them alive in the furnace of their boat. However, I found that manufacturers of atrocity stories have little imagination, for as soon as I was on Romanian soil I heard this particular charge brought against the Bulgarians in precisely the same terms.

The train left Sofia at 8.40 a.m. on the last day of November, and I was more than pleased to have a good view of Plevna, from where one could gather quite a reasonable idea of the siege. The only other occupant of my compartment was an elderly chemist from Frankfurt-am-Main, very much of Second Reich vintage, who, when he was quite certain that we could not be overheard, warned me that 'Hitler had unleashed the underworld on Germany and would assuredly unloose it on Europe'. The name of my companion I did not discover, but he must have been a man of some importance because he was treated with considerable deference both by the Nazi officials who saw him off at Sofia and by those who met him at the Romanian capital.

We got to Rustchuk about six in the evening where the Mayor greeted me and saw me through the various formalities. It was a beautifully mild evening, although the winter was destined to be a severe one, and I sat on the deck of the boat without an overcoat as we crossed the Danube to Giurgiu. Only four of us, the German chemist, a French diplomatist and his wife, and I were allowed by the Romanian authorities to land. Then from Giurgiu I took a slow train, which took three hours to do the sixty kilometres to Bucharest, but once I arrived I was soon duly settled at the Splendid Parc Hotel.

'Un ilot latin au milieu de l'océan slave et finnois qui l'environne', so Baron Jean de Witte described Romania a century ago; rather less complimentary was the Frenchman who said, 'I have often heard Bucharest described as a small Paris, but, thank God, nobody has ever called Paris a big Bucharest.' It would, of course, be absurd to claim that the Romanian race is of pure Latin stock – and in some parts of the country there are large racial minorities of very different origin – but no one can be in Romania for twenty-four hours without realizing that in all the essentials of civilization it is Latin. For myself, I have the most pleasant recollections of my visit, particularly of the people, but then I can always get on better with the Latins than with the Teutons or the Slavs. Certainly the Romanians did not deserve the tragic fate which has overtaken them.

On arriving in Romania I found the country even more disturbed than the Bulgaria I had left, with the government engaged in the suppression of the Iron Guard. Like many another political organization, this body had in origin been innocuous; having started primarily as a movement for the regeneration of Romania. It had, however, always demanded strong measures against the Jews, who are particularly numerous in Moldavia, being at the time supported by the Orthodox clergy, and having its greatest following among patriotic citizens who saw no hope in the existing political system. Its subsequent deterioration was largely due to the fact that it failed to produce a capable leader, for Codreano was little more than a gangster, and so had fallen under the control of extremists. When these started murdering their opponents in hospital, the moderate element left in disgust, and the Iron Guard became a purely terrorist organization.

This, however, is not the whole story, for international politics also came into the picture. The German Government viewed with considerable disfavour the increasing inclination of Romania towards the Western Powers, seeing in the Iron Guard a useful instrument with which to blackmail King Carol II and his ministers into dependence upon the Rome-Berlin axis. Codreano was in due course arrested by the authorities, and a day or two before I left Sofia for Bucharest he and several of his followers were shot trying to escape – or so it was officially announced – while being transferred from one prison to another. By way of reprisal the Iron Guard promptly murdered the Rector of Cluj University by shooting him in the back from behind a hoarding one foggy morning.

At first I took a purely objective view of these events, but I soon realized that they were to concern me more closely. The chairman at my lecture in Bucharest (which went off much better than the one in Sofia) was to be Professor Jorga, the historian, whom I had first met at the Convegno Volta six years before, and he had received a threat from the Iron Guard to the effect that he would be murdered while presiding on this occasion. He took this intimation very seriously indeed, so that I had great difficulty in persuading him to take the chair at all; in fact I only succeeded in doing so by stressing the fact that the Iron Guard was extremely unlikely to create an incident when there were to be foreign diplomats on the platform, though I was by no means convinced of the strength of my own arguments. However, all went off well, probably helped by the fact that the approaches to the building where the lecture was delivered fairly bristled with armed police. Never did any audience have a more attentive lecturer; at the first sign of any man moving a hand in the direction of hip or breast pocket I should have gone down behind the rostrum from which I was speaking, for after all it was no quarrel of mine. Poor Jorga's fears, it may be added, were by no means groundless, for eventually the Iron Guard did get him.

On the following day, half-way through a lunch that the Minister of Propaganda was giving for me at the Capsa Restaurant, a servant brought a telegram for the Minister. He glanced at it, then remarked to me quite casually, 'A couple more of the Iron Guard shot while trying to escape.' I murmured my congratulations as I felt decency required, but I was sorely tempted to say, 'I have never shot Iron Guard. Do you call that a good bag for so early in the season?'

All this was in the heyday of the personal rule of King Carol II, on whose behalf there is a great deal more to be said than is always appreciated. His energy was to be remarked in every direction. New roads were being constructed, fine public buildings were being erected, and the greatest attention was being devoted to agriculture in all its branches, while there was a considerable development in stock-raising, notably in sheep-breeding in Bessarabia. Eighty per cent of the Romanian population of twenty million was on the land, mostly as peasant proprietors, and three-fifths of the country was under cultivation, which is a high ratio when its configuration is taken into account. No one could be in Romania at this time for twenty-four hours without realizing that the inspiration came from the throne; nor could there be any question of the popularity of the monarch or the then Crown Prince Michael. The King's private life aroused neither the interest nor the disapproval in the country that was the case elsewhere. The real tragedy of the last two kings of Romania was that they were not given time to complete the task of national regeneration to which they set their hands, and which will have to be started all over again when the yoke of Russia is lifted.

Although there was more to see in Bucharest than in Sofia, I had much less time in which to see it. The churches of St Spiridon and Stavropoleos specially attracted me, also the Museum of Religious Art. It was very interesting to note the way in which national characteristics managed to make themselves felt in the framework of Byzantine convention, and there is a great deal of history to be learnt in the religious art of the countries where the Orthodox Church is predominant. Those who expect to find uniformity in Smyrna, Athens, Sofia, and Bucharest will be disappointed. Socially, I still recall an extremely pleasant dinner with Sir Reginald and Lady Hoare at the British legation as well as an equally delightful afternoon with Princess Marthe Bibesco at Mogosoaea; it was at this time, too, that I first became acquainted with that admirable Romanian drink, *tuica*.

From Bucharest I went by the Arlberg Orient Express to Cluj – Kolozsvar to the Hungarians – in Transylvania, the journey taking from 1.58 p.m. to 12.15 a.m. On the platform to meet me was Professor Grimm, well known to readers of Walter Starkie's *Raggle Taggle*, who took me to the extremely comfortable flat which the university had placed at my disposal. Once again, however, I was to be reminded of the activities of the Iron Guard, for the university authorities, mindful of the recent fate of their Rector, were determined to leave nothing to chance where their British guest was concerned. Accordingly, both a soldier and a *gendarme* were stationed under my window, and as they were relieved at alternate hours the latest comer had always plenty to tell his companion, with the result that my defenders had a great deal of conversation while I had very little sleep. However, the fault of my hosts, if it were a fault, was on the right side.

From the moment of my arrival I was attracted to Transylvania with its mosaic of races and religions, and as the various races even dressed differently from one another I was soon able to distinguish them at a glance. There were the Romanians, who belonged either to the Orthodox or to the Uniate Church, the latter being in communion with Rome; Hungarians, I discovered, were either Roman Catholics or Calvinists; while there was a German minority which represented about ten per cent of the total population of the province: these people were known as Saxons, but they were really of Rhineland origin and came to Transylvania in the days of the Saxon emperors. It is even said that the legend of the Pied Piper of Hamelin refers to their migration, but however remote the date when they left the Reich they were nevertheless being subjected to intensive Nazi propaganda. Nor was this all, for I actually came across some Unitarians who had a bishop: I forget their racial origin, but they were strongly Anglophil owing to their admiration for their co-religionist, Neville Chamberlain.

The countryside I found as attractive as the people, the day I enjoyed most during the whole of this visit being Tuesday, 6 December. The weather was still mild, and it was hardly daylight when Professor Grimm called for me at eight o'clock and we motored along excellent roads by way of Turda to Aiud, where there was an excellent example of the fortified churches which are so prominent a feature of Transylvania. From Aiud we went to Alba Julia where the Romanian sovereigns were crowned, and on to Sibiu, otherwise known as Hermannstadt. This is one of the most attractive places I have visited. Peopled largely by Saxons in the Transylvanian sense, it recalled a small German town of the early nineteenth century, an illusion which was heightened by the magnificent uniforms of the Romanian officers in garrison there. I left Sibiu after lunch with very great regret, and a determination to return at the earliest possible opportunity; though I now fear that opportunity will never present itself, and if it does Sibiu will be considerably changed for the worse.

That night I passed on to Hungary. Budapest was not new to me as I had been there for a couple of days with my father and mother in 1912. Together with Paris, St Petersburg, and Washington it is the most impressive capital, from an external point-of-view, that I have ever seen; nowhere is the Danube more majestic. Its social life, however, I thought vulgar; certainly it could not compare with Vienna in the days of the monarchy; they were like two different types of woman, the aristocrat and the courtesan. Vienna took a great deal of knowing, and would not allow the visitor to take it by storm, whereas in Budapest everything was in the shop-window, and like things in shop-windows could be bought at a price. Personally I had nothing except an excess of nationalist propaganda of which to complain, for in addition to the doors opened to me by the British Council I received a very warm welcome from a circle of Legitimist friends. Chief of these was Count Maurice Esterhazy, who had been Prime Minister of Hungary under King Charles, and who died in time to be spared the ultimate degradation of his country, brought about by those who had spurned his advice.

I saw little of the countryside except for a visit to Szeged where I lectured in the Great Hall of the University. I doubt if I have ever got through, or been put through, so much in a single day. The train, on which I breakfasted, started at 7.30 a.m., and took three hours to get to Szeged; immediately on arrival I was taken on a sight-seeing expedition which included a children's clinic, a training centre for district nurses, and a farm, the last of these being miles away and not far from the Yugoslav frontier. Then, in equally rapid succession, was a lunch at the Hotel Tisza, a visit to a Franciscan monastery, and tea at the Horthy College. I got back to the Hotel Hungaria in Budapest just before eleven, and not surprisingly the first line of my diary for the following day read, 'Got up late'.

In one respect Budapest resembled Sofia and Bucharest, namely that nobody really believed war could be avoided. The shadow of the Third Reich fell everywhere. As the Czechs were so unpopular nobody regretted their fall for their sake; what everyone wondered was who would be next. Chamberlain was generally admired because he had managed to postpone the evil day, but it was hoped that in consequence Britain would look to her armaments in such a way as to redress the Balance of Power. Nevertheless, the atmosphere was very different from what it had been when I was on the Continent a few months before the First World War, and it was not until I was back in London that I heard the idea of another conflict scouted by responsible people.

On Thursday 15 December I caught the Orient Express from Budapest at 9.58 a.m. I had not the heart even to get down to the platform in Vienna, having seen the city in its greatness under the Habsburgs, and when Dollfuss was working for the revival of his country; I did not wish to see even the station with the swastika triumphant. So the train took me across Hitler's Reich to Aix-la-Chapelle, where the authorities turned all the Jews off the train, presumably to stop them getting out of Germany, though as the Nazis did not want Jews in Germany it seemed illogical in the extreme to prevent them from getting out. Incidentally, this caused considerable commotion in the next sleeper to mine, where a Yugoslav diplomat on his way to Brussels was sharing his couch with a young Jewess whom he had met in the dining car on the previous evening. However, his protests were in vain; he was told quite firmly that his diplomatic immunity did not cover his bed-fellow; and the girl was removed in her night-attire in tears.

At 4.20 p.m. on 16 December I arrived at Victoria, having crossed by Ostend to Dover. It was to be my last visit to the Continent before the outbreak of the Second World War.

CHAPTER XII

The Second World War

My experiences in the Balkans, particularly listening to the gloomy forebodings of the King of Bulgaria, had convinced me that it would be a wise precaution to move ourselves down to Lillington, out of the way of the deluge of bombs which was predicted for London should war break out, so by the middle of June 1939 we had cleared our house in Kensington of its furniture and were wholly settled in Dorset.

The year had started badly so far as we as a family were concerned, for at the beginning of March I had a sharp attack of gastric 'flu and at Easter my wife was for a few days seriously ill with bronchial pneumonia. So deciding that a change of air would be good for us, we took what proved to be the last carefree holiday for many years. We wandered round Devon and Cornwall, staying at the Imperial at Torquay, the Falmouth Hotel at Falmouth, and the Golden Bay Hotel at Westward Ho, also paying a call on the Dalrymple Hamiltons at the Royal Naval College at Dartmouth, and finally ended up at Chevithorne Barton where for a few days we were the guests of Pat Heathcoat-Amory and his mother, who were admirable hosts. Pat, who was later killed in North Africa, was one among the younger generation whose loss the country could ill afford.

During the spring and summer I did a good deal of lecturing both at Portsmouth and Dartmouth, and at neither place did I come across the easy complacency regarding the prospect of war that was still to be found in many circles in London. It has been stated that little use was made by Britain of the twelve months' respite that Neville Chamberlain gained at Munich, but whatever truth there may have been in this accusation it did not apply to the country districts: in Dorset, at any rate, where we were utterly unprepared for war in the autumn of 1938, by September of the following year we were able to handle the problems of A.R.P. (Air Raid Precautions) and the evacuees quite efficiently.

When the war finally came it was paradoxical from the start, and it was not long in giving the lie to the prophets. For years it had been confidently asserted that never again would there be war in Western Europe, yet when Hitler's ambition falsified this prophecy the pundits were not slow to declare that the conflict would be precipitated without warning given, so that civilization might well perish overnight in a hurricane of gas and incendiary bombs. In actual fact it would be diffi- cult to find a precedent for a struggle of which the approach was more clearly heralded in advance, since it had been latent for many months before the first actual blows were struck. Indeed, there were not a few people in Great Britain who felt definitely relieved on 3 September to know that the tension was over; as for myself, as early as 24 April, I had noted in my diary, 'At times this suspense is almost unbearable, and even war itself would be preferable.' Finally, it was widely stated that there could be no repetition of the strategy of twenty-five years before, inasmuch as no British government would dare to send a large army to fight on the mainland of Europe; yet had anyone said in the early days of the Nazi regime that Great Britain would be given two years to make her preparations and then eight months to put them into practice, he would equally have been laughed out of court.

All this had a considerable effect upon public opinion. Far from bursting upon the country in full intensity from the first moment, the war, from the military and aerial standpoint, came gradually, and only at sea was it waged à l'outrance from the moment it was declared. Had it not been for the precautions necessitated by the new danger of attack from the air, by the restrictions upon the consumption of petrol, and by the dislocation of the population due to evacuation, the ordinary citizen during the first few months of the conflict had been far less aware of its existence than his father had been of its predecessor. All this was not without its influence upon the popular mind, which became perplexed at finding that events did not take the turn which had been so confidently expected. On the other hand no British government ever had a more docile people with whom to deal. Restriction was placed upon restriction to an extent and with a rapidity for which there is no parallel in English history since the time of Cromwell, and yet all were accepted with scarcely a murmur. Official interference with the life of the individual citizen was practised to a degree which was unknown in the First World War, or which would only have been possible after the most careful preparation of the public mind. Even outstanding blunders, which might have been expected to force the resignation of the minister concerned, were condoned. Never had a Prime Minister been so powerful as was Neville Chamberlain between September 1939 and the German invasion of Scandinavia.

This brings me to the man himself, but before I write about him I had better give my qualifications for doing so. In the early years of the century he and my father were respective custodians of the finances of Birmingham and Liverpool, and they met in that capacity; then I heard a great deal about him from Austen and Ivy Chamberlain; and lastly when I was writing my biography of Austen he gave me a great deal of the most valuable help.

His real tragedy was that circumstances involved him in problems, namely those of foreign policy, for which he had neither previous training nor special aptitude. I have a letter from him, dated 11 April 1939, in which, replying to some observation of mine about the Younger Pitt, he wrote, 'You were quite right in supposing that I have a great admiration for him. Indeed, he has always appealed to me more than any other of our Prime Ministers.' Although the Younger Pitt was a much better wartime Premier than Neville the two men had a great deal in common, both having regarded foreign affairs as an unwelcome distraction from the more congenial task of domestic reform. Had Neville been born in less troubled times he might have become another Peel, for he was an outstanding success as Minister of Health and Chancellor of the Exchequer; again, had Austen lived, Neville might have turned to him for advice in matters of foreign policy, though this is by no means certain.

Admittedly as Prime Minister he proved himself on occasion a poor psychologist, with regard to both the individual and the mass, and some of his appointments were incredibly bad. Among the many great qualities which he inherited from his father one would search in vain for Joseph Chamberlain's almost uncanny ability to appeal to the popular imagination. Nor is the reason difficult to find, for Neville came into national politics relatively late in life, and in his business career was associated with those branches of industry which require the least advertisement; had he been connected with one of the myriad businesses which depend on publicity, his outlook, for better or for worse, might have been very different. Then again Prime Ministers are essentially lonely men, Chamberlain having been no exception to this. As their colleagues are in many cases their rivals, they have to be extremely careful what they say to them. It might be answered that a Prime

Minister can confide in his wife – if he has one. But unfortunately few Prime Ministers' wives are intellectually capable of sharing their husbands' cares and worries; Margot Asquith was probably the only one in this country down to the outbreak of the Second World War. The breach has usually been filled by men like Monty Corry, Jack Sandars, and Horace Wilson, who, not being politicians, do not arouse the jealousy of the senior members of the Cabinet. Certainly Horace Wilson owed much of his influence to the solitariness of his chief.

Neville's reputation is unquestionably vulnerable on the score that he entertained a touching belief in Hitler's sincerity in spite of the Fuehrer's proved duplicity over a long period of years, but then so did Stalin. One would have thought that the German's changed attitude between the conversation at Berchtesgaden and that at Godesberg would have reminded him of his brother's warning to the House of Commons six years before, 'While something is refused to Germany it is vital. If you say, "Well, we will give it to you, and now our relations will, of course, be on a satisfactory footing", it loses all value from the moment that she obtains it, and it is used by her merely as a stepping-off place for a further demand.' Neville clearly sustained a severe shock when in March 1939 he realized that he had been duped: indeed, Iain Macleod once told me that it was by no means impossible that as a result of this shock Neville contracted the cancer of which he died. Never a good judge of character, he showed at his worst in this respect where Hitler was concerned.

Finally, his manner towards his political opponents was far from conciliatory. Once when he spoke in the House of Commons Oliver Stanley told him that he 'looked on the Labour Party as dirt', to which he replied, 'Their gross exaggerations, their dishonesty in slurring over facts that tell against them, and their utter inability to appreciate a reasonable argument, do embitter my soul sometimes, and if I seem hard and unsympathetic to them, it is the reaction brought about by their own attitude.'

The first impact of the war upon us in Dorset was the arrival of the evacuees, and until they came among us few of those living in the reception areas had realized the gulf which existed between town and country. The selfishness and dirty habits of a great many of the evacuees made the worst possible impression upon the countryside. One realized that the great weakness of an industrial civilization is the lack of resource of the mass of the population: deprive them of cinemas and remove them from the proximity of shops and they do not know how to use their spare time. In the Second World War they had not even television to relieve their boredom. On the other hand it was not always realized in the villages that many of the female evacuees were under considerable mental strain in being parted from their menfolk, who were either serving in the Forces or who had remained at their work in the towns exposed to the activities of the Luftwaffe.

Very soon, too, after the declaration of war troops began to arrive in the neighbouring villages, Lillington itself being too small for any to be billeted there. Their arrival was preceded by the most extraordinary rumours, for example, that a battalion of the I.R.A. was about to be stationed in Long Burton. When the unit in question did make its appearance it turned out to be the Royal Ulster Rifles. All this kept my wife fully occupied, for she was both Air Raid Warden and Billeting Officer for the evacuees, and in both capacities she gave, if I may be pardoned for saying so, evidence of the organizing ability she was later to display on a wider field as Mayor of Kensington, member of the London County Council, and United Kingdom Delegate to the fourteenth Session of the United Nations Assembly.

As for myself, I turned carefully over in my mind the best way in which I might be of use in view of the fact that I was too old to serve in the Forces. In due course I drew up the following memorandum:

MEMORANDUM ON THE INFLUENCE OF RIGHT OPINION IN EUROPE IN FAVOUR OF THE ALLIES

1. The understanding between Germany and Russia, and the Russian invasion of Poland, afford an excellent opportunity for mobilizing Right opinion against the Nazi regime. This will immediately be of great importance in many neutral countries, and ultimately will strengthen the centrifugal influence in the German Reich itself.

2. The Right elements in all Continental countries have long been suspicious of Nazism for its attitude towards monarchy and religion, but they disliked Bolshevism far more, and therefore they were tolerant of Nazism as the lesser of the two evils: now both their opponents are in the same camp. In these circumstances it should not be difficult to rally Right feeling to the side of Great Britain, which is a Christian and monarchical Power, in the struggle against Berlin and Moscow.

3. In Spain, and, to a lesser extent, Portugal, the Right was unfavourable to the Allies in the last war, but the position is very different today, and with a small expenditure of effort it could be made definitely enthusiastic. There is also great scope for similar work in Italy, Hungary, the Balkan States, and Latin America.

4. So far as the German Reich itself is concerned results would naturally be slower in manifesting themselves. The chief mistake of the Treaty of Versailles was that it attempted to undo the work of 1870, while there can be no real peace in Europe until the verdict of 1866 has been reversed. This can be accomplished only by encouraging separatist feeling in Austria and Bavaria to look once more to their old Royal Houses.

5. This analysis is the consequence of many years' study of, and in many cases co-operation with, Right movements on the Continent: it also proceeds from the conviction that in the present struggle Great Britain cannot afford to neglect any of her potential assets.

6. My concrete suggestion is that a bureau or department should be set up to establish contact with the Right elements in enemy and neutral countries; that it should work along the lines envisaged above; and that it should be staffed by people who are already known to, and respected by, those whom it is proposed to influence in this way.

20.ix.1939.

The fate of this document is an interesting commentary upon the point of view then entertained in high places. I sent it to the Prime Minister towards the end of September, and in due course he replied that he had 'read it with much interest' and was 'arranging for it to be brought at once to the notice of the appropriate Department'. This was apparently the Foreign Office, for although I heard nothing directly from that quarter I did eventually receive a letter from the Ministry of Information to say that my memorandum had reached them from Lord Halifax; the Ministry then proceeded to turn down my proposal on the ground that it was 'very anxious not to introduce any sort of class distinctions into our propaganda'. Not only had I made no allusion of any sort to class distinctions, but within two years Great Britain was working hand-in-hand with the Communists all over Europe with consequences of which we are still feeling the evil effects.

Whether it was my views or myself that were anathema to the Establishment I am not quite certain, but I shrewdly suspect the latter, though for what reason I have not the slightest idea. Anyhow, the war had not been in existence for more than a few weeks when the Greek Government indicated a desire that I should come to Greece to help to counteract Axis propaganda, and shortly afterwards Lord Lloyd asked me if I would be willing to go to Spain for the same purpose. In both cases I expressed the greatest readiness to do what was suggested, and in either country I feel that my connections might have been of use, but I never heard another word – someone high up in Establishment circles must have exercised a veto. A little later the B.B.C. used my services for a time to broadcast to Latin America, but this suddenly came to an end for no given reason, so I can only suppose that authority had again intervened. It is not only on the Left that one can come up against the Establishment, for Francis Yeats-Brown experienced the same treatment.

After the chilly reception of my memorandum I abandoned *la haute politique*, apart from giving a few talks on the war to various local organizations, to concentrate on finishing my official biography of Austen Chamberlain. Early in 1940 Oliver Stanley succeeded Leslie Hore-Belisha at the War Office, and as he did not share the doubts regarding my reliability which assailed his colleagues of the Establishment a request soon reached me to assist in the work of Army education, but of this more anon.

With the fall of France came the fear of invasion, which continued to affect the lives of the civilian population until at least 1942. We know now that save for a very brief period this fear was groundless, but at the time it had to be taken seriously, with the result that my services were now demanded by that same Ministry of Information which had spurned them in another capacity, so I spent a busy three months going round Dorset and Devon telling people what to do if the Germans came. There was no need to stress the danger in which we stood. Many of the French troops who had been evacuated from Dunkirk were repatriated through Weymouth, and their appearance, which I saw in company with Victor Raikes who was staying with us at the time, as they marched through the streets of that town told its own tale. Then, long before the raids on London started, we had enemy aeroplanes over both by day and by night, so that we became thoroughly used to the sound of exploding bombs. In the villages near the coast the threat of invasion stirred many a memory, however indistinct, of the stories told by an earlier generation of the day when one greater than Adolf Hitler lay at Boulogne waiting for the opportunity to land in Wessex.

Of course all these alarums and excursions had their comic side. One very nervous prospective visitor to Lyme Regis wrote to the landlord of the Royal Lion to enquire when the last enemy activity had taken place there, to receive on the back of a postcard the reply, 'June 11th, 1685' – the date of Monmouth's landing; but he was taking no chances, and nothing more was heard of him. At the Jolly Sailor at Salford, near Bath, during a particularly unpleasant air-raid, my friend, Gerry Face, who was the inn-keeper, found an old lady crouching in a corner of the lounge in the darkness clutching her deed-box and murmuring, 'All this for the sake of a few Poles.'

The actual events of those days may be read anywhere, but as there is a real danger that the mood of the country may be forgotten with the passing of the years here is a report by Mr Whiteside, local representative of the Ministry of Information at Exeter, and Clerk to the Justices in that city:

'Between September 9th and 14th, 1940, Sir Charles Petrie conducted a series of fifteen open-air meetings with loud-speaker van in Exeter. One meeting was abandoned after having been interrupted by an air-raid warning. It cannot be said with exactness how many people attended each meeting, but it is certain that at least 2,000 adults have heard Sir Charles during the week. The Mayor, the Sheriff and other people of local prominence have acted as chairman and, after a short introduction, Sir Charles spoke at each meeting for about half an hour on the general subject, "You and the War", after which he invited questions. In his speeches he supplied a commentary on the most recent B.B.C. news bulletin and dealt generally with some of the major aspects of the war: after the Prime Minister's speech on Wednesday he spoke particularly on the prospect of invasion and underlined the advice to "stay put".

'There was no hostility or heckling at any meeting; one rough-looking man was overheard before a meeting to say "More tripe, I suppose" – Sir Charles humorously referred to this remark, and the man sought him out afterwards to express his satisfaction with what he had heard. Audiences were rather diffident in putting questions, but after some encouragement questions were asked through stewards who mixed with the people. Not into a single question could be read the slightest trace of defeatism or of criticism of the war or of the country's leaders; indeed, the week's meetings confirm me in the view that the working-men are solid behind the Prime Minister and the Government. Certain questions were asked relating to local affairs but these were dealt with adequately by local people: the Chairman of the local A.R.P. Committee kindly attended one meeting to reply to certain questions which were foreshadowed. The questions asked of Sir Charles were varied and intelligent: questions relating to Japan, Spain, internal political opposition to Mussolini in Italy; support for General de Gaulle in un-occupied France; extent of air-raid precautions in Germany; evacuation of British Somaliland, to mention only a few. It was particularly notice-able that no question relating to war aims was put. One man was cheered when he asked if German prisoners might not be given the task of removing unexploded bombs, but a larger volume of applause greeted the explanation that we could not put German prisoners to work which we would not wish our own boys, prisoners in Germany, to be employed on.

'In brief, the series of meetings may be regarded as quite successful and I, who attended each of them, had an opportunity of studying the working man and the war which I would not willingly have missed.'

The bombing of Exeter was wholly unjustifiable, and is comparable only to the equally reprehensible bombing of Lübeck and Dresden by the Allies. There was no conceivable military objective in Exeter, for the Marine barracks were outside and the town was wholly undefended. To one arriving in Exeter a few hours after the last bomb had fallen, who knew and loved the city as I did, the scene was heartbreaking. It was an act of wanton savagery, after which there was only one consolation – to witness the efficiency and the humanity with which the authorities coped with the situation. On the other hand, if the bombing of civilians is ever venial, then the attack on Bath was justified, however much one may regret the material damage that was done. Authority, mainly in the form of the Admiralty, had packed the place with Civil Servants, and it must be admitted that in these days of total war a Civil Servant is a legitimate target. To send Civil Servants to Bath was to expose to destruction one of the architectural glories of England. It was indeed a miracle that not more of it was destroyed: certainly no credit for this is due to the Admiralty, which, having made Bath a legitimate object of attack, then took no steps to defend it.

In those days the memory of Lord William Cecil, who was Bishop of Exeter for the twenty years preceding his death in 1936, was still fresh, giving rise to many stories concerning his absence of mind. One of the best of these was to the effect that on a certain occasion he could not find his ticket on entering Exeter Central Station.

'That's all right, my lord,' said the inspector, 'it doesn't matter about your ticket.'

'But it does matter,' replied the Bishop, 'If I can't find my ticket, how am I to know where I'm going?'

At the same time Lord William was very popular throughout his diocese. He was one of the most approachable of men, though he had no great sympathy for, or interest in, the niceties of theological argument.

The See of Exeter was originally at Crediton, where it was founded in 909, but in 1050 it was transferred by Bishop Leofric to Exeter. To this day Crediton always seems to me not unconscious of the fact that it was once the seat of a Bishop. I spent a very happy week there at the Ship when I was working for the Ministry of Information in the summer of 1940. The town has had more of its share of fires in the past, which accounts for its relatively modern appearance, and the church is dominated – some would say ruined – by the memorial to Sir Redvers Buller. His merits as a general are likely to be canvassed for many years to come, but of his popularity in his native town there can be no question; it is said that Lord Roberts, who was locally believed to have behaved badly to Buller, met with a hostile reception on a visit to Crediton. Curiously enough, the same story is told about the first Earl of Iddesleigh. It is alleged that his neighbours, rich and poor alike, were so enraged against Lord Salisbury, then Prime Minister, that the police advised him to stay away from Iddesleigh's funeral.

Our first real experience of the war came on 30 September 1940, when in the latter part of the afternoon Sherborne was heavily bombed. Lenthay; Half Moon, Cheap, and Long Streets; round the cinema, and Newlands were the areas most affected and a large part of the town was a shambles. The final figures for the casualties were sixteen people killed and about forty injured, while 600 houses were damaged, half of them irreparably. There were complaints that the urban A.R.P. did not work any too well, and some people are said to have been trapped in the wreckage for nearly three hours before anyone came to dig them out.

My wife, incidentally, had a very narrow escape, for had she not looked in at the Rural District Council Offices on some A.R.P. business she would have been halfway down Cheap Street when one of the heavier bombs fell there, and could hardly have avoided being killed. After the tragic, however, soon came the comic. The rumour went round that a parachutist had been dropped in Honeycomb Wood, about a quarter of a mile from our house, to which proceeded the entire police force of Sherborne, headed by the superintendent with a revolver. My wife brought out in the car a young and unarmed Local Defence Volunteer, as the forerunners of the Home Guard were termed, to whom I lent a twelve-bore. When I asked him what ammunition he wanted he replied, 'Do you think I ought to use fives or sixes for a parachutist?'. In the event, the supposed parachutist turned out to be a British airman who had bailed out while attacking the raiders.

By this time it was generally agreed that the bulk of the British Army would have to remain at home until it was practicable to effect an invasion of Western Europe, whereupon the question arose as to the best method of keeping up the troops' morale during this trying period of suspense.

The answer of those in authority was education, which was, in due course, in one form or another to play a prominent part in the life of every unit until the landing in Normandy. It also had a revolutionary effect upon the life of the Petrie family.

As the war progressed the inconvenience of living in the depths of the country began to outweigh the amenities. My activities were such that Lillington became a very unsatisfactory base; my wife felt that A.R.P. work in a rural area, and the organization of concert parties for the troops, were not a sufficient outlet for her energies; and with our son Peter nearing the age of ten, something had to be done about his schooling. Accordingly, with the very greatest regret, we decided to move. We first let and then sold our house; my wife took on the work of personnel manager to a group of factories in the Bristol area; and Peter went to a preparatory school called Tormore, normally situated at Deal, but which had been evacuated to The Vyne, near Basingstoke. In this disruption of our family life we were typical of tens, if not hundreds of thousands of other families in the Second World War.

After trying one or two other experiments my wife settled down at the Jolly Sailor at Saltford on the Avon between Bristol and Bath, and I used to go down there whenever I could, while Peter spent his holidays there – though twice we all managed to have a few days at the sea together at Lyme Regis. In some ways the Jolly Sailor was a bit primitive, but any inconvenience resulting from this was amply compensated for by the unfailing kindness of the host and hostess, Gerry and Joan Face. I have only two unpleasant memories of the Jolly Sailor. The first was in May 1942 when the whole building, well-constructed as it was, shook like a jelly during the two nights of the so-called 'Baedeker raid' on Bath; several bombs were dropped in the immediate vicinity of the inn, next to which was a small paint factory which we all expected to see catch alight at any moment. The second unpleasant incident took place on Christmas morning, 1944, when a punt, on which several of us were crossing the Avon, sank, and my father-in-law, Peter, and I, with one or two others, were plunged into the river, an experience which sounds much more amusing in retrospect than it was at the time.

As a stranger to that part of Somerset I was struck by the extremely rural atmosphere of the district, which seemed unusual in view of the fact that it lay between cities of the size of Bristol and Bath. For example Kelston, lying at the foot of Round Hill, was in many ways as remote from the main stream of life as any Dorset village. One or two Bristol business-men lived there, but they were regarded with a mixture of tolerance and suspicion, and their merits were canvassed by the local inhabitants nightly in the Crown, then in the hands of Ted Trollope. The Crown had only one bar, and that was devoid of any illumination other than an oil lamp, while outside modern transport raced past on its lawful or unlawful occasions. This description, indeed, was typical of a good deal more than the external appearance of Kelston.

After we left Lillington I took up my residence at the Great Eastern Hotel in Liverpool Street, whence I conducted my numerous activities until after the war. During the years 1941–43 I delivered 637 lectures to the Forces, and in addition I did a certain amount of University Extension work both for Oxford and Bristol Universities; I gave a series of lectures on diplomatic history to potential Polish Diplomatists at the request of the Foreign Office; and, as has already been mentioned, for a brief space I broadcast a number of commentaries to Latin America. This work took me at one time or another over a very large part of the Kingdom: my furthest north was Catterick; my furthest east and west respectively were King's Lynn and Camborne; and my furthest south was Shoreham. In addition, I was editing the *Empire Review*, which had its office in the City.

The Service ministries very wisely decided to work through the extra-mural departments of the universities, for although these differed widely in efficiency the worst of them was probably better than any freshly created *ad hoc* organization would have been. For my part I was extremely fortunate in being mostly concerned with the universities of Oxford, Bristol, and Leeds, whose extra-mural departments were exceptionally good. In addition, of course, each Service had its own education officers, those in the Navy and Air Force naturally tending to be more technical in their scope than their counterparts in the Army. In view of the different, even contrasted, outlook which in normal circumstances obtains in the universities and the Services it was remarkable that there should have been so little friction among those associated in the great task of educating several million men and women in the middle of a war. That this should have been the case is a real tribute to all concerned.

Of one thing there can be no question, that never was so much done by individuals for so little financial reward. For a 'single lecture of academic standing' the lecturer was paid the sum of one guinea, and expenses were on what the War Office, no doubt, considered to be the same generous scale. The night allowance (covering twenty-four hours) was 23s 6d; for absence from home for over ten hours the allowance was 7s 6d; and for more than seven but less than ten hours it was 3s 6d. What sort of meals Whitehall conceived could be obtained for these niggardly sums it is impossible to imagine. I do not believe that there is any other country in the world where so many men and women would voluntarily have slaved away for so miserable a reward at a time when the Government was pouring out money like water in every direction. The financial treatment of Service lecturers was bare-faced exploitation of their patriotism.

On the other hand I am quite convinced that it would have been a mistake to put us into uniform: the idea of a commission, with the rank of full colonel, was mooted to me, but upon reflection I rejected the proposition though it would, of course, have considerably eased my financial position. I was, and still am, convinced that a lecturer in plain clothes carried far more weight with the troops than one in uniform, especially if he wore red tabs. Not only were people freer to discuss the various issues, but contact with a man in a lounge suit provided for them a link with that civilian world which the majority of every audience had most unwillingly left. It was certainly to the credit of the authorities that they were prepared to admit the force of these arguments.

Equally, my experience left me in no doubt as to the advisability, whenever possible, of sending the same lecturer to the same unit at regular intervals. In this way the men got to know the speaker, and he got on friendly terms with them, to the mutual advantage of both. Adult education of any sort was an entirely new thing to at least ninety-five per cent of those who thus came into contact with it during the war, so it is hardly remarkable that at first it should be regarded with a certain amount of diffidence. Men were naturally a little slow to ask questions when they had been made to look foolish for doing so at political meetings. The prerequisite of success is mutual confidence between the lecturer and the lectured, and sometimes this was a plant of slow growth.

Partly for this reason the academic lecturer was rarely a success with the Services. He was too inclined to forget that he was not addressing a university extension audience accustomed to hearing lectures, and who attended them of their own free will; also, his approach to his subject was often too laboured, for if one is to hold a Service audience one must plunge *in medias res*. In this connection an extreme instance was that of a Cambridge don whom one of the brigades in the 3rd Division invited to enlighten them on the subject of Greece when that country was attacked by Italy. The lecturer gave them a full hour, closing his survey with the end of the Peloponnesian War, after which date apparently Greek affairs ceased to interest him.

A very great deal depended upon the interest taken by the senior officers, my impression being that this was considerably less in the Air Force than in the Navy or the Army. A great deal of my time was spent in Southern Command with both the Guards Armoured Division and the 1st and 6th Airborne Divisions, and no one could have received more kindness and encouragement than I did from the senior officers of those formations. And I specially looked forward to a visit to Southern Command Headquarters, at Wilton, where first of all Field-Marshal Alexander and then Sir Charles Loyd were always ready to help. The Guards Armoured Division was commanded first by Oliver Leese and then by Allan Adair, to both of whom I am grateful for their continued support, as well as to John Marriott, Douglas Greenacre, Billy Fox-Pitt, Julian Gascoigne, and Henry Abel-Smith, to name but a few of the many Guardsmen without whose aid my activities would have been quite useless. In the 1st Airborne the initiative in education came always from the top, that is to say from its commander, 'Boy' Browning, as in the 6th Airborne it came from General Gale. The example which they all set was enthusiastically followed by those junior to them, and I would venture to say that nowhere was education, in the proper sense of the term, better conducted than in these formations.

So much for those with whom I worked. Those for whom I worked, namely the troops, came from all parts of the British Isles, and I got to know the British soldier far better in the Second World War than I did in the First when I was serving with him. Usually an army raised by voluntary enlistment inevitably produces a certain type of soldier, but this was by no means the case with the conscript forces of the last war. There was no type: resemblances and differences were based on locality to an extent which I never believed possible in the middle of the twentieth century; this applied even to the Brigade of Guards, though there was greater external uniformity there than elsewhere. In due course, therefore, I got to know what was likely to be the reaction to my remarks as soon as I learnt where the unit in question had been recruited.

From what part of the British Isles did you get the most intelligent audience? I have often been asked this, and it is really impossible to give a definite answer. The readiest audiences to take a point were those composed of Londoners or Welshmen, while those with the greatest amount of what may be termed background knowledge came from North of the Mersey and the Humber. For steady persistence in cross-examination when the time came for questions commend me to the Lowland Scot. The Irish, on the other hand, possibly because they were volunteers, partook of the attitude of the old regular. The instinctive reaction was not uncommon in all four nationalities. On one occasion when I was lecturing to a unit in the 50th division on France, a sergeant, a typical North Countryman, showed himself extremely critical of General de Gaulle.

When the lecture was over I sought out the sergeant and asked him the reason for this hostile attitude towards the French leader.

'Don't trust him, sir,' was the immediate reply.

'But why?' I persisted.

'Never trust a fish-face, sir,' was the crushing retort, after which there was clearly no more to be said.

My work also brought me into quite close contact with the W.R.N.S., the A.T.S., and the W.A.A.F. In their case it seemed to me that national and regional differences were less marked than with the men, but generally speaking the whole standard of education, intelligence, and interest was immeasurably lower, in the officers as well as the women. Although I do not profess to understand the reason for this, I am convinced that it is a fact. It is also true, however, that the women were much more alert and receptive when they were working with men, something that I noticed particularly on the mixed anti-aircraft gun sites in the Bristol area which I visited frequently. When the girls first arrived they were dumb from a lecturer's point of view, but after they had been on the site for a few months they took a much greater interest in general subjects. But I will not attempt any deductions from this.

Among the best audiences I had during the whole of the war were the Australian division, most of whose units I visited when they were still in England, in the Salisbury plain area. Not only were they most attentive, but they displayed a surprising knowledge of British and Continental politics. Of the Czechs I had only one experience. At the request of the British Council the extra-mural department of Bristol University arranged a Brains Trust on the working of the British Constitution for them at Yeovil, and I was one of those asked to assist. When, however, the questions began to come up we soon appreciated the fact that we had stern realists before us, for instead of 'Has the House of Lords any powers over a Money Bill?' or 'Is there ever a division on the First Reading of a Bill in the House of Commons?' we were asked, 'Why have you such an antiquated system of weights and measures?' and 'Why aren't your houses centrally heated?'

American audiences were probably the most difficult, possibly because I had not then been in the United States and had little idea what was going on in the men's minds. Somewhat to my astonishment they were reluctant to ask questions; those who did ask questions certainly asked good ones, but a very much larger proportion of every audience remained silent than was ever the case with British troops. My impression is that to some extent this was due to the fact that their officers did not feel the same responsibility towards their men as did the officers in the British Army, and consequently their influence was a great deal less. This, however, is pure speculation; the American troops with whom I was concerned had not been in action. As to American efficiency, at any rate in military matters, I was driven to the conclusion that it is vastly over-rated, while I formed a low opinion of the junior officers – a point-of-view which I find is shared by my friends who have more recently come across them in Vietnam.

Finally, looking back on the many thousands of men and women with whom I came in contact during these years, my impression is that it would have been impossible in any age or in any country to have met a more friendly set of people than these sailors, soldiers, and airmen. I was more than ever strengthened in my belief in the innate decency of my fellow-countrymen of every class whenever the politicians leave them alone. Certainly I have never been engaged in any work where there was less friction among those with whom I was working, and the number of questions which might be described as 'fast ones' could be numbered on the fingers of one hand. If a lecturer plays fair with a Service audience they will play fair with him, but God help him if he indulges in propaganda or tries to pull wool over their eyes.

It is often said that education in the Forces was almost entirely in Socialist hands, and that in consequence the Service vote was overwhelmingly Socialist at the General Election of 1945. The latter statement requires a great deal more proof than has yet been adduced in its support, indeed there is much evidence to the effect that the proportion of votes cast in the Forces was relatively low in comparison with that of the civil population. The causes of the Conservative defeat are to be found elsewhere, chiefly in Churchill's neglect of the advice of Ralph Assheton, then Chairman of the Conservative Party – on how to run the election – in any case it is often forgotten that the electorate only did what it had done in 1918, that is to say reject the party which had been in power when the war began. As for Socialist propaganda under the guise of education, no doubt this did happen, but the remedy was in the hands of those who complained. There was an overwhelming Conservative majority in both Houses of Parliament, and the Under-Secretary at the War Office, in whose hands lay the control of education in the Army, was none other than that redoubtable Old Tory, Lord Croft. Perhaps, too, if the critics had taken more pains to see that those who were engaged in the day-to-day work of Service education were adequately remunerated these latter would have been more inclined to stress to their audiences the merits of the Establishment.

It was spiritually a far cry from this atmosphere of youth and confidence to that of wartime London. It is true that in the First World War the capital had been crowded, but that was because it became the Mecca of all who wished to amuse themselves: in the Second World War it was crowded because the bombing to which it was subjected steadily diminished the number of places in which it was possible to eat, work, or sleep, while the increasing shortage of man-power resulted in the closing of hotels and shops, and the restriction of means of transport, which placed great strain upon anything that continued to function.

Indeed, London went through several distinct phases between September 1939, and May 1945. After the alarm of the first Alert of war, and the excitement of the evacuation, there was a lull during which, except for the black-out, conditions were almost normal. Then came the retreat to Dunkirk, and the days of anxiety when no one knew who was alive or dead – days which recalled to the older generation that anxious week-end in August 1914, when it was rumoured that the entire B.E.F. had been compelled to lay down their arms. In September the concentrated bombing began, and continued at intervals until the German invasion of Russia in June 1941. Those were the days when everyone who could left London, or at any rate spent as many nights as possible in the country, and hotels, clubs, and restaurants were empty. One afternoon I was on the platform of Exeter station when, hours late, the train from Paddington came in, and out of one compartment stepped a young woman who had nothing on beyond pyjamas, a fur coat, and a pair of bedroom slippers. During the previous night a raid had driven her to a shelter, and when it was over she found that the block of flats in which she lived had been completely demolished; as she had relations in Exeter she had very sensibly caught the next train there.

Piloted planes never gave so much trouble again, though there were one or two minor 'blitzes', and people began to sleep in London once more. All the same each morning most of us felt like the old lady in the contemporary *Punch* cartoon, who remarked to her sister at breakfast, 'Well, dear, we're still here.' So London filled up again, to the intense discomfort of all concerned, for it soon meant that to get a meal in a public place required the guile of Odysseus combined, very often, with the strength of Hercules. Even worse, to go to a place where one was not known was to court disaster, and there was a general lowering of every kind of standard, both moral and material. The Cities of the Plain must have been the quintessence of respectability compared with the streets of the West End.

Then in the middle of June 1944, when the Allied troops were tightening their grip on the French coast, came the first of the many flying-bombs. Once more every Londoner had his or her pet bomb story, and we tried to disguise our fear of this new menace by giving the emissaries of death silly names. This particular nuisance lasted only a few months owing to the success of the Allied operations across the Channel, but enough damage was done to show that had the Germans perfected the weapon sooner, then London and the south-east of England might well have been rendered untenable. After the V1 there came the V2, and concerning their respective demerits there soon grew up a sharp controversy. For myself I have no doubts on the subject at all: at least the V1 gave notice of its approach, so one had time to do something about it. The V2 came without any warning; there was nothing whatever one could do except assume a sheeplike expression in the expectation of being plunged into eternity. I grew to tolerate the V1, and the V2 always terrified me: it seemed the epitome of what I dislike most, namely anything in the nature of a sudden shock, and I never got used to it.

Since the war came to an end volumes have been written concerning the morale of the country during it, and there are doubtless many more to come: I cannot say that I paid any particular attention to the matter except when I was lecturing or speaking for the Ministry of Information, but I have no doubt whatever that once the immediate danger of invasion had passed away the attitude adopted in high places did little to hearten, and much to perplex, the ordinary citizen. Never was there a government in which less attempt was made to co-ordinate the speeches of its members. One minister would tell us that victory was just round the corner, then a day or two later a colleague of apparently equal standing would talk gloomily of the long struggle that lay ahead. To give Churchill his due he was generally consistent, but his Cabinet spoke with a perfect babel of conflicting voices: 'Uncle Fred' Woolton was an exception, and he was in consequence one of the very few ministers who carried any weight with the mass of the population. It was the same in every field. One day patriotism demanded this or that course of action, but on the next we were assured that entirely different conduct was required of the loyal citizen. Fortunately the older generation, as a result of its experiences in the previous war, entertained a healthy suspicion of anything that savoured of propaganda which it communicated to the younger generation, so most people quietly did the job that came to hand, and in doing it helped to win the war.

What will hardly be denied is the widespread decline in manners and courtesy, which did not improve until the war had been over for two or three years, if in London it improved very much at all. Yet it must be admitted that in the capital the Cockney good humour was never far below the surface. One excellent specimen of it dates from the later days of the war. A would-be bus passenger, a naval officer, had been waiting for some time on a cold street corner for a Number 11, when, as is by no means uncommon on that route, three came along together. The officer commented rather sourly on this to the conductor as he got on to the bus, only to be told, 'I'm sorry, sir, but you'll appreciate that since we've been going in convoy, we've never lost a bus.'

During this period I spent my spare time in London at the Carlton and Pratt's, mainly in the very pleasant company of Charles Rhys, Guy Kindersley, Shakes Morrison, Geoffrey Cox, Wade Hayes, Jay Llewellin, and Allan Chapman, all, alas, now dead. Those were the days when the clubs were full at week-ends with members whose families were in the country, and in the process of cheering each other up I fear that on occasion a considerable amount of alcohol was consumed, but our excuse – surely a reasonable one – must be that in one way or another we were all under very heavy strain.

The end of the Second World War was as protracted as its beginning. Whether the conflict could have been terminated earlier had the Allies not insisted upon unconditional surrender, and whether in that event the recovery of Europe would have been accelerated, are problems over which historians are likely to argue for many a long year. Whereas 11 November 1918, was a date which nobody was likely to forget, what is certain is that when it did come the end of the war was an anti-climax – whereas none of the older generation were likely to forget 11 November 1918, not one person in ten today knows exactly when the last shot was fired in 1945. Nor was this all, for there was no sudden relaxation of tension as in 1918. Everyone had been expecting the collapse of Germany for the greater part of the preceding twelve months, and at any rate in the south-east of England, the real relief had been the cessation of the V2 activities, which had already taken place.

The generation of 1945 was, too, not subject to the illusions of its predecessor; nor, to give the politicians their due, was it encouraged to harbour any – there was no talk this time about 'a land fit for heroes to live in'. In the main the country expected nothing and hoped for nothing. Moreover, there was still war with Japan, and the general belief was that this would last at least for another year. So the crowds which thronged the streets of London those May days were animated by a very different spirit from that which moved their predecessors of twenty-seven years earlier. They did some of the same things, it is true; they cheered the Royal Family, and they made bonfires of any combustible material they could find; also the weather was more propitious than on the earlier occasion. Yet behind this restrained rejoicing there was anxiety and disillusionment. In November 1918 even thinking people felt that the worst was over; in May 1945 only the unthinking did not fear that the worst was still to come.

It was in such an England that people once more began to pick up the threads of normal life. The task was much more difficult than before, though the older generation had the advantage over their younger contemporaries that for them the course was not wholly uncharted.

PART THREE

Third Look
1945–1971

CHAPTER XIII

London Politics in the Fifties and Sixties

As soon as we could get it rendered habitable, my family and I returned to 14 Tregunter Road, and not long after that, in the Michaelmas Term of 1945, Peter started at Westminster as a King's Scholar. Almost immediately both my wife and I became immersed in Conservative politics – she in a big way, first as member for the Queen's Gate ward of the Kensington Borough Council and then as the representative of South Kensington on the London County Council, and I to a much lesser extent as Chairman of the 1900 Club. To one who was brought up in the fierce clashes of North of England politics those of London have always struck me as amateurish in the extreme; certainly Kensington is no exception to this; both its main parties, but especially the Conservatives, I thought very tame.

Having first come to Kensington from Horley in 1931, at the end of the Second World War we were by modern standards comparatively old residents. In the years before we bought the house at Lillington I had for a time been Vice-Chairman of the South Kensington Conservative Association, where I saw nature in the raw so far as the Royal Borough was concerned. My official colleagues – Lords Lloyd and Danesfort, and the Countess of Limerick – were office-bearers of whom any organization could be proud, but there was far too much log-rolling and back-biting among the rank-and-file. Because South Kensington was a safe seat Conservatives felt justified in quarrelling among themselves, which they proceeded to do with an energy worthy of a better cause; the controversy over the Indian White Paper, for example, split the party locally from top to bottom. Largely in consequence of this factious approach to politics little was done to help the weaker neighbouring constituencies, such as North Kensington, while Parliamentary and Borough Council activities were insufficiently co-ordinated.

Of course all this time Kensington was changing. During the First World War, as I can testify from personal knowledge, it shared in the experience of the rest of London, and was as gay as it was possible to be when means of transport were extremely limited. It was certainly a very different place in the Second World War when one's footfalls echoed in the deserted streets; where practically every house had a large 'E' scrawled on its door; and the few people who had not been evacuated, or had not evacuated themselves, used to go to the Town Hall each morning to read the list of casualties from the previous night's raid. Kensington had profited by the boom which followed the Armistice in 1918. The late Douglas Jerrold has told in *Georgian Adventure* how the house in Red-cliffe Square in which he lived as a boy was divided into six flats, of which in 1919 he was offered the basement one at rather more than double the rent that his father paid in 1900 for the whole house. That was typical, not exceptional; my own similar experience I have related on an earlier page.

Nobody is likely to deny that there were revolutionary changes in the Royal Borough between the wars, but there may be differences of opinion as to their causes. Personally, I think there were two main reasons, namely the cost of living and the internal combustion engine. I can claim to have known something of the life of Kensington ever since my brother and his wife – incidentally a Miss Allen from whose family Allen Street gets its name – took a flat in Drayton Court on their marriage in 1912. In those days the outstanding feature of South Kensington was the number of retired people who lived there, particularly ex-officers from the Services, so that for some years we acquired a not-wholly-deserved reputation for being peopled almost exclusively by retired colonels. In due course, however, finding it too expensive to continue living in Kensington, they moved out into the country or abroad, leaving the large houses which they had occupied to be converted into the flats and bed-sitters which we know today, especially in the Earl's Court area.

With the development of the motor-car accelerating what taxation and inflation had begun, even for those who had not retired it became just as easy, as well as cheaper, to live out of town, and with the weekend habit spreading people began to prefer living on the fringe of the countryside rather than making long journeys to it on Saturdays or Sundays. In these ways there came about a great change in the character of the Kensington population, though for some reason the Royal Borough would always seem to have been popular with those from overseas, for in the census of 1901 it figures high in the list of Metropolitan Boroughs with an alien population, the vast majority of the aliens then being German or French.

The changed Kensington required someone out of the ordinary as its head, and it found such an individual in Robert Jenkins, who was Mayor during the war years and Leader of the Council after the war had terminated. He set an example of devotion to duty which was in itself an inspiration: people began to take an interest in a local authority which could produce men like him, and to which he thought it worthwhile to devote so much of his time. With a better type of Conservative candidate for municipal honours now coming forward, the choice of the selection committee was no longer confined to dug-out Poona colonels on the one hand and dubious local manipulators on the other. As the new generation of councillor lived and worked in the Royal Borough, its members were known to the ratepayers, which could do much to improve people's confidence in them. On the Labour side, too, there was a stirring of dry bones, for Jenkins was matched by Frank Carter, and it can only be a source of great regret that he felt unable to accept the mayoralty when it was offered to him by the Conservative majority on the Council; Carter, it may be added, was also supported by a number of able councillors of his own persuasion.

This happy state of affairs was not, however, destined to continue. For better or for worse in 1965 Kensington and Chelsea were amalgamated, and in a landslide in 1968 the Conservatives swept the Borough in an election which left Labour with only the Golborne Ward. As always on such occasions, whether parliamentary or municipal, the successful candidates, thinking that their victories were due not to any swing of the pendulum but to their own superior merits, proceeded to behave as if the Borough had only begun to exist when they entered the Town Hall: the experience of those who had gone before them was openly flouted, and all the old bickering of pre-war years reappeared. To make matters worse although they lived in the Royal Borough, as indeed they were bound to do by law, few of them worked there, so they only made contact with their constituents in the evenings, whereas their predecessors in the time of Robert Jenkins were to be seen about the streets at any hour of the day. Retribution came in 1971 when the Conservatives lost every seat in North Kensington, and most of the new councillors returned to the shades from which they had emerged three years earlier.

Today it would probably be true to say that, at any rate on the Conservative side there are two more weaknesses. The first is the absence of men during the day: the average woman councillor is more useful to the ratepayers than the man. Not having to commute to an office in the City on five days in the week, she is able to spend most of her time in the Borough, which is, as we have seen, a great advantage. The other real weakness of Conservatism in the Royal Borough is the absence of a club where its supporters could meet informally to discuss the problems that are common to them. The establishment of one has been discussed for at least forty years, it may be added, but nothing has ever been done about it.

On many scores it is to be regretted that local elections are coming increasingly to be fought on national issues, but it was probably inevitable, and it is by no means wholly the fault of Labour, as is often alleged. As the Central Government extends its influence to questions with which in the past it was quite unconcerned, so these questions must assume a different significance. When a certain view is held by one of the parties at Westminster, this view is naturally supported by that party's followers on the local authority, just as it is opposed by its opponents there. So the question becomes a party issue on national lines. The reason why this was not the case in the past was that there were very few local problems, apart from the maintenance of law and order, that concerned the Central Government. It is not easy to see how this trend can be reversed, and it may well be that in another twenty years no candidate will come forward, even for election to a parish council – if such continue to exist – save on a straight party ticket.

Soon after Richard Law became M.P. for South Kensington he asked me to take on the chairmanship of his Association. But I had to decline owing to other political commitments, notably the 1900 Club, and a nobleman with more spare time on his hands was persuaded to step into the breach. Whatever may be the case on the Labour side, and I doubt if there is much difference between the parties in this respect, the chairman of a Conservative constituency organization requires to devote a great deal of time to the work, that is to say if he is to do the job properly, as, for example, it was done by Charles Rhys in Westminster and Charles Ritchie in South Paddington. It is no mere question of taking the chair at a monthly meeting of the executive; what is required is daily acquaintance with everything that is going on in the division. And when an election, parliamentary or local, is in progress the chairman will be lucky if he gets two or three hours a day to attend to his private affairs – if he does get more then he is neglecting his work as chairman.

My pre-occupation with the affairs of the 1900 Club was due to the fact that in September 1946 I was elected its chairman, a position which had been held by the late Lord Gretton, who will not readily be forgotten by his contemporaries. In the late summer of 1946 he had a stroke, and quite unknown to me my colleagues on the committee decided that I should succeed him.

The 1900 Club is (for it still flourishes, though in a somewhat different form from what it was in my day) a typically English institution in that its name gives no clue to its constitution or its activities. It was not founded in 1900, and it has never had 1900 members. Its origin dates from 1905, when a number of Conservative Members of the 1900 Parliament, not standing again at the impending General Election but desirous of preserving ties of friendship formed with many of their fellow Members, resolved to form a club at which to meet and dine periodically. Soon, however, its scope was enlarged to include Conservative candidates and 'such other persons as the Committee think suitable for membership by reason of their services to the Conservative cause'. As its early records were not preserved we are dependent upon newspaper accounts of its activities; but everything goes to show that from the beginning its influence on the Conservative Party was great.

The club originally had modest premises in Pickering Place, just off St James's Street, and on various evenings of the week Conservative Front Benchers would attend there to exchange views with the members. In the Tariff Reform *versus* Free Trade controversy, as well as in the dissensions leading up to Balfour's resignation of the Conservative leadership, the 1900 Club played a prominent part, the majority of its members being critical of the party machine: indeed, independence of thought has generally been the outstanding characteristic of the Club. From Pickering Place it moved to Ryder Street, where it was extremely active during the years of the National Government in the thirties.

When the Second World War came the Club disposed of its premises, put its furniture into store, but – largely owing to Gretton's zeal – carried on its activities, though on a reduced scale. Speakers of the calibre of Rab Butler and the American Herbert Agar came to discuss various aspects of the struggle with the members, and more than once the proceedings were disturbed by a flying bomb. The Club met where it could, and a journalist in consequence described its members as 'the Bedouin of Clubland'. Yet it continued to meet, and when peace came was still in being, its energy unimpaired.

Once during my chairmanship when Winston Churchill came to the annual dinner, which was a mixed affair, he was naturally seated next to my wife. It so happened that our son, Peter, had just won the Public Schools Fencing Championship for Westminster, and Winston asked his mother to congratulate him. 'The only time Harrow ever won it, he went on, 'I won it for them': then there was a pause, and he added, 'But, Lady Petrie, I never fought a duel.' As my wife never thought he had she was somewhat surprised at the observation, but Winston was of course alluding to the old rumour that he had killed Earl Percy in a duel in France in 1909.

Verbosity at the Club's meetings was sternly discouraged; in fact the ideal member was he who remembered Sir William Harcourt's advice to a speaker, namely to think of his first sentence and his last, and to bring the two as close together as possible. In the Club's earlier days this rule was apparently not always observed. There is a legend to the effect that a speaker was holding forth at inordinate length on one occasion when Arthur Balfour was present. A member left the room, and returned ten minutes later.

'Hasn't he finished yet?' he inquired of A.J.B.

'Oh yes,' came the reply, 'some time ago, but he hasn't sat down.'

Another story of Balfour at the 1900 Club is about the time he asked some new and pompous M.P. how he liked the House of Commons. He went on, 'My dear fellow, there is no reason whatever to be frightened. In that place, all you have to do is to speak as long as you like and as often as you like. You will rapidly acquire that contempt for your audience which every bore always has.'

In normal circumstances the Club met after dinner some fifteen to twenty times a year, when it was addressed either by some leading member of the Conservative Party or by a recognized expert on a particular subject. From the moment I became Chairman I was determined that it should be neither an old man's nor a rich man's club, and we made a most successful drive for members at Oxford and Cambridge. These young men joined because, if they so desired, it need cost them nothing beyond their subscription – all they had to do was to walk into a meeting, dressed in their everyday clothes, and take part in a discussion which had been opened by some first-class authority. The Club's use to the Conservative Party in those days may be gauged from the fact that at the General Election of February, 1950, no less than 54 of its 318 members (of whom 38 were peers and so ineligible for the House of Commons) stood as Conservative candidates, and of these 44 were elected. I was certainly not alone in building up the 1900 Club after the Second World War; I should like to put on record the help I received from my fellow office-bearers, that is to say the present Lords Gretton and Tweedsmuir, and Ronnie Warlow.

During the years that I was Chairman of the 1900 Club I naturally saw a good deal of politics from the inside. My impressions of the time may not be without interest, not least because as a historian I always regarded them from a slightly different angle from the politicians themselves.

While he lived Churchill dominated the political scene. Different assessments of his character will continue to be made for many years to come, but the one that I believe comes nearest to the truth was made to me by one of his colleagues who eventually succeeded him as Prime Minister: 'Never forget that Winston was by birth half an American crook and half an English aristocrat – and the aristocrat was a Churchill.' Beaverbrook always maintained that Lloyd George was the greater man in that, apart from his leadership during the war years, Winston contributed nothing to English history, whereas Lloyd George laid the foundations of the Welfare State. His earlier career lies outside the scope of these pages, and has in any case been brilliantly dealt with by Robert Rhodes James in *Churchill, A Study in Failure, 1900–1939*, but a few remarks on his later activities, derived both from my own observation and from what his colleagues have told me, may not be out of place.

From the moment that he became Prime Minister he was criticized for actions which were not his fault but his misfortune, or for policies which were forced upon him owing to events beyond his control. He was accused of surrounding himself with small men; in fact they were often the only ones available, but in so far as he did not care to have potential rivals round the throne there is something in the charge. Once Neville Chamberlain was dead the only possible alternatives to himself were Halifax, Hoare and John Simon. Churchill decided that their talents could most suitably be displayed in Washington, in Madrid, and on the Woolsack. For the rest, it is true that his Cabinet was infinitely weaker than that of Asquith or Lloyd George in the First World War, and though it would be an exaggeration to describe his team as a second eleven, he had few ministers of the calibre of Grey, Milner, Balfour, or Austen Chamberlain, simply because they did not exist.

Again, Churchill could not be held responsible for the fact that as the war drew to a close Britain counted for increasingly less, and Russia and the United States for progressively more, in the councils of the Allies. He was himself under no illusions on this score. 'It is not so easy as it used to be for me to get things done,' he wrote to Smuts on 3 December, 1944, while of the last months of the war he has left on record, 'I moved amid cheering crowds, or sat at a table adorned with congratulations from every part of the Grand Alliance, with an aching heart and a mind oppressed with forebodings.' The war might be finished, but Britain, exhausted and bankrupt, was almost finished too. Churchill was no longer on the same footing as Roosevelt and Stalin, though few of his critics made any allowance for the fact.

The relations between Winston and the Beaver gave rise to many a speculation; it has even been argued that the great press lord was Churchill's evil genius. The Beaver could be a man's best friend or his worst enemy: I always found him the former, but in all our relations I could see how easily he could become the latter. I sometimes wonder whether he really understood the British people. The national press is always inclined to exaggerate its political influence, and Winston may easily have taken it at its own valuation – actually, he was in a much stronger position so far as the public was concerned than was Lloyd George in the First World War in that the radio enabled him to speak to the country direct. In the earlier conflict the Prime Minister had been able to reach the man-in-the-street only by means of the printed word, which accounted in no small measure for the enormous power exercised by newspaper proprietors such as Northcliffe: the Beaver was far from realizing that times had changed.

Where Churchill's critics are right is when they accuse him of unduly neglecting the home front, and in so concentrating upon winning the war that he gave no thought to the peace which was to follow victory – a mistake of which Stalin was certainly not guilty. In this he showed himself as a wartime leader definitely inferior to the Younger Pitt, who never committed the error of ignoring the future in his dealings with the present. Then again, too many of those who have written of Winston's life have surely made the mistake of separating his wartime activities from his peacetime career. There was in many quarters throughout the war always a readiness to criticize and a reluctance to take him at his own valuation, an attitude which was of much earlier date: the Tories never really forgave him for crossing the floor of the House over Tariff Reform, or Labour for many actions when he was Home Secretary; at the time of the Abdication his reputation had reached its nadir. In these circumstances there was always a section of public opinion ready to believe the worst of him which, when things went wrong, as at the time of the fall of Singapore, became extremely vocal. Like Canning and Disraeli in an earlier day, for all his virtues Churchill inspired a profound feeling of mistrust, the most fatal handicap an English politician can have.

It must also be admitted that he possessed to the full that pettiness which is so often a characteristic of great men. When, for instance, General Weygand announced his intention of passing through London on his way from Paris to Dublin Winston indicated that he would not receive him, so although this was years after the end of the war the General was obliged to fly from France to Ireland direct. The repeated sneers at Attlee were not only in bad taste but were wide of the mark: to refer to him as 'a sheep in sheep's clothing' was a travesty of the facts, for Attlee was one of the ablest Prime Ministers of the twentieth century.

I make no claim to have known Churchill well. Although I met him formally on a number of occasions, only a few times did I converse with him intimately. One such occasion was a Saturday at lunch at Charles Rhys's house in Eaton Square, when he could not have been more friendly. I remarked to him that had he remained a Conservative he might have become leader of the party in 1911 instead of Bonar Law, and in that case he could hardly have failed to succeed Asquith as Prime Minister, to which he replied that it was an interesting speculation, but an impossible one as 'Free Trade came before everything else.' Not long afterwards I related the conversation to Joe Chamberlain's widow, by this time Mrs Carnegie, who told me that she had been present at a dinner at which the only other diners were Chamberlain and Churchill, when Winston said that as Balfour had not given him office he would join the Liberals. She added that her husband observed on this, 'In your place, Winston, I should do the same.'

Most of our talk that afternoon was on the subject of history, about which I found him exceptionally well-informed. We shared a dislike of Bolingbroke, Winston making no secret of his views where that statesman was concerned. What he would say if he knew that today his portrait and Bolingbroke's hang on the same wall in the Carlton Club I tremble to think.

There can be no disputing the fact that the greatest blow the Conservative Party has sustained since the late war was the premature death of Oliver Stanley. He was one of the most gifted men of the century, and would have made a very great Prime Minister. Whether Winston Churchill should or should not have taken on the Premiership again in 1951 is not easy to decide even in the light of Lord Moran's disclosures, for by that time Stanley was dead, but had he been alive he would have been a far better choice. Of all those who addressed the 1900 Club during my chairmanship he made probably the greatest impression. He was as brilliant a conversationalist as a public speaker, while in the House of Commons I am told he was in the first flight.

Another prominent post-war figure and one whom I had known since Oxford days was David Maxwell Fyfe, subsequently Lord Chancellor and Earl of Kilmuir: indeed, we and the Maxwell Fyfes used to go on holiday together in the Isle of Wight so well did we know each other.

While the Conservatives were in Opposition during the Attlee administration David was the most sought-after speaker on the Tory side, especially by the Young Conservatives. There seemed to be no heights, not excluding 10 Downing Street itself, to which he might not rise, and his ambition seemed equal to his prospects. When I was a director of the publishing house Eyre and Spottiswoode I persuaded him to sign a contract to write the biography of Spencer Perceval, the only Law Officer who has ever become Prime Minister. As David had himself been Attorney-General the idea specially appealed to him, and when I jokingly reminded him that Perceval was also the only Prime Minister to be murdered he replied, 'I'd willingly be the second if I could first of all be Prime Minister for three years.' When the Conservatives came into office again in 1951 Winston made him Home Secretary, and from that moment David's ambitions seem to have waned, until he finally put himself out of the running by accepting the Lord Chancellorship. Had he been the David of earlier days he would have remained in the Commons, in which case he might have come in between Butler and Macmillan as Bonar Law did between Austen Chamberlain and Walter Long.

The Macmillans are also friends of long standing, for my wife served on the old Kensington Borough Council with Maurice at the start of his political career. Harold always seems to me to have been, like Asquith, the prisoner of a phrase, for 'The Wind of Change' taken in its proper connotation was as unobjectionable as 'Wait and See', but both have been extensively used against their coiners by their enemies. What Harold's critics forget is that it was entirely due to him that the Conservative Party did not break up altogether in the late fifties. He could not have succeeded Eden at a worse moment than the morrow of Suez; three of the outstanding members of his government, namely Lord Salisbury, Thorneycroft, and Enoch Powell, proceeded to resign; the by-elections went badly against the government; and there was widespread industrial unrest. Yet after little more than two years of Harold Macmillan's leadership the Conservatives were returned to power with an overall majority of 100 seats.

There is one other respect in which Harold has not received the credit he deserves, and that is in his patronage of the arts. Recent Prime Ministers have been very niggardly over this – and Churchill and Attlee could not have cared less. Macmillan on the other hand was at once a generous and discerning patron.

At this point I had better declare my interest, as I certainly have every cause to be grateful to him, for not only did he include me in his first Honours List but when I resigned the Chairmanship of the 1900 Club, he and his Cabinet came to a dinner which the Club gave in my honour at the Dorchester.

As the war had drawn to a close Douglas Jerrold and I both felt that the time had come for the revival of the *English Review* as the only satisfactory medium for propagating the views which a number of us held on the outstanding topics of the day. For certain legal reasons it proved impossible to resurrect the paper under its old name, so we called it the *New English Review*, a title which was subsequently, in 1949, altered to the *English Review Magazine*. If ever there was a venture of faith it was this, for those were the days when paper was strictly rationed, and it was forbidden to publish any new periodical. Our difficulties were eventually surmounted with the assistance of the Conservative Central Office, who made over to us the allocation of paper for a defunct publication of theirs called *Home and Empire*, and in this connection a tribute is due to successive Chairmen of the Conservative Party, notably Ralph Assheton and Lord Woolton. On not one single occasion was there the slightest attempt to interfere with the running of the paper or to dictate policy although views of the most unorthodox nature were often expressed in its pages; I doubt if any other party organization would in similar circumstances have allowed the same free hand as was accorded to Jerrold and myself.

In one respect we were probably lucky, for only one or two numbers had appeared before the Conservative Party went down to disaster at the General Election of 1945, and a party in opposition is much more receptive to suggestions than one in power. However that may be, the ideas put forward in the *English Review Magazine*, either as part of the editorial policy or by outside contributors, received much more careful consideration in high places than those which were ventilated by its predecessor of pre-war days. Persuaded largely by Lord Woolton, the hierarchy began to think that perhaps it was not after all the repository of all knowledge.

Looking back on the Second World War and its immediate aftermath one can now appreciate how it accentuated a number of tendencies, mainly in the social and economic field, which had really been operative since the early years of the century. Culloden had finally established the position of the English landowner both large and small, a position which was not seriously threatened again until after the death of Victoria. From then owing to the steady rise in taxation it began to be undermined at an ever-increasing pace: in any event it would not have been easy for the landed gentry to maintain themselves in a predominantly industrial community, but they were not helped by the ineptitude of their Conservative allies on more than one occasion. Today the spectacle of a landowner, be he peer or commoner, residing upon his property is far from common, and it is becoming rarer; one would have to go back to the sixteenth, if not to the fifth, century to find a parallel for the revolution which has taken place in the English countryside, where 'the stately homes' are going the same way as their predecessors the monastery and the Roman villa, except in such cases as their owners manage to live on, rather than in them.

Rarely in history has a governing class at the end of its dominance abdicated its position so quickly or so readily. Whether this is a subject for praise or censure is a matter of individual opinion, but that it is a fact cannot admit of question. For generations the landed gentry fought with the utmost ferocity for its position and its possessions; in its defence one King was sent to the scaffold, another was driven into exile, and a foreign dynasty was placed upon the throne; at the end of the social scale any attempt to disturb the existing order was crushed with equal remorselessness, and even in the relatively tolerant nineteenth century, when the wretched labourers of Wessex burnt a few ricks to call attention to the fact that they were starving, seven of them were hanged, four hundred were imprisoned, and four hundred and fifty-seven were transported. Yet within the last generation these once-privileged classes have meekly abandoned the fight, and have left their hereditary acres for the suburban boarding-house or the foreign watering-place. Their ancestors in the Elysian Fields must indeed be puzzled to account for so rapid a change of outlook.

CHAPTER XIV

The Twilight of the West End Club

HAVING been a member of the Carlton Club for more than fifty years, having served on its committee on two occasions and been Chairman of the Library Committee when we had a library, I think I can claim to have some knowledge of its working. What I am going to say about the Carlton is *mutatis mutandis* applicable to all West End clubs, for the Second World War and its aftermath marked the beginning of the end for many of them. Although the First World War had not affected them so adversely, there were signs that had it lasted much longer some of them at any rate would have found themselves in a position of considerable difficulty: indeed, in the early autumn of 1918 there was serious talk of amalgamations in certain quarters. The younger members were serving overseas, and although London was very full of people, the people who filled it were not those who used clubs. The subaltern back from the Somme or the Ypres Salient for a few days' leave was unlikely to spend it in the morning-room of his club even if he had one. The Armistice brought relief, the return to normal conditions being much more rapid than was to be the case after the Second World War. Although a club here and there, the Isthmian was a notable example, was compelled to close its doors, in the main the clubs resumed the even tenor of their pre-war way.

The Carlton was no exception. During the continuance of hostilities one breach with tradition had taken place, namely the employment of waitresses who first made their appearance in the summer of 1915, but the girls proved so satisfactory that they remained after the Armistice: the only member who was never really reconciled to their presence was the late Lord Winterton. For the rest, the Club retained its prestige undimmed, and it was still a very important political centre. There can, too, be little doubt that its standing was further enhanced four years after the war by the famous meeting when the fate of the Coalition was decided within its walls.

There was, nevertheless, one social revolution during the war years which did affect the Club, and that was the growing tendency to entertain away from home. The Carlton has always had a large number of members living in the country, many of whom now found that they could no longer afford to run a London house so that when they came to the capital it was to stay either in a flat or in a hotel. The pressure of taxation was also increasingly driving town members to move into smaller quarters, while others moved out into the neighbouring countryside. On all hands, members were ceasing to entertain their friends at home, and were clamouring for a place to do so where the atmosphere would be more personal than in a hotel or restaurant.

The Carlton still shut its doors to all guests, thereby creating a slight air of mystery, which proved a definite asset. Nor was it a cause of much inconvenience before 1914, for the more sociable member had only to join some other club or clubs where visitors were permitted. After 1918, when he was too often driven to realize that he could no longer afford several clubs, the question arose of what the Carlton could do to meet his requirements.

In 1925 No. 7 Carlton Gardens was purchased from the Earl of Dudley, and became the Carlton Club Annexe. This not only enabled members to entertain guests, but it also afforded bedroom accommodation. All this was made financially possible first by the issue of Bonds to the amount of £60,000 which were taken up by members, the final repayment being in 1941, and then by raising the standard rate of subscription to seventeen guineas – it is now fifty-five. The prices charged in the new building were also slightly higher than those charged in the Club itself. The annexe immediately obtained widespread support among the members; and during the fifteen years of its existence it was one of the most important social centres of London. Both the cooking and the service were of the very best, and invitations to lunch or dine at 7 Carlton Gardens were eagerly accepted. Evening-dress was compulsory, which reminds me of a story. One September night when the Prime Minister, Stanley Baldwin, and his wife entered the annexe in day clothes, and sat down to dinner, Bartlett the steward came over to them to call their attention to the rule. At this Baldwin got up and went to every occupied table in the room apologizing for his unorthodox attire, excusing himself on the ground

The Queen Mother with Lady Petrie,
Mayor of the Royal Borough of Kensington, 1956

Chatting with Professor Johnston of the University of Wales and Don Alfonso Vallejo Franco de Espés at the Diputación Provincial of Zaragoza

The author, with his wife, the Spanish Ambassador to the Republic of Ireland, and the Señora Iturralde, at the Annual Dinner of the Military History Society of Ireland at the Shelbourne Hotel, Dublin, November, 1956

that 10 Downing Street was closed and that he was himself only passing through London.

The end came with the bombing of the Club itself on 14 October 1940. The annexe was not directly hit by high explosive bombs it is true, but it was extensively damaged by incendiaries. At various times suggestions were put forward that it might be used as temporary premises by the Club, or re-opened as the annexe, but they proved impracticable chiefly because the building had no separate kitchens. The more immediate problem of where the members should go was temporarily solved by the generous and spontaneous offers of hospitality which at once came in from the other West End clubs. Such an attitude was the more commendable as both food and drink were, as the saying went in those wartime days, 'in short supply', and no club relished the prospect of sharing its meagre store of either with the members of another.

The question of the ultimate future was far more difficult. The most cursory examination showed that the restoration of the Club and the Annexe would be a very expensive business, certainly could not be possible while the war lasted, nor in all probability for several years after it had finished. Fortunately Arthur's old premises at 69 St James's Street, the original home of White's, were empty, and so the Carlton was enabled to establish itself there. Arthur's would appear to have been founded in 1811, but it had closed its doors early in the Second World War when many of its members had been absorbed into the Carlton, so they welcomed the idea of returning to their old home.

No mention of Arthur's, however brief, would be complete without at least an allusion to Kitty Fischer, of whom an engraving used to hang in the hall (it is now to be seen in the committee-room of Pratt's, for it was bought by the late Duke of Devonshire after Arthur's closed down). The lady in question was the daughter of a German stay-maker, who at an early age became one of the leading *demi-mondaines* of the day, or, to put it less brutally, 'her companionship was eagerly sought by many men of wealth and fashion'. There was a story to be heard in Arthur's that Kitty Fischer was for some time kept by subscription of the whole club, but unfortunately for romance the relevant dates do not tally with this attractive legend. Kitty died in 1767 'a victim of cosmetics', and Arthur's was not founded until the beginning of the following century. There was, however, an establishment called the Miles Club at 69 St James's Street between the removal of White's and the foundation of Arthur's, so it may have been the members of this club who jointly subscribed for the enjoyment of Kitty's favours.

Sex has played little part in the life of the Carlton, though until the bye-laws were strengthened it was not unknown for members to take ladies of the town to their bedrooms in the Annexe. Then there was the case of the waitress who complained of the excessive attentions of a member, and when asked to tell the committee what happened began by saying, 'He didn't do anything much at first.' Then, looking at the chairman, she added, 'Just pinched my bottom, same as you do, my Lord.' When I first joined there was a story going round of a member who had actually complained to the Secretary that he had contracted venereal disease from a female member of the staff, but this is surely apocryphal.

The decision to house the Carlton permanently at 69 St James's Street was not taken until many other possibilities had been examined, including a return to the old premises in Pall Mall. My old friend Roy Wise and some others still feel that the committee made a mistake, but with the whole future of West End clubs so obscure it would have been too great a risk to rebuild on the scale of the plans which were drawn up, even if the money had been available, and the subscription would probably have had to be raised to a figure far beyond the pockets of those who would be called upon to pay it. And as nothing today is on the magnificent scale that existed in the past, the Carlton could hardly expect to prove an exception. What particularly distressed me personally was that among the amenities that had to be sacrificed was the library, which had been one of the glories of the old Carlton.

For many years the Carlton Club combined for the Conservative Party the roles of rallying-point and melting-pot, which it was enabled to do because its members used it as a club, and not merely as a restaurant. They met there to discuss the problems of the day, and after any big event the leaders of the Conservative Party went there to hear the views of their followers. Of late years, and particularly since the Second World War, this state of affairs has largely passed away. The M.P. of today has perforce to spend most of his life either at the House of Commons or in his constituency, so that even if he has the inclination he has little time to converse with his fellow-members in the Carlton Club. What is true of the rank-and-file applies with even greater force to the leaders of the party – in this present year of Grace 1971 the Lord Chancellor and the Foreign Secretary are the only senior ministers to be regularly seen in the Club. This development is to be regretted on every score for it means that the politicians are being increasingly segregated and kept away from contact with any but other politicians, and in the case of the Carlton it is depriving the Club of one of the main spheres of its usefulness and interest.

The fact has also got to be faced that the internal combustion engine brought about a greater social revolution than has even been effected by the doctrines of Rousseau or Marx. The present generation is removed by centuries from the age when the committee of the Carlton found it most convenient to meet on a Saturday afternoon. Seventy years ago the normal member was either in the country or in London. If he was in the country he did not use the Club; if he was in London he probably spent a large portion of his time there. Today he possibly lives anything up to forty miles out of London, and comes up to town on five days of the week. When he is in London he may have his lunch at the Carlton, but he does not sit over it, neither is he to be found there in the evening very much, because he only stays up in town as the result of some special engagement, whether of a business or a social nature.

Another factor which has done a great deal to modify the old traditions of club life as it was lived in Victorian times has been the change in the position of women in just that section of the community from which clubmen are drawn. The days are gone when a man went down to his club for a few hours while his wife remained at home engaged either in looking after the children or servants, or in sewing a fine seam. Children and servants are now in short supply, as the wartime phrase had it, and husbands and wives tend to go about more together. Whether this is a good or a bad thing is a matter of opinion, but it has adversely affected the clubs. To some extent the challenge has been met by the institution of an annexe, but this does not really touch the root of the trouble, which is that on holidays and at weekends members and their wives tend to go out of London in their cars.

Then there is the question of finance, which requires to be considered under two separate heads, namely the monetary resources of members, and the vastly increased cost of running a club.

Broadly speaking, the class from which most of the members of West End clubs are drawn has been the hardest hit by the two World Wars of this century, and by the social revolution and the galloping inflation which have followed in their wake. It is true that there is a small minority of business-men who either have their subscriptions paid for them by their firms, or are able to show this expenditure, and a certain amount of business entertaining, as legitimate expenses, though this is by no means as easy as it was. But they represent an inconsiderable proportion of the total membership; seventy years ago, it is safe to say, the vast majority of the members of the Carlton were men whose income was wholly or largely indirect. For reasons which it would be out of place to discuss here that class has ceased to exist. Admittedly the Carlton was never a poor man's club, but today there are very many members who can barely afford the subscription, and who have to look very carefully indeed at every penny they spend within its walls, and in particular does this apply to the young married men in the professions. To make it worth their while to join a club they are liable to require such amenities as will meet all their requirements in the matter of recreation, including facilities for their wives to share these with them. Some club committees have gone out of their way to meet this demand by the provision of swimming baths, cocktail-bars, and squash-courts, but it is still doubtful whether they have solved the problem, for many of the younger men, paradoxically enough, seem to hanker after membership of the clubs where these amenities do not exist.

This leads me to my second point, namely the ever-increasing cost of running a club, which of late years has been accentuated by the Catering Wages Act and the Selective Employment Tax. Not only has this increased cost militated against the provision of fresh amenities, but it has made difficult the maintenance of existing ones, with unfortunate effects upon membership. It is not that the clubs were bad employers in the past; in fact the opposite was the case, and the wages paid by the Carlton at any rate were normal for the period. What has happened has been that the internal purchasing power of the pound has gone down, but whereas wages have been raised until they more than compensate their recipients for this fall, the income of the average club member is far from having risen correspondingly.

One last word about the Carlton. When all is said and done it is as a political club that the Carlton will stand or fall, and such being the case it is no exaggeration to say that its future rests with the Conservative Front Bench in the two Houses of Parliament, the Whips, and the Party machine as a whole, as well as with the committee for the time being. The days when their connection with the Club was close over a long period were the days of its greatness. Granted all the difficulties of running any club in the latter years of the twentieth century I find it impossible to resist the conclusion that if the old and close connection with those responsible for the destinies of the Conservative Party can be revived then there is no reason why the Carlton should not play an important part in the political life of the country for many years.

Before I was elected to the Carlton I was for a few years a member of the Oxford and Cambridge, but as I could not afford the subscription to more than one club I had to take my name off. During the time that I was a member I was told a good, and not very widely known, story about the Duke of Wellington. As Chancellor of Oxford University he had been made an honorary member of the Club, which he apparently used as a refuge from purely military society. In those days the Guards Club was next door to the Oxford and Cambridge, and when it was cleaned the members were entertained by their neighbour. On one such night a young ensign, who had certainly not stinted himself at dinner, threw himself into a chair next to an elderly gentleman whose face was hidden by the newspaper he was reading, and observed in a somewhat patronizing manner, 'You fellows in the middle classes do yourselves well, and no mistake.' The paper was slowly lowered to reveal the visage of the Iron Duke to the young officer's startled gaze.

Mention of the Guards Club prompts me to mention the fact that when I became Editor of what was then termed the *Household Brigade Magazine* the committee very kindly elected me an honorary member. After the First World War the club moved from Pall Mall to the never-satisfactory premises in Brook Street; it was later fortunate in securing Mrs Ronnie Greville's old house in Charles Street, and where after a number of vicissitudes which do not concern us here it would appear to be as comfortably settled as any club in London. The move from Pall Mall, however, involved one breach with tradition, for when it was there the officer of the guard at St James's Palace was allowed to use the club as he could watch his sentries from its windows.

Another club for which I had a very great affection during these years was the Authors'. Douglas Jerrold, who was a member for many years, rather sneers at it in *Georgian Adventure*, maintaining that none of its members belonged to the 'writing classes', or 'played much part in the literary life of their times', – his favourite appellation for it was 'the seedy club' – but then sneering at institutions and people to whom he was in reality greatly attached was one of Jerrold's less attractive characteristics. For myself, I can only say that some of the happiest hours of my life were spent within its walls when it was housed in Whitehall Court, and the staff were not only our servants but also our friends. Two in particular of whom I am thinking are 'Trina' (Miss Wyler), the stewardess in the club's later years, who controlled us all with a firm but gentle hand, and Willie, the barman, who administered to our alcoholic needs.

Why Jerrold should decry the literary standing of a club which at one time or another since the Second World War has contained writers of the distinction of Graham Greene, Malcolm Muggeridge, John Betjeman, Osbert Lancaster, Laurence Meynell, Steven Runciman, Frank Swinnerton, Lord Dunsany, Compton Mackenzie, C. S. Forester, and Henry Williamson is not easy to understand, but one thing even he could not question was the brilliance which marked the conversation at the long table. It would be invidious to particularize among those who contributed to it, at any rate among the living, but of those who are no longer with us I would single out Hugh Kingsmill as an outstanding spontaneous wit. I remember an American professor arguing in his presence that Marlowe had written Shakespeare; asked to prove his point he maintained that the man killed at Wapping was not Marlowe at all, but that the whole affair was a deliberate hoax to create the impression that Marlowe was dead, before, as a member of Walsingham's secret service, he was sent to the Continent to unravel one of the numerous conspiracies against Elizabeth I. 'When that assignment was ended, what could Marlowe do as he was officially dead?' asked the professor. 'I'll tell you,' he went on, 'He wrote plays under the name of William Shakespeare. What do you say to that, Mr Kingsmill?' Like a flash came the crushing reply, 'Damned annoyed Bacon must have been.'

Then there was John Munro who, by a single interjection, killed long-winded speeches in the club. One of our leading bores was proposing my health in a wearisome discourse mainly consisting of extracts from *Who's Who*, and when he reached the sentence 'For several years Sir Charles and Mr Douglas Jerrold collaborated in the publication of the *English Review*', John Munro shouted out, 'And serve them both bloody well right.' It was some minutes before the laughter subsided, and we never had a vote of thanks again. Of the more recent wits I would put Harold Brockman, the architectural correspondent of *The Financial Times*, very high indeed: he never repeats a story unless pressed to do so, but he has several in his *repertoire* which, when produced, show that like a vintage wine they have improved with keeping. Waveney Girvan was of the same ilk; his early death of cancer was a real blow to the club, of which he was one of the most notable conversationalists.

Perhaps the most delightful aspects of the Authors' Club in those days for most of us was that it represented a cross-section of the professional classes. Taking a few names at random, there was Guy Schofield, one of the ablest editors the *Daily Mail* ever had, and the kindliest of men; Dr Arthur Maiden, one of the real influences in the British Medical Association, and with a charm that defies description; and, above all, Dr Nathaniel Micklem, who combined in his person all that is best in Oxford and Nonconformity. Before his death there was also Kenneth Hare, who was always good company, even if some of us were not prepared to take him at his own valuation as a poet or as a lover.

Informality and friendliness were the outstanding characteristics of the old Authors' Club. If a stranger, waiting for his host, came into the bar he would be assured of a welcoming word and probably a drink from any member who happened to be there at the time. Pretty regularly we had dinners, addressed by various speakers of eminence in different fields, which we kept as informal as possible, abandoning evening-dress at an early date – not so much as a concession to democracy as because many of our members lived out of London, and had a long way to travel after the dinner was over. Then there were small lunches of which two in particular are fresh in my mind, one being to Harold Wilson and the other to George Brown: on these occasions there were no speakers.

As the sixties wore on the Authors' Club began to run into financial difficulties. Not only did it have to compete so far as membership was concerned with the Garrick and the Savile but there was a change of ownership at Whitehall Court, and the new proprietors did not view the clubs which were under its roof with anything like so friendly an eye as the old. The future was becoming so uncertain that we did not feel justified in making any great drive to recruit new members. Then began that weary quest for amalgamation with some other institution which those responsible for the management of West End clubs in modern times know only too well. A few years earlier the Chemical Club had joined us with the happiest results, and we hoped that the experiment might be repeated with some other club, but it was not to be. That the Authors' did not have to put up its shutters then and there is due to two of its members, Gavin Thurston and Kenneth Garside, and to the Secretary, Michael Lindsay, for whom no praise could be too great. They came to an arrangement with the National Liberal Club whereby the Authors' had a room of its own on the National Liberal premises, of which the members were also to have a free run.

So the identity of the club was preserved, and the National Liberals proved admirable hosts, while the amenities they provided were much appreciated, but it would be idle to pretend that the atmosphere was any more the same than it is in the case of the Carlton in St James's Street compared to what it was in Pall Mall. As the years have passed a generation of Carlton members has arisen who knew not the old regime, and if it survives the same will be the case with the Authors', so this will cease to matter, but as long as there are some of us who did know it there will be an irrepressible feeling of nostalgia. Talleyrand once said that only those who had lived before the French Revolution knew what living was: I would adapt his adage to modern times by saying that only those who were members of a West End club before the Second World War know what club life is really like.

It is a relief to pass from the clubs which, successfully or not, have fought, or are fighting, for life to one of which the future seems reasonably assured, that is to say from those of the West End to Hurlingham, which possesses all the advantages of a country house with none of its drawbacks, and to go there is like a visit to the country. It may not be so fashionable as in the days when it was the centre of polo, but it is very definitely an oasis of rest and relaxation for those whose commitments give them little leisure to go far from London.

An early, if not the original, owner of the house was Charles Ellis, who had hereditary connections with Jamaica, of which his grandfather was Chief Justice, and who had inherited a considerable fortune. For many years Ellis was a fine rider to hounds, but the nerve he displayed in the hunting field forsook him when he acted as Canning's second in the famous duel with Castlereagh: so anxious did he feel for the fate of his friend that his hand is said to have shaken to such an extent that he was unable to load the pistol, which had to be done for him by the other second, Lord Yarmouth. Although Ellis sat in the House of Commons for many years he was not a brilliant speaker; his importance at Westminster rested principally upon the fact that he was the acknowledged head of the then powerful West Indian interest. Canning was a frequent visitor to Hurlingham, which he is said to have been able to reach from the House of Commons in twenty minutes in a gig with a fast-trotting horse. When in 1826 the Prime Minister gave Canning the nomination of a friend to the peerage his choice fell on Charles Ellis, who duly took the title of Lord Seaford.

Hurlingham became a club just over a century ago, and for many years after that its chief attractions were polo and pigeon-shooting. The latter pastime ceased to be practised in 1906, partly because the age was becoming more humanitarian and partly because the croquet players, by this time a formidable body, resented the steady shower of dead and dying birds which interfered with their game. There was also an unfortunate incident when the German ambassador was peppered in the posterior, an event which added force to the arguments of those who stressed the undesirability of the continuance of pigeon-shooting in the club. As for the polo, that came to an end in 1939, for after the Second World War a covetous London County Council cast its eyes on Hurlingham which in consequence looked for a time like sharing the fate of Vauxhall and Cremorne; but largely owing to the efforts of the late Sir George Peplar this catastrophe was averted, though the polo-ground had to be sacrificed in the process. Whether in any case it would have been a feasible proposition to play polo in London in modern conditions on the old scale is very doubtful.

In its earlier days Hurlingham was only open in the summer, so that when, after the Second World War, it was decided to keep it open throughout the year, a great deal of reconstruction was necessary: matters were not made any easier by the fact that a V1 had disintegrated overhead, though the resulting war-damage payment, as well as the price paid for the abandoned polo-ground, provided the necessary finance for the alterations. The result is a club almost without a rival in the world. Nor is this all, for what may be termed the social atmosphere is extremely pleasant; it is true that there are cliques composed of the devotees of the various sports, but there is also a cross-section drawn from them all which centres round the bar in the winter and the rose garden in the summer. This happy state of affairs is very largely due to the present Chairman, Major Jack Rivington, for whom there can be no higher praise than to say that he is all a good chairman should be.

On the other hand if the old-fashioned West End clubs have made heavy weather since the Second World War the dining clubs have flourished like the proverbial bay tree; even the staid old 1900 has turned itself into one, and its members now dine in state and evening-dress at the Dorchester instead of drinking beer in pubs in their day attire. One of the oldest dining clubs is the Pitt, which had its origin in the dinner at the Merchant Taylor's Hall which Canning organized on 28 May 1802 in support of Pitt, who was then out of office, when the song was sung whose last lines are the well-known:

> *And, oh! if again the rude whirlwind should rise,*
> *The dawning of peace should fresh darkness deform,*
> *The regrets of the good and the fears of the wise*
> *Shall turn to the Pilot that weathered the Storm.*

At one time there were Pitt Clubs all over the country, but today they are to be found only in Cambridge, Chester, and London, and the London one cannot claim an unbroken descent from 1802, for it has lapsed and been revived on more than one occasion.

The London Pitt Club did me the honour of electing me its Chairman when Charles Rhys (by then eighth Lord Dynevor) died in 1962, and I can claim without any exaggeration that we are a very happy band. It would be difficult to find two more delightful colleagues than Ralph Clitheroe, the President, and Esmond Warner, son of the immortal 'Plum', the Honorary Secretary. The Club holds its dinners twice a year, usually at the Cavalry or the Turf, which are attended by fifty or sixty of our hundred members. Two other famous London dining clubs are Grillons,

of which Arthur Bryant is one of the leading stalwarts, and The Other
Club which Winston Churchill founded in his earlier years.

If the clubs have changed during the past generation so have their
denizens. The real eccentric, of the type described on an earlier page,
is becoming increasingly difficult to find. One who was definitely not an
eccentric, a leading clubman of the fifties was Hugo Wortham, who
operated, if that is the right word, from the United University. He was
'Peterborough' of the *Daily Telegraph* – easily the best-informed
columnist I have ever met, as well as one of the most charming com-
panions. If he did not know a thing or a person he always knew where
to find out all about them, and the food, drink, and conversation at his
parties were among the best in London. Then there is Sir Harry Brittain,
who at rising ninety-nine is still very much alive, the patriarch of the
Carlton, and the best company in London: he is, indeed, a link with
the past, and he has the happy knack of making that past become very
real.

It has been well said that the history of the West End Clubs is the
history of London manners since the Restoration, that the changes in
taste, habits, and customs are plainly reflected in club life. Even during
the half-century or so of which I can speak with any authority there
have been many such changes, most of them for the worse. It is true that
clubs, like every other human institution, must prove adaptable if they
are to survive, but there is no need for their committees to bend over
backwards to cater for what are alleged, often without proof, to be the
desires of the younger generation. For the rest, an existence of three
hundred years has shown these clubs to be at all levels an essential part of
modern British life, and he would be a churlish fellow who would not
admit that they constitute one of the most attractive elements of it.

CHAPTER XV

Ireland Again

1938 was the year of my last pre-war visit to Ireland, after which I looked forward greatly to the day when I would return. Although this was not possible until 1946, I was fortunately able both to revive many of my old friendships and to make new ones.

My first impression, which has been confirmed by every successive visit, is that the war produced more changes in what is now the Republic than is generally believed, and most of these have been for the better. This is not, of course, to suggest that all is well with the country, though – economics apart – there are fewer things wrong with it than most Irishmen would care to admit. There is certainly a greater homogeneity than there was forty or fifty years ago, and this is particularly noticeable among the younger generation. Personally, I find it difficult to resist the conclusion that this is in no small measure due to the common experience of the 'emergency', which brought together those who had hitherto been divided by conflicting loyalties of ancient date.

In this connection there is still a great deal to be done, and much for the older generation to forget. There are still a number of the descendants of the old 'Ascendancy' families who look askance at the Republic, and regret the severance of the constitutional link with Britain; but for them to think that they can put the clock back would be most unrealistic; too much water, and not a little blood, has flowed under the bridges for that. These people have a definite contribution to make to the Ireland of the future, but they will never make it if they are continually looking over their shoulders at what is after all only the recent past, and not a particularly creditable past at that. As for the British connection, history has proved that the two countries can never really be dissociated: direct political links are unlikely ever again to be forged, but is it too fanciful to look forward to the day when both nations will work side by side as members of a European federation?

Equally, no Irish purpose is served by sneering references to 'West Britons', and by the contention that patriotism and political wisdom are the monopoly of those who defended the Dublin Post Office and Boland's flour mills in the Easter Rising in 1916, as most of those who took part in these actions would readily admit. If a 'West Briton' means anything it means an inhabitant of the Celtic kingdom of West Wales after the Saxon victory at Deorham had cut off the Cymry of Cornwall and Devon from their brethren north of the Bristol Channel, but it is not in this connection that the term is now employed. A little back-biting and mud-slinging there will always be, for human nature is far from perfect even in Ireland, but it will be better for the country if it is confined to the minimum; what happens if it is taken too seriously we have seen in the North.

In Ireland there is, and always has been, a marked tendency to inter-pret the country's history as a series of episodes which bear little or no relation either to what went before or to what followed after: the Flight of the Earls, the Treaty of Limerick, the Union, and the Easter Rising are regarded as boundary-marks rather than as milestones, with the result that Irish history has not been looked upon as a continuous whole. This weakness is far from being completely eradicated even now, but until it is eradicated many Irishmen will continue to view their country in the wrong perspective. The Irish, like the Spaniards, are very conscious of their past, but until recently they have tended to look at it in the wrong light: the past should surely serve as the interpreter of the present and the guide-post to the future. If it is, on the contrary, used to keep alive old hatreds it will merely perpetuate the modern divisions which are based on them, as is happening in Belfast and Derry. One can hold the view that the wrong side won the Battle of the Boyne – I hold that view myself – without wishing to disparage the valour or the sincerity of those who fought for William of Orange and, more important, without ani-mosity towards their modern descendants.

One of the changes for the better which have occurred in the twenty-six counties since the British left is that old hatreds are being increasingly forgotten: there is far more Christian charity and far less hatred and malice between individuals and classes, while, as is certainly not the case in contemporary Britain, people still have time to talk and think. What is to be regretted is that there are so few outward and visible signs of that continuity of history which to a historically-minded people would be an encouragement to the centripetal forces operating in their midst. Why, for instance, should not the battlefield of the Boyne be made into a National Park on the same lines as that of Gettysburg? It would also provide a considerable tourist attraction within easy reach of Dublin.

There is no country, certainly not excluding England, where there is more tolerance for an opposing point of view than in the Republic of Ireland. The foreigner, particularly the Englishman, may be surprised at this statement, for he judges by appearances which are proverbially deceptive, and nowhere more so than in Ireland, but coming of a family which has now been connected with that country for nearly two hundred years, and which has always belonged to a small minority, I feel that I am entitled to speak with some authority in this matter. So long as Irishmen do not lose this attribute, and do not take their politicians too seriously, they cannot go far wrong.

What has unfortunately not changed for the better during the past fifty years has been the standard of those same politicians. Ever since the murder of Michael Collins there has been a great lack of political leadership, which, sad to relate, has not been compensated for in the religious field by either the Catholic or the Protestant clergy. Few countries have sustained so grievous a loss as Ireland did in the death of Collins, for had he lived the history of the country since the Treaty would undoubtedly have been very different. No one has proved capable of bending the bow of Odysseus – not even De Valera, as those who have read the masterly biography of him by Lord Longford and Mr Thomas O'Neill will readily realize. Although he has been the outstanding Irish personality for the last half-century, De Valera has never, strange as it may appear to the Englishman, become a father figure in Ireland, and he never will: too much is remembered against him, and too much been passed on even to a generation too young to have been contemporary with the events which made him odious to their parents. At his second election as President he got a majority of a mere 20,000 out of a million votes cast, but even that was largely due to the support of the old Unionists who have never forgiven Fine Gael for taking Ireland out of the British Commonwealth, and so would not vote for O'Higgins.

One of the organizations which I feel can justly claim to be helping the centripetal forces in Ireland is the Military History Society, which has recently celebrated its twenty-first anniversary. It was not until it came into existence that we realized how great was the need for it. Soon after the conclusion of the Second World War, when I was starting work on the second edition of *The Jacobite Movement*, I became more convinced than ever that there was a great deal more going on in

Ireland at the end of the seventeenth and the beginning of the eighteenth centuries than is usually recorded by historians. I therefore decided to see for myself what was to be found. For this purpose I sought the advice of two people: the first was my old friend Aodh de Blacam, who put me in touch with a number of people whom I did not previously know, but whom I have since numbered among my friends; and the second M. J. MacManus, whose tragic death was a great loss to Irish letters.

Not unnaturally this brought me into contact with the Irish Army to which I should like to take this opportunity of paying a tribute. The finest institution in the Republic today, it has in recent years been Ireland's shop-window on the world. Under the banner of United Nations it has kept the peace in the Congo and in Cyprus in the most difficult circumstances, and its prestige is everywhere very high indeed. Yet never was the truth of the old adage, that a prophet is not without honour save in his own country, more forcibly proved than in the case of the Irish Army which has never been honoured at home to anything like the extent to which it is abroad. Among the politicians, indeed, I have even detected a suspicion of it in some quarters – perhaps because they realize that it is respected while they are not.

However this may be, once I had talked matters over with Major-General Aodh MacNeill and Colonel A. T. Lawlor, we came to the conclusion that although there was a growing interest both inside and outside Ireland in military history no organization existed to keep the workers in that particular field in touch with one another. Out of our conclusions was born the Military History Society of Ireland in January 1949, of which its members did me the great honour of electing me President. Among the earlier stalwarts who are no longer with us were Richard Hayes, Henry Mangan, Colonel Lawless, Commandant G. S. Cox, and Lieutenant-Colonel Justin MacCarthy, while the continued existence of the Society during its teething troubles was largely due to that very remarkable figure, Diarmuid Murtagh of Athlone.

Our first task was to state the Society's objects in such a way as to make them clear without giving offence in any quarter; we finally decided that they were to further the study of Irish military history, which was defined as 'the history of warfare in Ireland, and of Irishmen in war'. The next step was to ensure that no charge of political or religious bias could be brought against us, which we felt we achieved by enrolling among our earliest members Mr de Valera on the one hand and Lord Rathcavan, then Speaker of the North of Ireland Parliament, on the other. Both, though now of advanced age, have continued to take an interest in the Society's activities. I well recall Dev's presence at the annual meeting in 1966 when Major-General Hally read a masterly paper on the military aspects of the Easter Rising. At its close I said from the chair, 'Mr President, would you like to say anything?' to which the reply came,

'Sir Charles, in the circumstances I think I had better not.'

At first we limited our terms of reference to the period ending in 1900, but we have recently extended them to the Treaty.

During the two decades of the Society's existence it can really claim to have made its contribution to the ends which it has in view, and its membership now stands at over a thousand scattered about the world: a link between these members is its official organ the *Irish Sword*, which has always maintained the high standard set by its first two editors, Professor G. A. Hayes-McCoy and Captain Kevin Danagher. We have during these twenty-odd years explored many of the well-known battle-sites in which Irishmen have been engaged, not only those in their own country, but others such as Culloden, Fontenoy, Almansa, and the Flanders battle-fields of the First World War.

At the moment of writing (July 1971) the Society continues to go on from strength to strength. Death has taken its toll of many of the original members, but they have been replaced by others of equal zeal: Major-General Aodh MacNeill, for example, has been followed by his brother Olaf, who is a tower of strength; the Irish Army still gives its warm support through a number of officers whom it would be invidious to mention by name; Father Crean, who has served as a chaplain in three armies, represents all that is best in his Church; Dr Simms brings us the scholarship of T.C.D. As for Professor Liam O'Brian, he is the personification of eternal youth though he was 'out' in the Easter Rising. It would also be ungenerous not to mention our great indebtedness to the Cultural Relations Committee of Ireland, to University College, Dublin, and to External Affairs for their continued support during all the years of our existence.

The Department of External Affairs, like the Army, seems to be another of the institutions of modern Ireland which never receives the credit that is its due. All over the world the Irish ambassadors are to my personal knowledge always at hand to help Irish people or an Irish cause, and in London in particular the Irish Ambassadors from the far-off days of Freddie Boland have always been men of a high standard, which has redounded to the credit of their country. Did an unknown Irish artist have a show of his pictures in Fulham, or was an Irish firm launching a new line of products, the ambassador would be there on the appropriate occasion to give a helping hand.

I happened to be in Madrid soon after the foundation of the Military History Society, and to celebrate the event the ambassador, Macaulay, gave a party to the Spanish descendants of the Wild Geese. As the members of the noblest families in Spain were announced a young female Irish journalist whispered in my ear, 'These Wild Geese seem to have done pretty well for themselves.' When I had conveyed the ambassador's invitation to the late Duke of Alba and Berwick he asked, 'Whom am I expected to represent?'

'James II', I replied.

'Admirable', he said. 'I have another engagement so I shall have to leave early.'

I suppose I go to Ireland two or three times a year, and have done so ever since the late war; in Dublin I base myself on the University Club and my wife on the Shelbourne Hotel. The University Club is what the London Clubs were, but no longer are; that is to say it is run like a civilized man's home, and not like a restaurant for all who can afford the charges. This is due largely to its excellent Secretary, Colonel McAlister. When he first became associated with it the club was in very low water indeed; there was even talk of its amalgamation with the Kildare Street, but McAlister pushed up the membership, and now, in its renovated premises, it need not fear comparison with any club in the world. Of course the problems facing a Dublin club are very different from those confronting a London one: the Irish capital has changed and is changing as the business element becomes predominant over the professional. But even so life proceeds at a more leisurely pace than in London, and as the city itself is so much smaller it does not take people so long to move about it. Men are therefore more inclined to drop in at their club on their way home of an evening, and even to meet their wives there for a drink or a snack.

Munster as a whole is a very happy hunting-ground for a historian such as myself, though one has to be on guard against the interpretations too often put on the past. The Algerine raid on Baltimore in 1631 is a case in point. All that most Irish people know about it is derived from the poem of Thomas Davis on the subject. Now he wrote some very stirring verse, though I will not say that he was a great poet; but whatever the quality of his poetry he was very definitely not a historian, and not a little of his history is inaccurate. From his poem one would gather the impression that the prisoners who were carried off by the Algerines into captivity were Irish, a fallacy which has been repeated in one guide-book after another right down to our own times. Yet if one reads the list of those who were taken away there is hardly an Irish name: they were nearly all English Protestant families who had been planted in Baltimore in the reign of James I. This may well explain why when the news of what had happened reached the Irish town of Skibbereen it seems to have aroused no great interest, though one would have thought that the English administration might have done better in the matter of patrolling the Munster coast. Actually, Baltimore remained predominantly English for many years after the raid, for as late as 1698 there were only two Roman Catholics in the town.

It must be confessed that the Irish Tourist Board, for understandable if reprehensible reasons, is by no means guiltless where the propagation of bad, though often colourful, history is concerned. The legend that there was a Major of Galway who hanged his own son for murdering a Spanish merchant because he could find no one else to do it, is completely untrue, but visitors to Galway are attracted by it, so it is still going the rounds.

In Ireland more than in most countries I can claim to know there is much for the historian to learn from local tradition, though of course this has to be carefully checked against the established facts. My grandfather, living so close to Killala, and having been born in the reign of George IV, had met many men and women who remembered the landing of the French in 1798. He often told me that Humbert and his troops were by no means so popular locally as some modern chroniclers would have us believe: the French had come without horses, and as the United Irishmen rolled up to strike a blow for their country they were harnessed to the French guns which they then had to pull across the bogs at the foot of Mount Nephin to Castlebar: nor was their abandonment by their allies at Ballinamuck readily forgotten. Of a different type are the rumours that Bonnie Prince Charlie visited Ireland, Donegal, Galway, and Cork being among the counties where he is said to have been seen at one time or another. In Donegal in particular various local legends tell in detail how he landed at Glencolmcille. My friend the late Dr Richard Hayes once had a farm-house near the place where the prince was said to have been in hiding, pointed out to him. It need hardly be said that none of these stories have documentary or other concrete evidence to support them.

More reliable is some information about the flight of James II after the battle of the Boyne which Billy Wicklow very kindly unearthed for me during one of my visits to Shelton Abbey before he sold it.

James stayed only one night in Dublin after his defeat before going on to Duncannon, where he took ship to Kinsale: at this port he embarked on a French frigate which took him to Brest. In the king's own account of his journey to Duncannon he mentions having gone 'to the house of a gentleman of the name of Hatchet, near Arclough [Arklow]', where he rested his horses. Just over a century later, in 1791, Hugh Howard, brother of the first Viscount Wicklow, wrote of this visit:

'Formerly the road from Dublin to Wexford was not through the town of Arklow, but across the river by a ford. It led by the herd's house, on the brow of a hill called Stringers Hill, at the end of Shelton avenue across the river to Polehony, Lord Carysfort's seat, and so into the county of Wexford; or into the county of Waterford through Carlow and Kilkenny. This road to the ford has ever since been called King James's Lane; it is now impassable. The avenue was at the foot of Stringers Hill, about a quarter of a mile from Shelton House, to which it led straight up to the door, through a double row of beech trees, having a hill to the right and the Hall Meadow to the left. At the door was a porch made of wood, with seats.

'An old man, one Richard Johnson, who was son to the gardener at Shelton, told me that just after the battle of the Boyne, being then a young boy, as he was standing one evening in company with a labouring man of the name of Coghlan in Shelton avenue [this must have been the evening of 2 July 1690] he saw two tall gentlemen, grandly mounted and all covered with dust, ride down Stringers Hill on their way to the ford; but instead of proceeding onwards, they turned up the avenue, whither he followed them, not knowing then who they were.

'When they came to the house, which was at that time in the possession of one Mr Hacket [he was the sequestrator] they alighted, and sat down in the porch, where they had some cold meat and a jug of strong beer. While they continued there, which was only for a few minutes, one of them was seized with a violent bleeding at the nose, which stained the post of that side of the porch where the gentlemen sat. When the bleeding was stopped they mounted their horses again, and rode down the avenue and across the ford [probably the short cut way to Duncannon Fort]. He afterwards knew for certain in that the person whose nose had bled was King James II, and that the other was a person of distinction ... The porch was afterwards taken down, and the post with the blood on it [which I have seen] long carefully preserved, but it has been since burned by the carelessness of servants.'

One wonders if James's companion, whoever he may have been, recollected that during a previous period of stress, namely at Salisbury in the autumn of 1688, the King had similarly been afflicted with a bleeding of the nose.

Wicklow is an extremely attractive county: I have paid, and still do pay, frequent visits there, mainly to Coollattin where Olive Fitzwilliam always makes a home from home for my wife and me. So far as I know there are no special historical or ghostly associations connected with Coollattin. There is, however, a ghost at Humewood, in the shape of a canon who is reputed only to present himself to Roman Catholics. Humewood was the home of the Right Hon. W. W. F. Dick who was M.P. for County Wicklow from 1852 to 1880. He would appear to have been far from vocal in the House of Commons, for he addressed it but once, and that in support of a Bill prohibiting pigeon-shooting, when he spoke for three minutes.

This is not the place to write at length about the future of Ireland, but perhaps a word or two may be said by one who is devoted to her. Not long before he died Lord Carson confessed to me in the Carlton Club that he was worried at the course events were taking in the Six Counties. His words were: 'I fought to keep Ulster part of the United Kingdom, but Stormont is turning her into a second-class Dominion.' And that was too long the case, not least under the rule of the late Lord Craigavon with the unhappy consequences we see today. That successive British governments down the ages must bear their share of the responsibility is only too true, for the curse of Ireland has been that so often its affairs have become the sport of party politics at Westminster. One must, however, give a word of praise to Mr Heath and Mr Wilson for their objective approach to Irish problems at the present time.

In spite of the protests of various groups of interested politicians in Belfast, Dublin, and London there can in the long run be no solution other than a united Ireland. It may be fifty years before this consummation is reached, and an intervening period of federation of some sort may prove necessary, but it is the goal to which all must strive who have the best interests of Ireland at heart.

CHAPTER XVI

The Latest Look Round

In recent years my overseas activities, apart from my involvement in Ireland, have been mainly concentrated on Spain, the United States, and France, and it is to them that I propose to dedicate this chapter.

Spain, apart from my experiences there described on an earlier page, will always be associated in my mind with Jimmy Alba, namely the tenth Duke of Berwick and sixteenth Duke of Alba, by whose death in 1953 the world unquestionably lost one of its most interesting personalities. Few men of our time, or of any other, have played so many parts. He was a large and extremely progressive landowner in the South of Spain; he was one of the most cultured men of his age – a veritable Maecenas to writers and painters; although no politician in the ordinary sense of the term he had been Minister of Education and of Foreign Affairs; and, in addition to a number of business interests, he was a governor of the Bank of Spain. Moreover, he was in his earlier years an enthusiastic polo-player, though he never attained to the proficiency of his brother, the late Duke of Peñaranda, who was murdered by the Reds in the Spanish Civil War.

Alba was an aristocrat to his finger-tips, and during a friendship of more than twenty years I never saw him anything except completely self-possessed; yet by nature he was, like all true aristocrats, one of the most courteous and kindly of men, as a single instance will suffice to prove. He was, until his disagreement with General Franco, President of the Patronato of the Prado, the present arrangement of the pictures there being largely due to his efforts. Even after he ceased to hold office he frequently visited the gallery, where he knew all the staff from the highest to the lowest personally, and he treated them all alike. As he passed from one room to another he would pause for a word with the attendant, calling him by name, and inquiring after his family. He showed the same interest in the country people during a journey I made with him in the east of Spain a few weeks before he died.

If Alba possessed to the full the pride and chivalry of the traditional Spaniard he was also the perfect cosmopolitan, which made him the most interesting of talkers; there was nothing narrowly nationalist in his outlook, devoted as he was to his country. Yet he had a second love, and that was England, where he had been educated at Beaumont, and where he spent much of his time. Indeed, when he was Spanish ambassador in London his more chauvinistic critics in Madrid used to declare that Britain had two representatives, one in the British embassy in Spain, and the other in the Spanish embassy in London. He and Churchill always referred to each other as cousins, in view of their common descent from an earlier Winston Churchill of the seventeenth century, though they were by no means always agreed with regard to that Sir Winston's son, the great Duke of Marlborough. Alba could never forgive what he considered to be John Churchill's treachery to his own ancestor, James II. On one occasion when he was denouncing it in no measured terms to Sir Winston, the British Prime Minister, as he then was, attempted to defend the Duke on the ground that for him the Protestant religion had always been the primary consideration. This line of defence only added fuel to the fire. Alba replied contemptuously, 'The Protestant religion! My foot!'

Alba's relations with Franco varied; at one time in particular they were very strained, namely in 1947 when he did not invite the Caudillo to his daughter's wedding, Franco retaliated by clamping down a censorship on all descriptions of the ceremony in the press, and soon after that, when Eva Perón visited Madrid, she was told that a call upon Alba would not be regarded at all favourably in official circles. On another occasion Alba's passport was taken from him so that he could not leave the country; yet he had been Franco's representative in London for six years. It was primarily their divergent views about the monarchy that estranged the two men, for Alba thought that when the Civil War and the Second World War were over it was Franco's bounden duty to call Don Juan to the throne.

With King Alfonso XIII he was on terms of intimacy, indeed it would be no exaggeration to say that he and the monarch's mother, Queen Maria Cristina, were among the few really responsible advisers the King ever had. On the other hand the Sovereign's indifference to danger could be an embarrassment to those who accompanied him. For example, in his first attempt to drive Alba's car – before he possessed one himself – and after a cow and a donkey had already become casualties, the Duke observed, 'Hadn't I better take the wheel?'

'If you feel afraid,' was the royal reply, 'get out.' Alba remained, but they were soon both in a ditch.

He was an admirable ambassador to Great Britain at a very difficult time, and it was as much his personality and British connections as anything else that prevented Anglo-Spanish relations becoming even more strained than they were. In those days, when Churchill declared that Spain 'seemed to hang in the balance between peace and war', to Alba must go most of the credit for the fact that there was no open breach with Britain: it was largely due to his wisdom and untiring efforts that Spain did not, like Italy, espouse the losing cause. His country's – and Britain's – debt to him is very great indeed.

In the years immediately following the Second World War the enemies of Spain, including those in Great Britain, did everything in their power to ostracize her. Today it is scarcely credible that in 1946 the General Assembly of the United Nations not only called upon the member States to withdraw the heads of their missions from Madrid, but went so far as to declare that the Security Council should consider what measures might be necessary to overthrow the Spanish Government. This threat of subversion organized from without was no doubt meant to appease Russia, although the Russians were then, as now, posing as the champions of unconditional national sovereignty. In effect there was neither sense nor consistency in a resolution which did Franco no harm at all, but on the contrary gave him an uncovenanted bonus of support among his own people.

Even Spaniards who had no great liking for a dictatorship preferred the dictatorship of another Spaniard to that of the outside world – Franco's bitterest enemies abroad proved his best friends at home. Furthermore, the conduct of the Spanish Government during the Second World War neither explained nor excused the boycott at the hands of the victors. Admittedly that conduct was equivocal and ambiguous as seen by the average Englishman, but first it was necessary in the circumstances, and secondly, so was the conduct of many another nation which was readily forgiven. The truth is that the policy enshrined in the funest resolution of the United Nations was inspired by the Left, which heaped praises on other dictatorships but denounced that of Franco as unclean.

Hardly had the bitterness aroused by this ill-fated action at New York died down than Anglo-Spanish relations took a turn for the worse as a result of the rival claims of London and Madrid to the ownership of

Gibraltar. Where the Rock is concerned it has always seemed to me that the best solution would have been the compromise which was once suggested by King Alfonso XIII. His idea was that Great Britain should recognize Spanish sovereignty, and in return should be granted a ninety-nine years' lease of the fortress for the annual payment of one pound sterling, which the King of Spain would come in person to Gibraltar to collect; on this occasion the British and Spanish flags should fly together over the Rock. Furthermore, there should always be a British officer attached to the staff of the King of Spain, and a Spanish one to that of the Governor of Gibraltar. Unhappily, this eminently reasonable idea was never pursued.

Spain, like Ireland, has of late been extraordinarily fortunate in her ambassadors in London, although it may be argued that Miguel Primo de Rivera was an exception. He was, however, a man of great charm and of unquestioned patriotism, in spite of the fact that, being an amateur he was not always the master of a difficult situation. In some respects he was more sinned against than sinning, and it did no credit to those who were so often entertained by him at his embassy that so few of them took the trouble to attend his memorial service. As for the present Spanish ambassador, Pepe Santa Cruz, and his wife, it will suffice to say that they are in the great tradition, and while never neglectful of the interests of their own country they are always mindful of ours as well: any move to improve Anglo-Spanish relations is sure of a warm welcome at 24 Belgrave Square.

It is well that his high standard of diplomatic representation should have been maintained, for relations between Britain and Spain have never been easy. It has always seemed to me that Englishmen have neither forgiven nor forgotten the Armada: they may flock to the Costa Brava every year in their tens of thousands, but on the slightest provocation, or on none at all, they are always ready to believe the worst of Spain and Spaniards, an attitude in which they are only too often encouraged by the newspapers. These hostile feelings do not exist in Ireland, nor should they, for Ireland has owed more to Spain down the ages than any country has ever owed to another. The Armada was a very long time ago, while the Spanish-American War was only at the end of last century, but there is no latent hostility to Spain in the United States. This bitterness is certainly not reciprocated by Spaniards, but to ignore the fact that it exists would be to get one aspect of European politics today very definitely in the wrong perspective.

Since 1945 I have visited every part of Spain, except for the north-east. In particular I have maintained close contact with its cultural life, a fact which has been officially recognized on several occasions by the Spanish Government; one of my greatest satisfactions was to be given an honorary degree by Valladolid University – the first ever granted since its foundation in 1346. In the matter of historical research the amount of work being done in Spain today is most gratifying, though it is to be feared that where the printed word is concerned the traffic is largely one-way, in that far more English books in translation reach Spain than Spanish books are published in England. Turning to personalities, perhaps the greatest link between the English-speaking and the Spanish-speaking worlds where literature is concerned is Walter Starkie, who was for so long Director of the British Institute in Madrid. If any foreigner knows his Spain, Walter does; to walk with him through the streets of any Spanish town is to secure a personal introduction to a large number of its inhabitants.

I remember in particular a visit we paid to Salamanca, when he introduced me to the then Rector of the University, Dr Antonio Tovar, who could not have been kinder: he had been the interpreter at the famous meeting between Franco and Hitler at Hendaye, and was reputed to be very Anglophobe: indeed when I told the late Lord Halifax, who was staying in Madrid at the time, that I was going to see Tovar he said that nothing would induce him to meet the Rector, which I thought rather small-minded for a man in his position. I am told, however, that not long afterwards Tovar was presented in New York to Queen Elizabeth, the Queen Mother – the last person to harbour narrow prejudices – with the happiest results.

When speaking of the future of Spain, as of any country's future, the historian must weigh his words. As a convinced monarchist I am naturally well pleased that Franco's successor is to be the Infante Don Juan Carlos: the history of the last hundred years proves that the monarchy unites while the republic divides. The Infante has been brought up in the new Spain which has come into existence since his grandfather was forced to leave the country, and from the days when I knew him as a cadet at Zaragoza he has been trained for the throne with a thoroughness which has marked the education of few princes in history. Above all, he is married to a wife who has every qualification for the position she has to fill: she is a Greek, and with one or two exceptions the women of the Greek Royal House have of late filled their roles with distinction.

On an earlier page I have told how I nearly went with my parents to the United States in the summer of 1914, but it was not until the fifties that I first crossed the Atlantic. Since then the United States has meant a great deal to the Petrie family. My wife and I in 1953 were guests on the maiden voyage of the *Olympic* from Southampton to New York and back; in 1959 my wife was U.K. Delegate to the 14th Session of the United Nations Assembly; and since 1969 our son, Peter, has been First Secretary to the U.K. Mission to the United Nations: while my last visit to the U.S.A. was in November, 1970. So as a family we can claim to be in close touch at any rate with the Eastern seaboard.

It is common knowledge that the climate of American opinion is always changing, but in one respect in particular there has been a very great change during recent years, namely in the marked decline in self-confidence on the part of the average citizen, at any rate in the Eastern States. The arrogant Yankee whom an earlier generation of Europeans was wont to caricature has disappeared, and in his place there is an apologetic type only too desirous of seeing faults in his own country. In the old days one had simply to mention almost any sphere of human activity to be told that things were done a great deal better in the United States, but that is far from being the case today: mention, for instance, the inefficiency of the British postal service, and one's American friends will reply that theirs is a great deal worse.

There is also widespread realization of the lack of leadership in all walks of life, which is depressing to the Americans too, more particularly when they remember the great men who were to be found at the head of affairs earlier in the century: only the most rabid party politicians will deny that the last Presidential election was fought between two very second-rate men. In effect, the Americans are becoming almost English in their efforts to denigrate themselves. Whether this decline in self-confidence is due to failure in Vietnam is an interesting speculation, but it could well be the case. The United States has never since its inception lost a war until now, and the iron seems to be entering into its soul. The Nixon administration appears to have sensed this, for it is now using spectacular space flights as a means of boosting the national morale.

On the other hand the one thing that remains unchanged is the pathetic desire to be liked, which marks the North American off from all the great peoples of the world, past and present. In their heyday the Spaniards, French, British, and Germans did not care whether they were liked or not, nor do the Russians at the present time, but to the citizen of the United States it means a very great deal, and the fact that his country is loathed in Latin America puzzles and irritates him.

So far as Anglo-American relations are concerned I have always felt that they would probably have been better had the two nations spoken different languages. In the latter years of the eighteenth century there was a school of thought which held that German, rather than English, should be the official tongue of the new state, and on many grounds it is to be regretted that their views did not prevail. Because the Englishman and the American speak the same language they are inclined to take it for granted that they mean the same thing, with the result that misunderstandings arise. Of course this consideration also applies to the Irish: when an Irish waiter says he will carry out an order 'presently' the English visitor is inclined to think that he is being treated in a very off-hand manner, whereas what the man means is 'at once'. In any case the interpretation of words can have very serious consequences. I remember Austen Chamberlain telling me of a discussion he once had with Briand, when at intervals during the Frenchman's exposition of his theme Austen kept repeating '*oui*'. When Briand had finished he expressed his delight to Chamberlain that they were in agreement, only to be considerably taken aback when the other said that this was certainly not the case. 'But you kept on saying "*oui*",' said Briand, without realizing that whereas '*oui*' means to a Frenchman 'I agree', to an Englishman 'yes' merely implies 'I am listening'.

Actually there is no great national affinity between the two so-called Anglo-Saxon peoples, which is why men like Sir Harry Brittain with his Pilgrims' Club have performed a public service by fomenting a common interest which has proved invaluable on more than one occasion. The fact that Americans flock in their thousands to see London Bridge in the Middle West does not imply an interest in, or devotion to Great Britain; all it means is that they have cars and nowhere to go in them, so they make a pilgrimage to the nearest spectacle available. In effect, they are acting in the same way as their English contemporaries who swell the pockets of the owners of the 'stately homes': this distraction, rather than implying a devotion to the old aristocracy, merely shows that those who indulge in it have nothing else to do – it is *panis et circenses* again in a different form.

Even in their sense of humour the two nations have little in common, though the Americans are perhaps the better at coining a happy phrase: the late Adlai Stevenson excelled in this respect, and it will be long before his definition of a politician as 'one who approaches every problem with an open mouth' is forgotten. I rather like, too, the epitaph in Copp's Hill burial ground in Boston, Mass.:

> *Stop here my friend and cast an eye,*
> *As you are now so once was I,*
> *As I am now so you will be,*
> *Prepare for death and follow me.*

To which some wag added:

> *To follow you I'm not content*
> *Until I know which way you went.*

An American whom I knew very well in my youth was E. P. Warren of Rhode Island, who, after being an undergraduate at New College, Oxford, came to live in England, where he made his home in Lewes. During term times he always lived in Oxford, where he was made a Fellow of Corpus Christi. Warren's hospitality was lavish on the old-fashioned scale, with beer and cutlets for breakfast. He was a man of real classical culture, which was probably his reason for settling down in England, for he was very critical of the way of life in his own country. In particular he was scornful of the social and intellectual pretensions of the Bostonians, and one of his favourite verses was the following:

> *There was an old lady of Boston,*
> *And a great sea of doubt she was tossed on,*
> *   As to if it were best*
> *   To be rich in the West*
> *Or poor and peculiar at Boston.*

Warren was also fond of reproducing a saying of a Bostonian about Shakespeare: 'Yes, Sir, William Shakespeare was a very great man. I don't think there are twenty men in Boston who could have written what William Shakespeare has written.' The alleged Bostonian snobbery which he derided recalls the story of the young man from that city who in his application for a job in New York mentioned by way of recommendation that he was closely connected with the Cabot, Lowell, and Lodge families. The unsympathetic reply that he received was 'We propose to employ, not to breed from, you.'

As may be supposed Warren was no admirer of the free and easy ways of American democracy. Another verse of which he was very fond ran as follows:

> *This is the country of the free,*
> *   The cocktail and the ten cent chew,*
> *When you're as good a man as me,*
> *   And I'm a better man than you.*
> *O Liberty! How free we make!*
> *Freedom! What liberties we take!*

When Prohibition was introduced Warren was extremely scornful, and there was one story in particular about it which he often told. A traveller arriving by train at a town in the Middle West, on leaving the station asked a local inhabitant if he could direct him to a place where he could get a drink. The local inhabitant said he could. He told him to follow the street in which they were, take the third turning on the left, then follow that street for three blocks and turn to the left. Then, after turning, he would see a house painted white. 'Got it?' asked the native.

'Yes,' said the traveller.

'Well,' his companion replied, 'that's the only house in this town where you can't get a drink.'

In fact the modern American is very different from the parody which passes muster for the real thing in Great Britain and the Republic of Ireland. In both countries it is assumed that he is wealthy: a few are, but the majority cross the Atlantic on a package tour for which they have saved up for years. In consequence they are by no means free with their dollars, so that in some places they are even acquiring the reputation of being mean. A year or two ago I was in the bar of the Talbot hotel in Wexford when a coachload of American tourists arrived. I remarked to the barman that he would now be doing some business, to which he replied that he would be surprised if one of them came in: he had no call for surprise as none of them did. In many conversations with taxi-drivers, hall-porters, and barmen I have always been told that on holiday the man who is most free with his money is not the American but the tourist from the north of England or even the Lowland Scot, but they want value for what they spend.

Except for a small circle in New York and Washington the average American is ill-informed as to what is going on in the outside world, which is in no way surprising as even in the East the newspapers devote very little space to foreign affairs. Whereas the English press carries a great deal of U.S. news the North American neglects Britain almost completely, so that the Englishman travelling in the U.S. will have the greatest difficulty in finding out what is happening in his own country. As a result attention tends to be focused on the proceedings of the United Nations to an extent impossible to conceive in Great Britain, and it is not unknown in some places for employers to give their workpeople a paid holiday on United Nations Day.

This leads to a good deal of uncritical support for the U.N. especially in the Middle West. But even the most detached observer, both in the Old World and in the New, must surely admit that it is not a useless organization. To make such a charge is to forget what it has done in the economic and social sphere, to which is devoted eighty per cent of its Budget and ninety per cent of its personnel. FAO, WHO and UNESCO have between them made the world a better place for a great number of people through locust control in the Middle East, well-drilling in India, the improvement of the varieties of grain in Brazil, the provision of management consultants for work projects in Korea, and help for Pakistani refugees. On the political side, however, it has been unsuccessful in several respects. It has failed to maintain international peace and security; to develop friendly relations among nations based on respect for equal rights and self-determination; and to achieve international co-operation to solve problems of an economic, social cultural, or humanitarian nature. All the same it has a record of success in cooling major political crises before they attained the size of world-wide problems.

The real danger threatening United Nations today as my wife and I see it is an excess of politics and politicians. When my wife was a member of the Third Committee in 1959 its deliberations were conducted in a civilized manner, concerning themselves with the social problems with which its terms of reference authorized it to deal; when we went to its meetings in 1970 it was to find that they had become a battle-ground where Jews and Arabs hurled abuse at one another, and it is to be feared that the change is symbolic of what is happening elsewhere.

As I have already mentioned, with the exception of the visits to the United States which I have described, during the last twenty years my excursions outside the British Isles have been confined to Western Europe. France, however, and Spain saw a good deal of my wife and me during the troubled years when the Fourth Republic was giving way to the Fifth. Peter, having now passed through Christ Church and done his military service with the Grenadier Guards, had entered the Foreign Service, and with Frank Roberts as his ambassador, was for a time in Paris at NATO, where he married Lydwine d'Oberndorff. We also had friends in Champagne, Comte Robert de Vogüé and his family, whose guests we often were at the Château de Saran near Epernay, and in the South of France at Menton were Colonel and Mrs Rocke, so in one way and another I was brought into touch with a cross-section of French opinion.

France at that time was suffering not so much from the aftermath of the war against Germany as from the barely suppressed civil war which had followed in its wake, and of which the trial of Marshal Pétain was the outward and visible sign. The French people are lively in the extreme and full of sensibility, but every now and then the virus of politics enters their blood, as we were to see again in 1968, undermines their judgement, and renders them an easy prey to violence and excess; at such moments they become impervious to the evidence of fact. It need be no surprise, therefore, that a movement of hostility to the previous regime should have started in 1944, and won the support of a large part of the nation. Still less need we be surprised at the political trials immediately following the Liberation, for which there are many precedents in French history.

Of these trials the most notable was that of Pétain, and the feelings it roused have not died down even today. Whether de Gaulle really wanted him tried is open to doubt – he would quite likely have preferred that the Marshal should have lived in exile because there is less risk of an exile becoming a martyr than of a prisoner appearing in such a guise. Without doubt when France fell in 1940 both men believed that they were acting in the best interests of their country, but whereas de Gaulle felt that these would be most adequately served by throwing in her lot with Britain, the Marshal saw her only hope in co-operation with Hitler. Britain won the war and Germany lost it, which accounts for the subsequent careers of the two men. It was as simple as that. As for the trial itself it was a travesty of justice, for the real issues were ignored.

In short, the main charge against Pétain was that he asked for an armistice, but could he have done otherwise? The only reasonable answer must be in the negative, for the Marshal was no corpse-raiser, and morally France was dead before the campaign opened. It has been suggested by his critics that Paris should have been held as a little later Churchill proclaimed that he would hold London; that a *levée en masse* should have been made in the best revolutionary manner; and that, failing a continuation of the war in France, the French Government should have transferred it to North Africa. The first proposal was senseless. There was no use in attempting to hold the capital when the north of France was already lost, for without it no new French armies could be equipped. In fact Paris was in the same position in which London would have been had the whole of the Midlands and North been in enemy hands, and not in what would have been the much more favourable one had the Germans landed in Sussex and Kent. The second suggestion was in the circumstances equally fatuous, because a *levée en masse* with eight to ten million refugees choking the roads rendered any form of military *levée* impossible.

On the other hand Pétain could certainly have retired to Africa and raised his standard there, but it was extremely fortunate for Britain that he had neither the will nor the energy to do any such thing; for Italy's entry into the war on June 10 had given the Axis the command of the Central Mediterranean, and there can be no reasonable doubt that Hitler would have pursued the Marshal to his doom, with the result that before many months were over the whole of North Africa from Ceuta to Cairo would have been under German occupation. That in spite of Pétain's surrender the Fuehrer did not take this course was to prove the most fatal strategic blunder that he committed during the war.

The irony of the whole situation is that now both Pétain and de Gaulle are dead the resemblance between their essentially monarchist administrations becomes obvious. Yet far too often do Englishmen sneer at French justice. England was not invaded, but if she had been there might well have grown up the feuds and the bitternesses which have marked post-war France; while if the French politicians made a poor show during Pétain's trial with their lying, evasions, and refusal to face facts, it is unlikely that in similar circumstances English ones would have been any better.

There is one respect in which France appears to be unchanged down the ages – in the attitude that politically only Paris really matters. I remember one day in the spring of 1958, when the country was very much in a crisis and Paris was like an armed camp, going into Rheims with my wife and Sir Ralph Anstruther, who was also staying at Saran, and hardly seeing a single policeman – they had all been drafted into the capital. In England such a state of affairs would be impossible, but then in England most of the great movements have started in the provinces.

Since then de Gaulle has given place to Pompidou. When I attended a conference in Ghent in 1964 the Burgemester of Maastricht said to me, 'You British think it will make a great deal of difference when de Gaulle goes. It won't. You said the same thing about Richelieu, yet Richelieu was succeeded by Mazarin, who was merely much more subtle than his predecessor, and Mazarin by Louis XIV.' Was he prophetic?

CHAPTER XVII

Some Conclusions

WHAT conclusions have you drawn from your seventy-six years of life? That is a perfectly justifiable question, but one which is much easier to ask than to answer. Of one thing I am quite certain, that the First World War was the Peloponnesian War of Europe and that the Second carried the earlier calamities to their logical conclusion. If any previous century is to be compared with the twentieth it must be the seventh, when Rome and Persia exhausted themselves in their struggle for the mastery of the Near and Middle East, and left the way clear for the conquests of Islam. So in our own time have Britain and Germany exhausted themselves until neither has the power to stem the advance of Communism, with the force of Russia at its back. As I see it the only hope for the future is a federated Europe capable of holding its own in a world dominated by the Great Powers of China, Russia, and the United States.

Of one thing there can surely be no doubt – that the Second World War was the first conflict in English history, at any rate since the loss of France in the fifteenth century, which left the nation both mentally and physically exhausted. After earlier wars, even after its immediate predecessor, the general attitude was 'Well, that's that', and to turn to the next task that lay ahead. This was not the case after 1945. The mass of the population might have been disillusioned, but they continued to belong to a dead world with a wholly different standard of values. Of course the politicians were to no small extent to blame, in particular the Labour administration of Clement Attlee, though there is no evidence that if Churchill had won the General Election of 1945 he would have behaved any differently. The country was living on the dole from the United States, but this subvention was regarded as if it were the natural surplus

*Major-General Hally, the author, and Father V. de Paor
at the memorial to the Irish dead at Fontenoy, 29 August, 1965*

*Sir Charles and Lady Petrie being received by the Alcalde of Madrid,
Conde de Mayalde, November, 1960*

*The author in lighter mood with his son Peter at Epsom Races,
August, 1971*

of income over expenditure. To restore the national position in the world's economy and repair the ravages of war, it was clearly necessary to work longer and harder; instead, every opportunity was given – and taken – to work shorter and less. Far-reaching social services were introduced, and were proclaimed to be free, whereas the most crushing taxation had to be maintained to pay for them. Above all the pretence was kept up that the pound was still worth twenty shillings. The verdict of our descendants will be interesting and instructive, but it is hardly likely to be flattering.

Nevertheless it must be admitted that the prophets of gloom have proved wrong in the past. In 1783 Dr Johnson lamented that he had 'lived to see all things as bad as they can be', and two years later Cowper deplored the terrible state of society when

> ... *Discipline at length,*
> *O'erlooked and unemployed, fell sick and died.*

Then Lord Chesterfield wrote on the outbreak of the Seven Years' War, 'Whoever is in, or whoever is out, I am sure we are undone both at home and abroad: we are no longer a nation.'

Appearances are admittedly deceptive: the bankrupt and beaten Britain forced to sign the Treaty of Versailles in 1783, thereby acknowledging the loss of its colonies, hardly looked as if in a generation's time it would have successfully overcome the threat of Napoleon. Both points of view have clearly to be taken into consideration, but it must also be remembered that we have no precedent to tell us to how much strain an industrial civilization can be subjected to without completely breaking down.

Then there is inflation, which in the past was largely responsible for the downfall of both Rome and Spain. The Spanish parallel is not so applicable to British conditions today as the Roman, which calls for investigation by those who are worried, as I certainly am, about the future, being, to quote E. H. Carr, essentially the type of man who 'peers eagerly back into the twilight out of which he has come in the hope that its faint beams will illuminate the obscurity into which he is going'. A scrutiny of the economics of the later Roman Empire, of which the conditions were in many ways anticipatory of our own, should help us to avoid some of the tragic paths which led to its iron compulsions and controls.

From the death of Marcus Aurelius in 180 there was galloping inflation; there was also a black market in silver currency as we know from a decree of Caracalla forbidding it on the ground that the existence of illicit exchange rates and the wild speculation which was the result rendered it impossible for the ordinary citizen to secure the necessities of life. There were several reasons for this inflation, but most important was the steady depreciation of the currency.

The Empire had inherited from Augustus a magnificent coinage of a range never seen before. This included a gold piece (*aureus*) and the related silver one (*denarius*), both of which possessed a precious metal content worth as much, or very nearly as much, as the official valuations attached to the coins. Yet by the time of Gallienus in the middle of the third century the Roman government's coinage was mainly based on *antoniniani*, made almost entirely of bronze with a thin surface coating of silver wash. Of course a contributory factor was the ever-increasing cost of administration, particularly where defence was concerned, and the situation was not improved by the partiality of the government for policies it could not afford.

The collapse of the silver coinage produced catastrophic effects during the decades following the death of Gallienus. In Egypt, for instance, papyri tell us that thirty litres of wheat cost seven-eighths of the Greek currency unit (*drachma*) during the second century; from ten to twenty *drachmai* in the first half of the third century; and by the time of Diocletian the figure was as high as a hundred and twenty thousand. Between the years 258 and 275 prices in many parts of the Empire are likely to have risen by nearly 1,000 per cent with a resulting misery which even the harassed subjects of Queen Elizabeth II have not yet known. To avoid bankruptcy the Roman state turned to authoritarianism, which gave rise to a totalitarianism beyond anything which the ancient Assyrians or the Ptolemies had contrived. To quote that most eminent ancient historian, Dr Grant, 'The censor-ridden, standardizing police administration of Plato's *Laws* has arrived, and governments, even in countries with the most democratic traditions, are tempted to feel that the only way to meet their financial needs is by constantly intensifying regimentation.'

The truth is that in these latter days we are constantly deluding ourselves with the notion that we are confronted by entirely new situations, when in effect we are merely undergoing the experiences of former generations and treading the paths which they long since have trod. If inflation is one case in point unrest in the universities is another. Student power at Oxford manifested itself as long ago as 1258, when the papal legate had to be rescued by men-at-arms from the unwelcome attentions of the undergraduates: later, in 1715, it required a regiment of dragoons and one of infantry to prevent the young men there from seizing the city for King James III of England and VIII of Scotland.

More apposite at the present time was the student revolt in Germany a hundred and fifty years ago. It may be said to have begun with the Festival at the Wartburg in October 1817, which was held to celebrate the defeat of Napoleon at the battle of Leipzig four years earlier, and the tercentenary of the Reformation. At first the proceedings passed off soberly enough, but, as is not unusual on such occasions, in due course they got out of hand, and assumed what today would be termed a definitely anti-Establishment character. In imitation of Luther's burning of the Papal Bull unpopular books were solemnly committed to the flames — and not without professorial approval — while at the last moment there were added, as symbols of reaction, an Uhlan's stays, a pig-tail, and a corporal's cane.

This demonstration soon proved to be the beginning of a widespread student revolt all over the Reich. Young Germany was still effervescing with the enthusiasm of the War of Liberation: crowds of volunteers had returned from France, covered with a somewhat exaggerated glory, and naturally loth to settle down into the dull routine of German *Klein-staaterei*. So in odd clothes which they claimed were the old German costume, with long hair, and staff in hand, they wandered about the country as zealous missionaries of German unity — the catchword of the moment. The effect of this was out of all proportion to its intrinsic impor-tance, but as it was something out of the experience of the authorities it frightened them; and so the astonished members of students' beer clubs suddenly found themselves elevated into a power capable, apparently, of striking terror into the hearts of monarchs and statesmen.

These young men would not appear to have had any well-defined policy beyond a vague belief that the unification of Germany would somehow solve all their problems, so it is impossible to say where their movement might have led them had it not been halted by an act of violence which rendered strong action on the part of the authorities in-evitable.

A young student of Erlangen University, by name Charles Sand, noted for the gentleness of his character and the purity of his morals, had been present at the Wartburg Festival. What he had heard and seen there had powerfully affected his mind, enthusiastic to the point of fanaticism, so that he developed a zeal for popular government which did not rule out political assassination in the course of its attainment. Self inspired, or, as a paper found upon him suggested, selected by a group of fellow-fanatics, he prepared with some deliberation to assassinate August Kotze-bue, a native of Weimar with strong anti-revolutionary views who had long been in the service of the Tsar, and who combined the work of a well-known German playwright with the activities of a Russian spy. Introducing himself to his victim as an admirer, Sand seized a convenient moment in the interview to strike Kotzebue a mortal blow with a dagger.

A servant had been attracted by the noise, but Sand kept him at bay with his weapon, fled downstairs with cries of triumph, and on the threshold fell on his knees, thanked God for his success, and dealt himself two blows that caused a loss of consciousness though not of life. The papers found on him were evidence of the confusion of his mind, for they included an appeal to the Germans to shake off tyranny, to kill those who disagreed with them, and to complete the work of the Reformation by uniting Church and State.

To what extent the students enjoy public sympathy today is at least arguable, but in Germany at the time of Kotzebue's murder there was no doubt that the bulk of the educated classes were inclined to approve the motive while condemning the deed; in some circles voices were raised to declare that the motive excused the crime. One clergyman went so far as to write to Sand's mother saying, 'He held it to be right, and so he has done right . . . So, as this deed has been done by this pure, pious youth with this belief, with this confidence, it is a beautiful sign of the times.' By the students Sand was hailed as worthy to rank with Brutus, Harmodios, Aristogeiton, and other classic ridders of tyrants: when he paid the penalty of his crime his execution was made the occasion of a sympathetic demonstration, while the place of his death became popularly known as 'The Field of Sand's Ascension'. It all has a very modern ring.

It was not to be expected that authority would see the humorous side of a state of mind which could confuse Kotzebue with Julius Caesar, and the panic in high places was soon increased by another attempt, the work of the inevitable imitator, directed against the life of a senior civil servant. The result might have been expected, but was certainly not what the students desired. Rigid repression, especially where the universities were concerned, became the order of the day. For a time this policy appeared to be successful, chiefly because the Establishment had a plan while the students were without one, but in the end it would seem that revolutionary sentiments were merely driven underground, to make their reappearance in redoubled force in 1848, the year of revolutions.

What message has all this for us today? The most important would appear to be not to let matters go to extremes or we may well have another Kotzebue affair, with the inevitable reaction. If the students become the type of the enthusiasts of the Wartburg Festival the same results will follow, only possibly more quickly, because the modern taxpayer is affected more directly in his pocket: it is he who has to pay the students' educational grants; he has in consequence less sympathy than his great-grandfather with ebullient youth. Also it is by no means clearer today than it was in the early years of last century what the students really want, and it is never easy to negotiate with enthusiasts who lack a definite programme: youth would do well to bear this in mind. In too many cases its claims are as vague as were the slogans of Sand's contemporaries.

At the same time the Establishment must take care that authority is not too remote, as it seems to have been in early nineteenth-century Germany. In the small community of an Oxford or Cambridge college it is the easiest thing in the world for an undergraduate to bring his griev-ances, real or imagined, to the notice of the authorities: in the larger and newer universities, which have no college system, this is more difficult, and so a dangerous feeling of frustration is developed. One has also heard that the younger members of the teaching staff are not in as close touch with their pupils as were their predecessors a generation or so ago — except, of course, for the handful who aspire to be their ring-leaders.

It is not only in the academic sphere that authority seems to me to be becoming too remote, for the same state of affairs surely obtains in industry. On the one hand the Trade Unions are no longer in their old intimate touch with the workers, who are increasingly passing under the control of the shop-stewards, while on the other the individual firm is being absorbed into the big combine. It is here that I differ from a good many of my Conservative friends. They see a world divided between nationalization and its partisans on the one side and what they are pleased to call 'private enterprise' on the other, but to me there is little or no difference between them, more particularly now that the taxpayer is expected to put his hand in his pocket whenever an industry, national-ized or not, runs into financial difficulties. There was a time when the Tories stood for the small man, and looked after his interests; but that is a thing of the past, and the present position is one of the evil conse-quences of the intrusion of Big Business into the counsels of the Con-servative Party.

To pass to the more material changes of recent years, surely the greatest has been the coming of radio and television, which has been to the present post-war period what the internal combustion engine was to the earlier years of the century: yet although their influence is universally acknow-ledged it is by no means easy to define it. Most people will agree that a play seen on T.V. does not make the same impression as one seen in a theatre, while a speech heard on radio or television is unlikely to be remembered as long as one listened to at, say, the Albert Hall. My own experience – and I have broadcast off and on since the thirties – certainly bears this out. Time and time again I have been complimented on what I have said, but it is very rare for anyone to remember, even a few hours later, what I did actually say. All this may well be that there is a lack of concentration on the part of the listener or the viewer, who is probably doing something else like putting the baby to bed, preparing the dinner, or even making love, whereas if he or she reads a book or a newspaper, or seeks entertainment outside the home, much more concentration is required: the result would seem to be that the influence of radio and television, if momentarily considerable, is also ephemeral.

In one respect the period covered by the preceding pages can, however, afford grounds for unmixed satisfaction, and that is where the writing of history is concerned: this is not to disparage the work, particularly in the matter of research, of the historians of the latter years of the nineteenth, and the earlier years of the twentieth, century, but their successors are readable, while they were not. It is also a welcome sign of the times that in the van of this movement there should be four women, namely Veronica Wedgwood; Elizabeth Longford, and her daughter, Antonia Fraser; and Carola Oman: thanks to them and eminent male historians such as Arthur Bryant history is once again being read as literature.

Finally, the longer one lives the more impressed one becomes with the attitude of one's fellows towards life and death. It has always seemed to me that with the very old the will to live has often disappeared before death finally takes possession. For obvious reasons this theory cannot be supported by reference to the living or to those recently dead, but there are historical examples which may be cited in its favour.

Certainly in middle age the coming of death is resented much more than in later life. At fifty the dying Cecil Rhodes, who had long been familiar with the prospect of premature death, bitterly lamented his fate with the words, 'So little done, so much to do.' At fifty-nine the will to live is still strong. Cromwell, at the beginning of his last illness, burst out to his doctors, 'Do you think I shall die – say not I have lost my reason. I tell you the truth – I know it on better authority than any you can have from Galen or Hippocrates; it is the answer of God Himself to our prayers.' Even when he was compelled to abandon all hope of recovery he was still reluctant to go: 'I would be willing to live to be further serviceable to God and His people, but my work is done.'

As one nears the psalmist's three score years and ten a change comes, and though life may still be pleasant and placidly enjoyed, the tyrannical autocrat, death, gradually becomes a benevolent despot. At seventy-two Darwin wrote to Wallace, 'I have everything to make me happy and contented, but life has become very wearisome to me,' and at the same age Archbishop Tait confessed, 'It is better I should go now. Other men will do my work better. It isn't so very dreadful after all.' The eighth Duke of Devonshire was three years older when he spoke his last words, 'Well the game is over, and I am not sorry'; while at seventy-six the dying Disraeli was heard to murmur, 'I had rather live, but I am not afraid to die' – a remark which surely shows that hitherto unconquerable will on the verge of collapse.

Then there is the case of Louis XIV, dying within a few days of his seventy-seventh birthday. 'I have always heard it said,' he observed to Madame de Maintenon, 'that it is difficult to die; for my part, now that I have reached the moment so feared by men, I do not find that it is difficult.' To two pages who were crying at the foot of his bed he remarked, 'Why do you weep? Is it because you thought me immortal? As for me, I never thought I was that, and considering my age you ought long ago have been prepared to lose me.' When the doctors forced on him some particularly unpleasant medicine, Louis said, 'I take this neither in the hope nor with the desire of being cured, but in my present condition I must obey the doctors.'

What is resignation in the seventies appears from the evidence to become a wish in the eighties. On the last day of his life Tennyson at eighty-three said, 'Death? That's well.' John Wesley came of a long-lived family, and until he was eighty-four he enjoyed perfect health which he attributed to continual exercise, change of air and the will of God. Soon afterwards his strength began to fail, and this prompted him to comment, 'I feel no pain from head to foot; only it seems nature is exhausted.' Finally, when someone assured Gladstone, at the age of eighty-eight, that he would live for another ten years, he replied, 'I trust that God in His mercy will spare me that.'

A more recent example of this resignation of the old at the approach of death was the attitude of the late Sir George Arthur who died at the age of eighty-five. I had recently succeeded him as editor of the *Household Brigade Magazine*, and almost the last letter he wrote, or rather signed, for he was by then unable to write, was one of good wishes for the future: in it he told me that he knew he had not long to live, but that he was quite ready to go. He was a sincere Christian, and death held no terrors for him.

To me it has always seemed that life is like a visit to the theatre, when one has arrived after the raising of the curtain. By taking a little trouble and using a certain amount of intelligence it is possible to get the gist of what has happened before one arrived; by diligence it is not too difficult to find out what is taking place on the stage at the moment, though admittedly this is not so simple a task as it used to be; but one always has to leave before the end.

Index

Abel-Smith, Col Sir Henry, 175
Adair, Major-General Allan, 175
Agar, Charles, 75
Agar, Herbert, 189
Alba and Berwick, 17th Duke of, 129, 214, 218–20
Alexander, Field-Marshal, 175
Alfonso XIII, King, 101, 103, 105–7, 219, 221
Allenby, Viscount, 129
Amery, Leo, 42, 148
Andrew, Prince (father of Duke of Edinburgh), 149
Anstruther, Sir Ralph, 229
Aosta, Duke of, 135
Apponyi, Count, 111, 135
Arthur, Sir George, 237
Arundell of Wardour, Lord, 121 n.
Ashmore, Maj-Gen. E. B., 38
Asquith, H. H., 25, 43, 62, 89–91, 191, 193–4
Asquith, Lady Cynthia, 37
Asquith, Margot, Countess of Oxford and, 165
Assheton, Ralph, later Lord Clitheroe, 60, 63, 177, 195
Attlee, Clement, 95, 193–4, 230

Bainville, Jacques, 47, 100
Balbo, Marshal, 138
Baldwin, Stanley
  Conservatives and Big Business, 70
  fails to dress for dinner, 198
  Liberals hold balance, 90
  party loyal to, 117
  rejects dinner invitation, 120
  'Safety First' slogan, 110
  sketch of, 84–6
  Spanish press rumours, 108
  Tariff Reform election, 71
  uninspiring leader, 116

Baldwin, Lucy, 86
Balfour, Lord
  denies Churchill office, 193
  difference with Sandars, 62
  election defeat, 15
  literary parliamentarian, 93
  reaction to verbosity, 190
  resigns leadership, 189
  silence over Greece, 88
  sketch of, 82–4
Barclay, Neville, 63
Barrère, Camille, 120
Barrès, Maurice, 98
Bathurst, Lady, 76
Beaumont, Hon. Ralph, 57
Beaverbrook, Lord
  anti-Baldwin campaign, 85
  biography of Lloyd George, 82 n.
  Churchill and, 192
  difference with Salvidge, 14
  proprietorial power, 76
  secret of peerage, 89
  view on Ll. George, 191
Beckett, Joe, 82
Beechman, N. A., 57
Belloc, Hilaire, 93
Benes, Eduard, 146
Benoist, Charles, 100
Bergson, Henri, 33
Berthelot, P., 100
Bertrand, Louis, 135
Betjeman, Sir John, 203
Bettington, R. H., 57
Bibesco, Princess Marthe, 158
Birkenhead, 2nd Earl of, 13
Birrell, A., 27–8
Bismarck, Prince von, 47, 145
Blake, Robert Lord, 15
Bloomfield, Paul, 63
Blumenfeld, R. D., 76
Boland, F. H., 213

Borgia, Count, 137
Boris III, King, 153-5, 162
Bottomley, Horatio, 61
Boyd-Carpenter, John, 121, 127
Brannigan, Dr, 20
Breakey, Lt-Col., 40
Briand, Aristide, 97, 109, 121, 224
Bridges, Dr, 55
Brittain, Sir Harry, 208, 224
Brockman, Harold, 204
Brown, Lord George, 205
Browning, 'Boy', 175
Browning, Oscar, 64
Bryant, Sir Arthur, 208, 236
Bryan, William Jennings, 72
Buchan, John (1st Lord Tweedsmuir),
    46, 60, 91-3, 121, 190
Bull, Sir Stephen, 116, 119, 121 n., 127
Buller, Sir Redvers, 171
Burnett-Brown, A. D., 122
Burnham, Lord, 76
Butler, R. A., 189, 194

Cain, Charles, 14
Campbell-Bannerman, Sir Henry, 24, 27
Canning, George, 86-8, 192, 206-7
Carnegie, Mrs (formerly Mrs Joe Cham-
    berlain), 193
Carol II, King, 157
Carr, E. H., 231
Carson, Lord, 15, 27, 217
Carter, Frank, 187
Case, Tommy, 9, 54-6
Castiella, Fernando Maria, 99
Castlereagh, Lord, 87, 206
Cavendish-Bentinck, Lord Henry, 63
Cecil, Lord Robert (3rd Marquess of
    Salisbury), 75
Cecil, Lord William (Bishop of Exeter),
    170
Chamberlain, Sir Austen
    Allenby irritates, 129
    among best Foreign Secretaries, 79
    background on Neville, 164
    Baldwin's chicanery, 85
    butler and 'drunk' note, 118
    calibre absent in World War II, 191
    first meetings with, 42
    guest of Eighteen Club, 119
    memorandum minuted by, 46
    on University discussions, 113

'oui' misunderstood, 224
    out of office, 110
    sketch of, 86-90
    Spanish trains, 102
    warns Grandi on E. Africa, 142
Chamberlain, Ivy, 127, 142, 164
Chamberlain, Joseph, 6, 89, 102, 164
Chamberlain, Mrs Joseph, 193
Chamberlain, Neville
    admired in Budapest, 160
    assessment of, 164-5
    Birmingham finances custodian, 12
    brother could have helped, 88
    Buchan a supporter of, 93
    Conservatives and Big Business, 70
    guest of Eighteen Club, 119-20
    Munich respite, 162
    Sanctions abandoned, 138
    Unitarian, 159
    winning smile, 137
Chapman, Allan, 180
Charles, Emperor, 145
Chenevix-Trench, Richard, 103
Chesterton, G. K., 55
Chichibu, Prince, 64
Churchill, Lord Ivor, 60
Churchill, Winston
    Balfour replaces as First Lord, 62
    consistent war assessment, 179
    Cousin Alba, 219
    dines with Bonar Law, 15
    founds The Other Club, 208
    Gold Standard and, 109
    guest at 1900 Club, 189-90
    Indian reforms controversy, 117
    London to be held, 228
    nation's post-war exhaustion, 230
    1945 election, 177
    offered Chief Secretaryship in Dublin,
        27
    on Spain, 220
    Spanish press rumours, 108
    supports Salter's candidature, 72
    views on, 189-93
    Wavell and, 129
Ciano, Count, 141-2, 148
Clemenceau, Georges, 49, 97, 120, 145
Clitheroe, 1st Lord, 51, 207
Codreano, 156-7
Cohen, Alderman Louis, 14
Collins, Michael, 95, 146, 211

Colville, Lord, 4
Colvin, Ian, 76, 99
Comte de Paris, 98–100
Connell, John, 129
Constantine, King, 148
Cooke, Gresham, 119
Cooper, Capt. Bryan, 21
Coote, Sir Colin, 100
Coote, Denise, 100
Corry, Monty, 165
Cox, Commandant G. S., 212
Cox, Sir Geoffrey, 180
Craigavon, Lord, 217
Crean, Father, 213
Crichton-Browne, Capt., 38
Croft, Lord, 177
Curran, John, 5
Curran, Sarah, 5
Curzon, Lord, 42, 54, 88, 95

Danagher, Capt. Kevin, 213
Danesfort, Lord, 185
Darling, Lord, 61
Darwin, Charles, 236
Daudet, Léon, 98–9
Daviot, Miss Gordon, 91
Dawson, Christopher, 135
De Blacam, Aodh, 5, 212
De Gaulle, Charles, 100, 175, 228–9
De Guise, Duc, 99
Del Val, Cardinal Merry, 136
Del Val, Marqués Merry, 119
Derby, 17th Earl of, 9, 14–15
De Reynold, Gonzague, 81
De Rivera, General Primo, 105–7, 137, 221
De Rohan, Charles, 135
De Romanones, Conde, 37
De Ropp, Baron, 136
Deroulède, Paul, 98
De Valera, Eamon
    Irish are conservative, 27
    patriot, 146
    proposals, Boris asks about, 154
    silent on Easter Rising, 212–13
    takes Oath of Allegiance, 22
    voters' long memory of, 211
    winning smile, 137
De Vogüé, Comte Robert, 227
Devonshire, 8th Duke of, 237
Dick, W. W. F., 217

Disraeli, Benjamin, 62–3, 93, 141, 192, 237
D'Oberndorff, Lydwine, 227
Dodington, George Bubb, 133
Dollfuss, Engelbert, 160
Donaldson, Stuart, 51
Don Juan, 219
Don Juan Carlos, Prince of Spain, 222
Drummond, Lady, 139
Drummond, Sir Eric (Earl of Perth), 139
Dudley, Earl of, 198
Duff, Presbyterian Minister, 5
Dunsany, Lord, 203

Earp, T., 56
Eden, Sir Anthony, 57, 85, 142, 194
Edward VII, 9, 16, 30–2, 145
Edward VIII (see also Windsor, Duke of), 85, 94
Einzig, Paul, 135
Eley, Bert, 125
Eliot, T. S., 33
Elizabeth, Queen Mother, 222
Ellis, Charles (Lord Seaford), 206
Emmet, Robert, 5
Esterhazy, Count Maurice, 160
Eugénie, Empress, 97

Face, Gerry, 168, 172
Face, Joan, 172
Farquhar, Lord, 82
Ferdinand, King, 155
Fitzgerald, Lord Edward, 5
Flecker, Hermann, 55
Fleming, Dr Archibald, 91
Foch, Marshal, 49
Forester, C. S., 203
Forster, William, 119
Franco, General, 104, 140, 218–20, 222
Franz Josef, Kaiser, 32
Fraser, Lady Antonia, 236
Fuller, Boney, 130

Gale, General, 175
Gandhi, Mahatma, 146
Garside, Kenneth, 205
Garvin, J. L., 75–7
Gascogne, Julian, 175
Gaxotte, Pierre, 135
George II of Greece, 147–9

George V, 30, 46, 90, 93–4, 129
Gibbon, Edward, 92
Girvan, Waveney, 204
Gladstone, W. E., 22, 89, 93, 120, 237
Goering, Hermann, 135–6
Goicoechea, Antonio, 121
Gordon-Lennox, Victor, 139
Gordon, Lt-Colonel Hon. E. I. D. 41–2, 46
Gore-Booth, Brian, 21
Gore-Booth, Constance, 21–2
Gore-Booth, Paul, 21
Gore-Booth, Sir Josslyn, 21
Gough, Gen. Sir Hubert, 63, 129
Graham, Sir Ronald, 137
Grandi, Dino, 38, 119, 140, 142
Grant, Dr, 232
Graves, Robert, 57
Gray, Roger, Q.C., 119
Greenacre, Douglas, 175
Greene, Graham, 203
Greer, Lord Justice, 61
Gretton, Lord, 72, 187, 189–90
Greville, Mrs Ronnie, 118, 203
Grey, Sir Edward, 29, 31, 87, 191
Griffiths, Arthur, 25, 27
Grigg, P. J., 116
Grimm, Professor, 158–9
Guedalla, Philip, 121
Gwynne, 'Taffy', 76

Haig, Douglas 1st Earl, 14, 44, 50
Halévy, Elie, 135
Halifax, Lord, 153, 167, 191, 222
Hall, Sir Reginald, 71
Hally, Maj-Gen. P., 213
Hannay, Canon (George A. Birming-ham), 21
Hanotaux, Gabriel, 121, 135
Harcourt, Sir William, 190
Hare, Kenneth, 204
Harris, C. R. S., 60, 63, 141
Hayes, Dr Richard, 212, 215
Hayes-McCoy, Prof. A. G., 213
Hayes, Wade, 180
Heathcoat-Amory, P. C., 121 n., 162
Heath, Edward, 217
Henderson, Arthur, 79
Healey, Father, 22–3
Henley, W. E., 75
Herbert, A. P., 89, 92

Herriot, Edouard, 96, 121
Hewart, Lord Chief Justice, 144
Hitler, Adolf
    Allies paved way for, 47
    Boris on, 154
    Chamberlain duped by, 165
    completes *Mein Kampf*, 96
    French collaborators, 113
    meets Franco, 220
    Pétain cooperates with, 228
    second-rate leader, 138
Hoare, Lady, 158
Hoare, Sir Reginald, 158
Hoare, Sir Samuel, 63, 85, 191
Hogg, Quintin, later Lord Hailsham, 120–1
Holmes, A. B., 6
Hope, H. J., 60
Hore-Belisha, Leslie, 54, 56, 63, 121, 168

Houston, Sir Robert, 13
Howard, Hugh, 216
Howell, Miles, 57
Hughes, Richard, 57
Humbert, Crown Prince, 142
Hyde, Douglas, 25

Irving, Lady, 40
Irving, Sir Henry, 17, 40
Isaacs, Sir Rufus, 12

James, Robert Rhodes, 191
Jenkins, Robert, 187
Jerrold, Douglas
    authors poorly paid, 79
    character of, 116
    English Review, 69
    English Review policy, 116–17
    Kensington rents soar, 186
    Review revived, 195
    sneers for Authors' Club, 203
    toasts Oxford tradesmen, 51
Jinnah, Mahomed Ali, 146
Johnson, Donald McI., 85
Jorga, Professor, 157
Joseph Francis, Archduke, 145
Jowett, Benjamin, 64
Joyce, William, 115

Kindersley, Guy, 180
Kingsmill, Hugh, 204

Kitchen, Clifford, 57, 63
Kitchener, Lord, 17, 27
Knightley of Fawsley, Sir Rainald, 63
Kotzebue, August, 233-4

Labouchère, Henry, 99
Lancaster, Osbert, 203
Lane-Fox, Col, 63
Lansdowne, Marquess of, 15, 87
Lathom, Earl of, 9
Law, Bonar, 15, 61, 70, 84, 86, 193-4
Law, Richard, 188
Lawless, Col, 212
Lawlor, Col A. T., 212
Lee, Major-Gen. Alec, 128
Leese, Gen. Oliver, 175
Leighton, Lord, 84
Lenin, V. I., 128, 138
Lennox-Boyd, Alan, 121, 127
Lentaigne, Capt. E. C., 41
Levidis, Dimitri, 149
Liddell, Henry George, 64
Limerick, Countess of, 185
Lindsay, Michael, 205
Livingstone, Sir Richard, 56
Llewellin, Jay, 180
Lloyd, Geoffrey, 85
Lloyd George, David
  chapel and, 8
  Civil Service increased, 45
  foundations for welfare state, 191
  George V questions memorandum, 46
  golfer, 32
  initiates Cabinet minutes, 43
  nickname for Asquith, 90-1
  praise from Prince Sixte, 145
  press in World War I, 192
  surging crowd salutes, 48
Lloyd, Lady, 115
Lloyd, Lord
  backs *English Review* movement, 116-17
  considers joining Mosley, 115
  guest at Eighteen Club, 119
  heads British Council, 151
  offers Spanish trip, 167
  office with Kensington Conservatives, 185
  unreliable orator, 114
  world rushing to disaster, 110

Loyd, General Sir Charles, 175
Locker-Lampson, 147
Lohr, Marie, 63
Londonderry, Marquess of, 87
Londonderry, Theresa Marchioness of, 21
Long, Eric, 3rd Visct, 73
Longford, Elizabeth, Countess of, 236
Longford, 7th Earl of, 211
Long, Walter, 1st Visct, 14, 61, 73, 194
Loraine, Violet, 46
Louis II, Prince of Monaco, 144
Ludendorff, Erich von, 43
Lumley, Roger, later 11th Earl Scarbrough, 57
Lunn, Sir Arnold, 116
Lymington, Gerald (Earl of Portsmouth), 116, 135

McAlister, Colonel, 214
Macaulay, Lord, 93
MacCarthy, Lt-Col Justin, 212
MacDonald, Aeneas, 4
MacDonald, James, 4
MacDonald, J. Ramsay, 79, 90, 93-6, 142
McEwen, Jock, 144
Mackenzie, Sir Compton, 17, 203
Macleod, Iain, 165
McManus, M. J., 212
Macmillan, Harold, 194
Macmillan, Maurice, 121, 194
MacNeill, Major-Gen. Aodh, 212-13
MacNeill, Olaf, 213
Mahaffy, Sir J. P., 64
Maiden, Dr Arthur, 204
Mallins, C. W., 7
Mancroft, Stormont, later 2nd Lord Mancroft, 119, 121
Mangan, Henry, 212
Marconi, Guglielmo, 78, 135
Maria Cristina, Queen, 219
Marjoribanks, Edward, 57, 60
Markievicz, Count, 21-2
Marks, Sir George Croydon, 71
Marlborough, Duke of, 61
Marriott, Major-General Sir John, 175
Marriott, Sir John, 80
Masaryk, Thomas, 146
Masefield, John, 63
Maude, John, 57
Maura, Antonio, 121

Maurras, Charles, 98–9
Maxwell Fyfe, David, later Earl of Kilmuir, 57, 60, 63, 193–4
Maxwell, Herbert, 87
Mersey, Lord (Mr Justice Bingham), 6
Meynell, Laurence, 203
Michael, Crown Prince, 158
Micklem, Dr Nathaniel, 204
Milner, Alfred Viscount, 191
Milner, Lady, 118
Molson, Hugh, later Lord, 139
Mond, Mrs Emile, 139
Moran, Lord, 193
Morgan, Charles, 63
Morley, Viscount, 93
Morrison, Shakes, 180
Mosley, Sir Oswald, 113–15
Mowat, R. B., 55–6, 60
Muggeridge, Malcolm, 203
Munro, John, 204
Murtagh, Diarmuid, 212
Mussolini, Benito
  captured public imagination, 107
  defies League of Nations, 111
  good talker, 106
  interviewed, 88
  Mosley flirts with, 114
  sketch, 137–42
Mussolini, Edda, 141

Nicholas, Grand Duke, 33, 45
Northcliffe, Lord, 76–7, 80, 192

Oastler, Richard, 70
Oberndorff, Graf von, 47
O'Briain, Prof. Liam, 213
O'Brien, Toby, 121, 125–7
O'Broin, Dr, 28
O'Connor, T. P., 32
O'Hagan, Lord, 32
O'Higgins, Kevin, 211
Oman, Carola, 236
O'Neill, Thomas, 211
Otto, Archduke, 143, 146

Page Croft, Henry, 59
Paling, Mrs G., 72
Palmerston, Lord, 87–8
Paul, King, 148–9
Pearce, Edward Holroyd, Lord, 57
Peñaranda, Duke of, 218

Penson, Sir Henry, 60, 92
Peplar, George, 206
Perceval, Spencer, 194
Percy, Earl, 190
Percy, Lord Eustace, 63
Perón, Eva, 219
Pery-Knox-Gore, Mrs, 21
Pétain, Marshal, 227–9
Petrie, Alexander, 5, 19–20, 22
Petrie, Dick, 69
Petrie, George, great-great-grandfather, 4
Petrie, George, archaeologist, 5
Petrie, James, 5
Petrie, Margaret (née MacDonald), 4–5
Petrie, Peter (son)
  born in Kensington, 118
  ducking from punt, 172
  fencing champion, 189
  First Secretary at U.N., 223
  Foreign Office service, 21
  King's Scholar, 185
  marries in Paris, 227
  snipe shooting, 124
Petrie, Peter (uncle), 19–20
Petrie, Robert, 3–4
Petrie, Sir Charles (father), 6–8, 11–14, 16, 17, 26, 30
Pinto, V. de S., 63
Pius X, Pope, 98
Plá, Señor, 38
Plummer, Rev. Charles, 55
Plunket, Lord, 23
Poincaré, Raymond, 96
Pompidou, G. J. R., 229
Pope, Sybil, 128
Pope, Lieut-General Vyvyan, 128
Powell, Enoch, 194
Preston, Lady, 79
Preston, Sir Harry, 78–9
Pujo, Maurice, 99

Quickswood, Lord, 22

Raikes, Sir Victor, 59, 127, 168
Rathbone, R. B., 60
Rathcavan, Lord, 212
Redmond, John, 24–5, 27
Rees, Leonard, 76
Reitz, Denys, 46
Rendel, Sir George, 152–3

Rennell Rodd, Sir (1st Lord Rennell), 120, 135–6, 139, 141
Rhys, Charles (8th Lord Dynevor), 85, 118, 180, 188, 193
Ribot, G., 145
Riddell, Lord, 76
Ritchie, Charles, 187
Rivington, Major Jack, 207
Roberts, Sir Frank, 227
Roberts, Lord, 17, 27, 171
Robertson-Galsgow, R. C., 57
Robey, George, 46
Rocke, Colonel, 227
Rocke, Mrs, 227
Rommel, General Erwin, 128
Roosevelt, Franklin D., 192
Rosebery, Lord, 8, 69
Rosenberg, Alfred, 135–6
Rosenberg, Rose, 93–5
Ross, Sir Charles, 75
Rothermere, Lord, 76, 85, 115
Routh, C. R. N., 63
Runciman, Sir Steven, 203
Russell, Sir J. W., 60

Salisbury, Lord (Foreign Minister), 87–8, 95
Salisbury, Lord, 119–20
Salisbury, Lord, 194
Salter, Sir Arthur, 72
Salvidge, Sir Archibald, 13–14
Sandars, J. S., 62, 165
Sand, Charles, 233–4
Santa Cruz, Pepe, 221
Schacht, Hjalmar, 135–6
Schofield, Guy, 204
Sefton, Earl of, 9
Selby, Sir Walford, 143
Shaftesbury, Lord, 70, 126
Shuttleworth, Lord, 121 n.
Simms, Dr, 213
Simon, Sir John, 142, 191
Sitwell, Sir Osbert, 118
Sixte of Bourbon-Parma, Prince, 145
Smith, F. E. (1st Earl of Birkenhead), 6, 14–16, 61, 76
Smith, Janet Adam, 91
Smuts, Jan, 191
Squire, Sir John, 83, 115, 127
Stacke, Capt. FitzM., 42, 45
Stalin, Josef, 96, 138, 165, 192

Stamfordham, Lord, 95
Stanley, Oliver, 165, 168, 193
Starkie, Walter, 158, 222
Stephens, J. R., 70
Stevenson, Adlai, 224
Stewart-Mackenzie, F., 121 n.
Strachey, John, 114–15
Street, A. G., 125
Stresemann, Gustav, 109
Swinnerton, Frank, 203
Swinton, Lord (Philip Lloyd-Greame), 46

Taft, William, 72
Tait, Archbishop, 103, 237
Taylor, A., 91
Taylor, H., 91
Teck, Duke of, 128
Tellini, General, 111
Temple, Earl, 133
Tennyson, Alfred Lord, 237
Tepel, Abbot of, 32
Thomas, J. H., 115
Thomson of Fleet, Lord, 76
Thorneycroft, Peter, 194
Thurston, Gavin, 205
Tilby, A. Wyatt, 75
Tolley, Cyril, 57
Továr, Dr Antonio, 222
Townsend, Dr, 36
Townsend, Mrs, 36
Trauttmansdorff, Prince, 32
Tremaine, Lt-Col., 40
Trenchard, Viscount, 42
Trollope, Anthony, 21, 39
Trollope, Ted, 173
Trotsky, Leo, 138
Turner, H. Charlewood, 127–8
Tweedmouth, Lord, 60

Venizelos, E., 149–50
Venn, Lawrence, 144
Victor Emmanuel III, King, 142
Victoria, Queen, 10, 17, 27, 89, 103, 195
Villari, Luigi, 138
Villasante, Señor, 38

Walker-Smith, Sir Derek, 121, 127
Wallace, Alfred Russell, 236
Warlow, Ronnie, 190
Warner, Esmond, 207

Warner, 'Plum', 207
Warren, E. P., 225–6
Warren, Herbert, 64
Wavell, F-M. Earl, 128–30
Webster, Daniel, 118
Wedgwood, Veronica, 236
Wellington, Duke of, 202–3
Wells, Mrs, 9
Wells, Warden of Wadham, Oxford, 9
Wemyss, Earl of, 83
Wesley, John, 237
Westminster, Duke of, 75
Wethered, Roger, 57
Weygand, Gen., 192
Whitehead, George, 119
Whyte-Melville, 39
Wicklow, Billy, 8th Earl of, 215
Wilhelm II, Kaiser, 12, 30–2, 46–7
Williamson, Henry, 203
Willway, A. C. C., 60
Wilson, Arnold, 38, 116

Wilson, Harold, 84, 205, 217
Wilson, Sir Horace, 62, 165
Wilson, Thomas Woodrow, 37, 50
Windsor, Duke of (see also Edward VIII), 30, 64
Winterton, Lord, 197
Wise, Roy, 127, 200
Wolfe, James, 4
Woolton, Lord (Frederick Marquis), 14, 179, 195
Wortham, Hugo, 208
Wyler, Miss 'Trina', 203
Wyndham, George, 75
Wyndham, Mary, 83

Yarmouth, Lord, 206
Yeats-Brown, Francis, 115, 127, 168
Younger, Sir George, 64, 76 n.
Young, Kenneth, 83

Zaharoff, Basil, 149